PRELUDE TO
THE COLD WAR

PRELUDE TO THE COLD WAR

The Tsarist, Soviet, and
U.S. Armies in the
Two World Wars

JONATHAN R. ADELMAN

Lynne Rienner Publishers • Boulder & London

For Dora

Published in the United States of America in 1988 by
Lynne Rienner Publishers, Inc.
948 North Street, Boulder, Colorado 80302

Published in the United Kingdom by
Lynne Rienner Publishers, Inc.
3 Henrietta Street, Covent Garden, London WC2E 8LU

Library of Congress Cataloging-in-Publication Data
Adelman, Jonathan R.
    Prelude to the Cold War: The Tsarist, Soviet, and U.S. armies in the
two world wars / by Jonathan R. Adelman
       p. cm.
    Bibliography: p.
    Includes index.
    ISBN 1-55587-123-2 (lib. bdg.)
       1. United States. Army—History—World War, 1914–1918. 2. United
States. Army—History—World War, 1939–1945 3. Soviet Union.
Raboche-Krest´anskaia Krasnaia Armiia—History—World War,
1914–1918. 4. Soviet Union. Raboche-Krest´anskaia Krasnaia
Armiia—History—World War, 1939–1945. 5. Russia. Armiia—History—
World War, 1914–1918. 6. Soviet Union—History, Military—20th
century. 7. United States—History, Military—20th century.
8. World politics—1945–   I. Title.
    D570.2.A73   1988   88-2048
    355'.033'004—dc19   66321   CIP

British Library Cataloguing in Publication Data
A Cataloguing in Publication record for this book
is available from the British Library.

Printed and bound in the United States of America

The paper used in this publication meets
the requirements of the American National
Standard for Permanence of Paper for
Printed Library Materials Z39.48-1984. ∞

Contents

List of Tables   vii

1 Introduction   1

SECTION 1   WORLD WAR I

2 An Economic and Political Overview of World War I   27
3 Russian and U.S. Armies in Battle   47
4 Russian and U.S. Institutions in Wartime   77

SECTION 2   THE INTERWAR YEARS, 1919–1939

5 The Interwar Years   95

SECTION 3   PRELUDE TO GOETTERDAEMMERUNG, JUNE 1941–JUNE 1944

6 A Military and Political Overview   123
7 Soviet and U.S. Armies in Battle   149

SECTION 4   THE SOVIET AND U.S. DESTRUCTION OF THE THIRD REICH, JUNE 1944–MAY 1945

8 Soviet and U.S. Armies in Battle   169
9 Soviet and U.S. War Efforts   201
10 Soviet and U.S. War Economies   223

11 Conclusions   237

Bibliography   261

Index   277

About the Book and the Author   287

v

Tables

2.1	Sources of Weapons Used by the American Expeditionary Force in France in 1918	35
2.2	Sources of Weapons Acquired by the Russian Army in World War I	36
2.3	Number of German, Russian, and U.S. Infantry Divisions at the Front in World War I	39
2.4	Military Expenditures by the Great Powers in World War I	43
2.5	Economic Production of Russia, the United States, and Germany in 1913	45
2.6	War Production of Russia, the United States, Germany, and France in World War I	45
5.1	Soviet Industrial Production, 1928–1940	104
5.2	Soviet, U.S., and German Industrial Production, 1938	104
5.3	Soviet, U.S., and British Defense Expenditures, 1938–1941	107
5.4	Soviet Weapons Production, 1930–1940	108
5.5	U.S. Weapons Production, July 1940–December 1941	110
5.6	Size of the Armed Forces of the Soviet Union and the United States, 1931–1941	111
6.1	German Troop Disposition, June 1941–June 1944	131
6.2	The Share of British, U.S., and Soviet National Income Spent on Defense in World War II	133
8.1	Wehrmacht War Casualties, June 22, 1941–June 4, 1944	171
8.2	German Troop Dispersal Among Fronts, June 1944–April 1945	175
8.3	Comparison of Anglo-American and German Divisions Deployed on the Western and Southwestern Fronts, June 1944–May 1945	176

9.1   U.S. and Japanese War Production,
         January 1942–August 1945   203
9.2   Number of Divisions of Major Powers in World War II   212
9.3   Soviet and German Economic Production, 1941–1945   219
9.4   Weapons Production of the Soviet Union,
         United States, and Nazi Germany in World War II   219

10.1   Soviet and U.S. Economic Production, 1945   225

1

Introduction

The Soviet and U.S. destruction of the Third Reich in World War II marked an event of world-historical proportion. This rare and fleeting military cooperation between the two future superpowers produced results with enduring impact on the international order. The liquidation of Nazi Germany and ensuing political dominance of the United States and Soviet Union dealt a death blow to the European balance-of-power system that had characterized international politics for almost three hundred years since the Treaty of Westphalia in 1648. The improbable alliance destroyed the power of Germany, which had been unmatched on the European continent for seventy-five years since the final unification of Germany in 1870, and it smashed the twelve-year reign of the Third Reich that in June 1944 still dominated the European continent. So great was German power in World War I that even in November 1918 German troops remained on foreign soil. In World War II it took the Soviet Union, the United States, and the British Empire acting in concert almost four years of war to eliminate Nazi Germany.

The removal of German power from the heart of Europe—combined with the parallel demise of Imperial Japan, the exhaustion of Britain and paralysis of France emerging from four years of German occupation—opened the door to a new international order. This act avoided the possibility of a resurgence of German militarism that had plagued Europe in the 1930s and early 1940s, in the aftermath of a failure to decisively defeat Germany in World War I. The military prowess of the United States and Soviet Union, whose armies met on the Elbe in the heart of Germany in 1945, propelled these two hitherto peripheral actors, and seemingly unlikely arbiters of the destiny of the world, to center stage as nascent superpowers in a devastated world order.

The passage of over four decades has dimmed the sense of wonder one feels at the emergence of these two particular states as predominant actors in the postwar era. This is especially true, given that the events of World War II seemed to reverse the result of World War I—a politically active but militarily impotent Russia and a politically isolationist but militarily untested United States. In 1945, both powers seemed to be both politically and militarily powerful, at least on the surface.

WORLD WAR II AND THE EMERGENCE OF THE SUPERPOWERS

The United States had for several decades refused to accept the mantle of world leadership that would inexorably flow to the world's greatest economic and strongest naval power. After a belated and brief (but successful) intervention in World War I, the United States had largely withdrawn from the international arena (with certain exceptions, like the disarmament drive of the 1920s) in the wake of the 1920 League of Nations debacle. During the 1930s it refused to use its potentially awesome power to arrest the inexorable spread of fascism across the European continent in the wake of the Great Depression. This reflected U.S. disenchantment with the outcome of World War I, traditional U.S. avoidance of European conflicts, overwhelming preoccupation with the Great Depression, the safety inherent in the vast expanses of the Atlantic and Pacific Oceans, and the lack of any serious Axis threat to the United States until 1940. This also mirrored a generalized Western underestimation of the extent of the Nazi threat (one initially shared in 1933 by the Soviet Union) and lack of clarity about the true aims of Hitler until the late 1930s.

Having crippled itself with a tiny army (176,000 men in 1939) more appropriate to Bulgaria or Romania than a great power, the United States lacked not only the will but also the capacity to seriously intervene in Europe in the early years of World War II.[1]

Geographic remoteness from Europe and the delay in hitting full war production until 1943, caused by lack of military preparedness, would take its toll in the early years of the war. Not until June 1944, almost five years after the beginning of World War II, would the United States be able to launch a serious military campaign that would engage a significant number of German troops on the European continent and threaten vital German objectives. Until then, U.S. military moves were restricted to air and naval objectives, limited campaigns in North Africa and Italy, and Lend Lease. The bulk of the fighting, inevitably, fell to British and Soviet forces. From such material it would seem unlikely that a superpower could be fashioned.

Nor were things any better with the other prospective candidate for superpower status, the Soviet Union. Indeed, Moscow seemed an even more dismal candidate than Washington. The glory of the march of the Imperial Russian army into Paris in 1814 had long since been superseded by a series of Russian military disasters from the Crimean War to the Russo–Japanese War and early years of World War I. The abysmal performance of the Tsarist army in World War I, symbolized by the 1914 disaster at Tannenberg, hastened the disintegration of Tsarism, the twin revolutions of 1917, and the shameful Tilsit Treaty of Brest Litovsk in 1918. In the wake of the 1917 October Revolution a weakened Russia, battered by the trials of World War I (1914–1917) and the Civil War (1918–1920), yielded not only Finland and Poland but also such vital western territories as the Baltic states and Bessarabia.

During the interwar era the Soviet Union remained a political pariah and ineffectual political actor in Europe. The activities of the Comintern, housed in Moscow, to promote revolution were a dismal failure everywhere, even during the Great Depression. In conventional diplomacy Soviet Russia made little progress apart from attaining diplomatic recognition and carrying out limited economic relations with the West. The crucial military/political connection with Germany—symbolized by the Rapallo and Berlin Treaties and secret military relations—abruptly ended with the rise of Hitler to power in 1933. The shaky alliance with France never developed into the needed full-blown military coordination that might have had an impact on the coming war. Belated Soviet entry into the League of Nations in 1934 only led to the Soviet expulsion from that impotent body in 1940 in the wake of the Winter War with Finland. Soviet support of the Republican forces during the Spanish civil war terminated well before 1939 when it was apparent that the Fascists under General Franco were going to triumph. In short, the Soviet exclusion from the crucial 1938 Munich conference merely symbolized its isolation from the European political system and its perceived weakness by those same powers.

The image of Red Army impotence was strongly reinforced by the massive Great Purges (1937–1941), the poor performance in the Finnish Winter War (1939–1940), and the repeated disasters in 1941 and 1942 when the German army marched eastward. Even when the tide began to turn on the Eastern front in 1943, the enormous scale of the Soviet Union's human and physical losses and the weakness of its economic base seemed to call into question any Soviet preemptive claim to superpower status.

As these two countries, the Soviet Union and the United States, moved into the heart of Europe in the final year of the war, both the similarities they shared and the dissimilarities that separated them were striking. Both countries were huge land powers with great populations, enormous natural resources, and powerful economic capabilities. They both, as heirs of great revolutions, disdained the old European order, viewing themselves as prototypes of new progressive worlds, which would displace the decadent old world. Each had a strong vision of that new order centered around itself—for the United States a liberal international capitalist order, and for the Soviet Union an international socialist order. Both states were relatively inexperienced in foreign affairs and newcomers to the role of great power with bright hopes for the future.

In 1941 both the United States and Soviet Union had been reluctantly propelled into World War II by surprise Axis attacks that did serious damage to their best military services, the U.S. navy and the Soviet army. With their previous histories in the last half-century as relatively mediocre land forces winning victories only against weak enemies, the road back and onward to victory would be protracted, especially against the powerful German army. And World War II was the first and only total war that both the United States and Soviet Union have fought in this century.

Yet the differences between the two nascent superpowers in 1944 were far greater than the similarities, especially in the military, political, and economic spheres applicable to warfare. Economically, the United States was vastly more powerful than the Soviet Union, with the U.S. economy a staggering four times larger than the Soviet economy in 1944.[2] Politically, the United States was much more influential in the world, counting most of the world's major powers as its allies. Militarily, the United States was a powerful naval power; the Soviet Union was an awesome land power. While by June 1944, the Red Army had been bled white, having lost five million prisoners to the Germans and suffered almost six million battle deaths, the U.S. army had suffered less than one hundred thousand casualties.[3] While the United States had strong partners in the British Commonwealth, and later in France, the Soviet Union stood alone. The road to superpower status was protracted and diverse for the two nations.

The end of World War II, then, saw the emergence of two militarily powerful, nascent superpowers, which divided a prostrate Germany between themselves in the center of Europe. This new superpower order also soon developed several other features that differentiated it from the old balance of power system. The ideological rivalry between the capitalist West and socialist East soon reinforced the fracturing of the old international order into two power blocs, perpetually suspicious and hostile towards each other. These rigidities were reinforced by the advent of nuclear weapons, which would further set the superpowers apart from all lesser powers and heighten the dangers immanent in superpower rivalry.

World War II decisively decimated the old international political order and promoted in its place a new ideological and nuclear order dominated by the two superpowers. On the surface World War II bore a marked resemblance to World War I, which also left a strong impact on the international order. In one sense, they were two phases of one war. In both wars only a protracted struggle by an Allied coalition of states, including the United States, Russia/Soviet Union, France, and England, ultimately prevailed over a German-dominated coalition. In both wars the belated entry of U.S. power onto the European continent proved decisive for England and France, which were unable to dislodge Germany from Europe by themselves. And both wars saw the emergence of modern warfare on a vast scale.

But there were crucial differences between the two world wars, differences which were largely military in nature. In World War I, Germany, having knocked Russia out of the war, launched five great offensives in the spring and summer of 1918, and even Armistice Day found German troops remaining outside of Germany. In sharp contrast, the end of World War II saw Allied troops dividing Germany among themselves while an abject and humiliated German army agreed to the humiliation of unconditional surrender. Second, the Russian army, whose disintegration had led to the abasement of the Treaty of Brest Litovsk in March 1918 in World War I, in World War II stood triumphantly in Berlin, Prague, Vienna, and Budapest at the end of the war. Third, France, which had played a powerful role in the Allied cause in World War I, had to be liberated in World War II by Anglo–American forces after four shameful years of Vichy France, German occupation and collaboration, and memories of the military disaster of 1940. These military events effectively neutralized France as a great power. Fourth, while England played a major role in both wars, it exhausted itself by its supreme effort and had already begun its irreversible decline even before World War II ended. Finally, the liquidation of Japanese military power and Allied occupation of the islands ended a potentially serious threat to Soviet and U.S. dominance of the postwar era.

The military events of World War II had profound implications for the new international order after 1945. The great Red Army victories, from Stalingrad to Kursk-Orel to Berlin, and subsequent occupation of Eastern Europe, legitimized Soviet claims to great power status as the world's leading land power and second leading economy. Without these decisive military victories, the Soviet Union would have had no viable claim to such status (nor would it today). The destruction and occupation of Germany and Japan removed the only main military challengers to Soviet preeminence in Europe and Asia. The importance of the military aspects of World War II in this regard are difficult to exaggerate. Without World War II's denouement, the undeniable military capabilities of Germany and Japan, as demonstrated so graphically from 1939 to 1942, combined with their emergence as economic superpowers in the postwar era, would have severely limited Soviet aspirations. Only their elimination as military powers by 1945 opened the door for the Soviet Union, using its own military might, to become the world's second superpower.

For the United States the war was less important but still significant on its road to becoming a superpower. There had never been any doubt about U.S. economic power, which by 1945, in the wake of the destruction of Japan and Germany, accounted for nearly 50 percent of the world's GNP.[4] But in view of the United States' isolationist past and rapid withdrawal from Europe after World War I and the League of Nations debacle, there were serious questions about U.S. political capabilities and willingness to participate in the international order.

There were even greater questions about U.S. military capabilities. Until World War I U.S. victories had been won only against such military nonentities like the Indians and Mexicans and the decaying Spanish empire, and the U.S. had done poorly in the War of 1812 against the British, whose fleet burned Washington. Only in the American Civil War had the United States demonstrated impressive military skill and even advanced the art of military science. But in its aftermath, the United States had reverted to its traditional weak military posture and had once again fallen far behind the leading European powers.

In World War I, as we will see in Section 1, the United States' only important campaign came in the Meuse–Argonne battle in the last two months of the war (September-November 1918). Its 71,000 battle fatalities accounted for less than 1 percent of the battle losses in World War I.[5] This belated and limited military performance called into question U.S. power projection capabilities—although 1919 might have shown a very different picture. The U.S. retreat from political responsibility and massive demobilization to a miniscule army with weak technology in the interwar period called its capabilities into question. U.S. abstinence from the first two years of the war and weak U.S. military performance in 1942 and 1943, which we will see in Section 3, on the periphery of the European conflict did nothing to strengthen any claim to being a great military power. Thus, a moderately effective U.S. military performance and power projection in the last year of the war was vital to its postwar claims as a superpower, especially in light of the waning British contribution and weak French role.

IMPORTANCE OF ARMIES AND WARS

It is in this context that the study of armies and wars—and their nexus with politics and economics—becomes critical, for the fates of nations and great causes have traditionally been settled on the battlefield. Take the cases of the great revolutions. The outcome of the English, Russian, and Chinese Revolutions was resolved only in a series of bloody and protracted civil wars. The French

Revolution sparked a massive military struggle that lasted over two decades before the final defeat at Waterloo spelled the doom of the revolution.[6]

Similarly, World War I provoked the dissolution of four great dynastic empires (Imperial Germany, Tsarist Russia, Ottoman Empire, Austro–Hungarian Empire) and formation of a group of new European states. World War II liquidated fascism in Germany and Italy and militarism in Japan while it promoted the rise of a new world order dominated by two new superpowers. Wars have accelerated social change, with World War I helping to stimulate the February and October Revolutions in Russia, and World War II acting to establish socialism in Eastern Europe and later in China and Vietnam. On a less drastic level World War I promoted significant changes in English society after the war, while World War II brought major changes in U.S. society in the postwar era.

Military power, then, was a major factor in creating the postwar world as we know it. Internationally, wars are capable of rapidly transforming the entire international political order and even the economic order. Domestically, they reveal the strengths and weaknesses of a society; those found wanting may undergo radical changes or even perish. As Arthur Stein analyzed the impact of war on society,

> Wars are major determinants of change: they affect all aspects of a nation's domestic life and transform polity, society and economy...war alters critical facets of domestic life. At the extreme, war can simultaneously rend the national fabric, shift the balance of governmental power and narrow the gap between richer and poorer.[7]

Of course, wars and military power are not the only factors in creating the international order. The importance of economic, political, technological, cultural, and diplomatic factors in shaping the contemporary era is beyond dispute. But what we are trying to accentuate here is that military power, so often ignored or underrated, should also be seen as a major factor in its own right.

How are we to comprehend wars and military power? Military power cannot be reduced, in a form of primitive Marxism, to being merely a function of economic power. Economic capability is a necessary, but not sufficient, condition for military effectiveness. History in this century is replete with many examples of countries whose military power did not correspond to their economic power and of wars won by armies inferior in numbers and equipment to their enemies. The United States, though the predominant economic power in this century, was traditionally a weak land power until the last year of World War II. Many other examples leap to mind: the repeated Israeli victories in five wars against larger and better-equipped Arab forces, the triumph of the poorly equipped People's Liberation Army in the Chinese civil war (1946–1949), and the victory of the North Vietnamese forces over the better-equipped South Vietnamese Army in 1975.

Clearly, wars reflect far more than simply the quantity and quality of men and equipment. They include, as Martin van Creveld has ably demonstrated, the moral-organizational aspects which he labels as "fighting power."[8] These reflect the quality of military leadership, strategy and tactics, logistics, foreign interactions, and military technical capabilities. Military capacities mirror not only economic capabilities, but also overall societal capabilities, including governmental, political, and purely military capabilities. Thus, studying wars and military powers also tells us a great deal about the nations and societies involved in them—their strengths and weaknesses.

Armies themselves are not isolated from society—their structures and capabilities reflect those of the nations as a whole. Armies are a microcosm of the societies for they are created by the state as the ultimate, total institution to serve as its protector from domestic and foreign enemies. The human relationships in the army tend to reflect the class relationships in society. The nature of coercion in the military sphere is a heightened form of that extant in the civilian sphere. And the style of war tends to reflect societal morale and values.

Historically, then, wars and military power have been important forces shaping the international political order and domestic societies. They in turn have been shaped by a broad array of economic and noneconomic factors reflecting overall societal capabilities. In World War I German military superiority during the bulk of the war was not built on any corresponding economic superiority over the Triple Entente. In World War II the great German military victories of 1939–1942 were not matched by any concomitant German economic superiority; indeed in men and machines the Germans were only evenly matched with the French in 1940 and outnumbered by the Soviets in 1941. Similarly, the great Soviet victories of 1943–1945 on the Eastern front did not reflect any significant economic advantage over the Third

Reich—indeed the victories were built on an inferior base. The ultimate example, of course, is the Cold War. With a U.S. gross national product (GNP) four times that of the Soviet GNP in 1945, and with the disparity even greater when allies were counted, there was no basis for the continuing stalemate of the Cold War if only political and economic power were taken into consideration.

LITERATURE

The literature on the Cold War, while not yet rivaling that on the French Revolution, is increasingly voluminous and complex, as befits its subject matter. There are at least two ways to categorize this literature. One is through the often acrimonious debate over the causes of the Cold War between the orthodox, revisionist, and postrevisionist camps.[9] The other is by looking at the particular method of analysis, whether political, diplomatic, or economic in nature, or some combination thereof.[10] Both methods of categorization of the literature are extensively represented, with suitable changes over the decades reflecting political shifts in U.S. and Western politics and changing modes and styles in academia.

Despite this vast outpouring of work on an important topic, there remain some glaring omissions in the literature. The U.S., as befits the origins of the writers, the preponderance of academic specialization and available information (the Soviet archives are closed), is far more extensively and ably treated than is the Soviet Union. And, strikingly, although the political, diplomatic, and economic aspects of the origins of the Cold War are treated extensively and even exhaustively at times, the most obvious aspect of the dispute—the military—is routinely ignored. This is especially curious because it was precisely military events, that is, World War II, that finally liquidated the old order and created a new one, devoid of Japanese and German power. And it is even more curious since in 1945, as in 1988, it was only in the military sphere that the Soviet Union could properly be called a great power on the same magnitude as the United States.

Indeed, there is not a significant volume dealing with the military/political origins of the Cold War. The only real reference to military affairs comes in the concept, developed by Gar Alperovitz and the revisionists, of "atomic diplomacy."[11] Even here, though, the emphasis is on diplomacy rather than military events. And this concept seeks to wrench from a far broader and richer military context only one isolated and exceptional element of limited importance in the first few postwar years.

This volume seeks to restore balance in several ways. It stresses the importance of military events both in themselves and as reflection of greater economic and political variables. Only by considering military events as well can the other variables attain the necessary capacity to explain complex events. And, second, this volume focuses as much on the Soviet Union as on the United States. This can be done since there is no aspect of a country's behavior that is as externally visible or the focus of foreign interest as that of an army, especially in wartime. And, finally, we try to put this in a comparative and historical mode so as to provide the basis to ask some interesting questions as to how the United States and Russia, relatively peripheral actors in most of World War I, emerged as predominant forces on the European stage by 1945.

Given the impact of the war and military power on the modern world, one would expect a plethora of books dealing with the issues of comparative military power of the Soviet Union and United States (perhaps Germany, England, France, and Japan as well) and the military/political nexus at the end of World War II. Despite the many thousands of books written on the war, there are almost no works dealing with this question. In some cases the mere suggestion of such comparative study arouses indignation. Only the Soviet literature has tended to raise these broader questions, and this is generally quickly dismissed by Western academics as special pleading by the Soviets or reflecting peculiarities of Marxist analysis of no relevance to the West.

The great majority of Western work on World War II, as on the later Cold War, focuses on the diplomatic, political, and economic dimensions to the neglect of the military and security dimensions.[12] Richard Gabriel has written that "the study of military forces used to be at best an academic curiosity" and remains little examined, except by military specialists and military historians.[13] On a broader level there have been almost no comparative studies of the United States and Soviet Union since Zbigniew Brzezinski and Samuel Huntington's masterful study over two decades ago, *Political Power: USA/USSR.*[14]

The military specialists, mainly historians, have, of course, often refought the war on both sides, especially and naturally the U.S. side of the campaign.[15] The Soviet war effort has been recounted by far fewer Western authors in depth.[16] The broader problem here, though, is that just as Western political scientists generally are not interested in military questions, Western military specialists are usually not interested in politics, or even distrust it. They prefer the safer ground of reviewing operations and campaigns. John Erickson's two-volume set on the war on the Eastern front, for example, is a masterly, scholarly, and much needed work on the war. In the end, though, after 1,112 pages, one is still not clear why the Red Army slogged all the way to Berlin or why it got there before the U.S. army.[17]

The consequences of this are that the military aspects of World War II, especially on the Eastern front, have been largely neglected. This is particularly true of the dearth of good works on the subject.[18] As James Millar has asserted,

> The Soviet experience in World War II and its impact upon Soviet society have scarcely been charted by Western students of Soviet society. As a consequence, the war and immediate postwar periods are the least understood of the years since 1917.[19]

Why have important questions and aspects of World War II, that most formative of all modern experiences, been largely ignored and downgraded in the West in the more than four decades since 1945? Three main reasons suggest themselves. The first concerns the amount of information available on different fronts and specialists to interpret them. There are far more Western specialists who study the United States than study the Soviet Union. U.S. archives are open while the Soviet archives are closed. There are limits to this argument. After all, the Soviets have published over fifteen thousand volumes on the war. The result, though, has been clear as "outside the Soviet Union little has been published about the Soviet–German front in World War II compared with the rich literature about the war in the west."[20]

Second, Westerners, and especially Americans, have never felt compelled to reexamine the war because of their past history and great satisfaction with its outcome. For Americans, World War II was a "good war," and seems to pose no troublesome questions. After all, with relatively light casualties and no damage on the home front, the United States achieved superpower status, economic prosperity, and monopoly of the atomic bomb. The horror of the war—the Holocaust; the enormous loss of life in the Soviet Union (20 million people), Poland (6 million people), and

Yugoslavia (1.7 million people); the staggering destruction on the Eastern front—seemed very far away to a satisfied United States. Historically, the United States, unlike China, Japan, or the Soviet Union, has never known the horrors of war on its own soil except for the American Civil War. As Arthur Stein has well written,

> Americans tend to put their wars behind them; they are not continually confronted with the ravages of battle after peace has been restored. The natural defenses of the United States have often assured its security and insulation.... Europe has been a battlefield whereas the United States has escaped from conflict relatively unscathed during the last one hundred years. To Americans, war is something they go off to fight and come home to forget—it does not come to them.[21]

The final reason is that Western academics in general, and U.S. scholars in particular, do not wish to raise the troublesome questions that would inevitably come up in a comparative military history of the two world wars. To begin with, they generally lack any interest in either military affairs or comparative historical inquiry. If they were interested, there are many uncomfortable aspects of the war that a study such as this one would raise. Let us look at some of these questions which we hope to discuss and answer in this book.

IMPORTANT QUESTIONS

First, we need to understand the nature and role of the two future superpowers in World War I. At first glance it seems surprising that the U.S. role was so limited in duration while the Russian role, despite far greater involvement, was ultimately a failure. What factors, then, promoted this limited role for Russia and the United States? Why was there such a disparity between their degrees of success in World War I?

Second, if we glance back to 1939 as well as 1944, why did World War II last almost six years when the correlation of forces overwhelmingly favored the Allies?[22] Or to put it another way, what took the two future superpowers, aligned with the entire British Commonwealth and France (when unoccupied) such a long time to smash Germany and its weak allies in Italy and Eastern Europe?

The correlation of forces greatly favored the Allies (the United States, Soviet Union, and Great Britain) over the Axis powers (Germany, Japan, and Italy). The Allies had twice the population (372 million people: 186 million people), over 3 times the industrial production (60 percent: 17 percent of world production in 1936–1938), almost 4 times the steel production (113.4 million tons: 31.3 million tons in 1944), and almost 30 times the oil production (221.8 million tons: 7.5 million tons in 1944).[23]

The reason this question is unpalatable is obvious—there is no way the Soviet Union can bear the bulk of the blame for this failure. The Great Purges did harm the Red Army officer corps and the Molotov–Ribbentrop Pact in August 1939 weakened the Allied front against fascism for twenty-two months. But the four-year Red Army struggle on the Eastern front overshadowed these deficiencies. The major failings were not on the side of the Soviet Union. The biggest failure was the inability of the Western powers to stop Germany (and Japanese) imperialism in the 1930s, when it was still weak, and even to encourage it through appeasement, as at the 1938 Munich conference. Second, the war was prolonged because of the military unpreparedness of the Allies, most notably the United States, rather than the Soviet Union, which feverishly prepared for war in the 1930s. Finally, there were specifically military shortcomings such as overemphasis on strategic bombing, no second front in 1943, and weaknesses in U.S. land power.

A third, even more problematic, question concerns the final year of the war, from the Normandy landings in June 1944 to the storming of Berlin in May 1945. After June 1944 the two countries, at full mobilization capacity with enormous armed forces of over 11 million men each, sought to destroy Nazi Germany from opposite ends of the continent. And by May 1945 they had done so, dividing Europe relatively evenly between themselves, with the United States occupying France, Italy, the Benelux countries, and Western Germany, while the Soviet Union occupied all of Eastern and Central Europe, Eastern Germany, the Baltics, and Belorussia.

This, however, raises a key question of this volume: how could this relatively symmetrical division of Europe occur given the great asymmetry between the two countries in terms of their economic and political power, the state of the armies by D Day, and the degree and intensity of German resistance on the two fronts? Economically, by 1945 the United States was a colossus, totally unharmed by the war, with a GNP four times that of the

Soviet Union. During the 1939–1945 period the United States produced 8.6 times more oil (1,466.1 million tons: 171.1 million tons), 6.0 times more electricity (1,678.3 million kilowatts: 282.2 million kilowatts), and 5.5 times more steel (511.7 million tons: 93.2 million tons). And this gap widened further by 1944—the U.S. GNP increased 70 percent during the war as it emerged from the Great Depression while the Soviet GNP, devastated by the Germans, declined 20 percent in the course of the war.[24]

Second, the United States had a much stronger political position and aid from its allies than the Soviet Union. By May 1945 U.S. allies provided 2.1 million soldiers in Europe, Soviet allies .3 million—and the Soviet Union had to provide arms for its Eastern European troops while U.S. allies were largely armed without U.S. help.[25]

Third, militarily the two armies approached June 1944 in radically different states. The Red Army had been devastated in three years of continuous large-scale fighting from Moscow in 1941 to Stalingrad in 1942 to Kursk-Orel in 1943 that had cost it almost 6 million deaths and 5 million soldiers taken prisoner by the Germans. By contrast, the U.S. army was fresh and eager for combat, having suffered far less than 100,000 casualties in small scale campaigns in North Africa and the Mediterranean.[26]

Finally, German troop disposition and will to fight was stronger in the East than the West, except during the Battle of the Bulge. In June 1944 there were twice as many divisions in the East (189) as West (96); in April 1945 this situation was still roughly true (135:77) if to a lesser degree.[27] This German preponderance in the East was matched by a far greater German desire to fight the Soviets than the Americans. The battles in the East, as for East Prussia, Budapest, and Berlin, were more savage than in the West, taking the lives of 1.2 million Soviet soldiers and .2 million Allied soldiers.[28] By April 1945 German resistance in the West had disintegrated so much that the final official casualty report for 11–20 April 1945 stated that these were 43,000 German casualties and 25,800 Germans missing (largely POWs) on the Eastern front but 2,500 casualties and 268,200 soldiers missing (largely POWs) on the Western front.[29]

By contrast, the disadvantages borne by the United States in the last year—supply of weapons to its allies, longer supply lines, and second front against Japan—were relatively less. None were potentially catastrophic, as the Soviet disadvantages nearly were for Moscow. U.S. Lend Lease shipments to the Soviet Union in the last year of the war accounted for 2 percent of the U.S. war budget and bore direct fruit. Apart from trucks and specialized items such as aviation fuel, these shipments never accounted for even 10 percent of Soviet war production, although they did help to relieve bottlenecks.[30]

Supply lines were a major U.S. problem but mitigated by the use of England as a supply base and substantial English help in controlling the Atlantic. The Soviets had their own supply problems, caused by German scorched-earth policies pursued in the East and not in the West.

The war with Japan did use significant U.S. resources, especially given the great distances and often primitive bases available at the other end of the supply line. But, as we will see in Section 3, Japan was then a very weak power which had gained great victories over weak and isolated Allied and largely colonial forces in 1941 and 1942. Early Japanese victories and subsequent Japanese fanaticism on the battlefield have obscured the true weakness of Imperial Japan. As a small island it would prove uniquely vulnerable to U.S. air and naval power. Overwhelming United States economic superiority, as seen by the fact that from 1939 to 1945 the United States produced twelve times more steel and seven times more electricity than Japan, would prove decisive. During the last nine months of the war Japan suffered 897,000 fatalities, including heavy civilian casualties, the United States 32,000 fatalities. The Red Army also had to maintain large forces in the East numbering almost 1 million troops against 1 million Japanese troops in Manchuria.[31]

In short, how did the Soviet Union make such great gains in Europe, equal to the United States in the final year of the war despite these massive disabilities? This implies and involves several other related questions. Why was World War II considered a "good war" by Americans and a "disaster" or "catastrophe" by the Soviets? Why was the Soviet Union (and Great Britain) exhausted and spent by 1945 while the United States was fresh and eager for the postwar era that would lead to Pax Americana?

These questions, in turn, lead to important questions about both the Red Army and the U.S. army in the war. On the Soviet side the key question is: how could the Red Army perform so effectively in the last year of the war, despite its enormous human and material losses earlier in the war, the German devastation of the Soviet Union, and the relatively weak economy, which was further harmed by the war? The answers, such as good Stalinist political leadership, a transformed economy, politically mobilized masses supportive of Stalin, newly literate population, capable army officers, strong Communist role in the army, are likely to be displeasing to most Western specialists reluctant to acknowledge the great role played by the Red Army in the Allied victory and the high degree of effectiveness of the Soviet system. Devotees of "totalitarian" theory, unable to reconcile themselves to such positive images of the Soviet Union, prefer to console themselves that only German errors, Russian winters, and U.S. economic, political, and military power were the true prods to victory.

They are even more distraught by a second question drawn also from comparative historical inquiry. Simply put, how can we explain the great Russian/Soviet military improvement in World War II over World War I? In World War I, after humiliating defeats, the Russian army had disintegrated, Russia had undergone two revolutions and was forced to pay the price of weakness in the humiliating Tilsit peace of the 1918 Treaty of Brest Litovsk. Yet in World War II, this time against a far larger German army (with France eliminated, the Germans could deploy three times more forces in the East), and with less Allied aid than in World War I, the Soviet army not only ultimately expelled the German army from the Soviet Union but occupied half of Europe in the aftermath. How can we adequately explain this striking change in Russian/Soviet power between the two world wars?[32] Obviously, this question is even more distasteful to many Western Soviet specialists loath to see anything positive arising from the Soviet experience, and especially the Stalin era. For as Stephen Cohen has written in his provocative book, *Rethinking the Soviet Experience*, about the development of these views,

> Counter-Communism found a natural home in academic Soviet studies. . . . Simple anti-Communism—the assertion that "Communism is evil"—was not enough. The larger scholarly purpose was to show that the evil had unfolded inexorably at every historical turning point since 1917 and that professed Soviet achievements were not only empty but the antithesis of real progress.[33]

There are some equally disturbing questions on the U.S. side. First, why was the United States unable or unwilling to mount any significant military challenge to the German army until June 1944, and why did it rely heavily on British and Soviet military power to contain German expansionism? And what was the cost of this delay after June 1944? This question goes to the heart of U.S. unpreparedness for major war, reliance on air and naval power rather than land power, deferral of the second front in 1943, and diversion of resources to the Pacific. It also entails the contrast between the United States, whose homeland was not directly threatened by the war, and the Soviet Union, almost half of whose territory was overrun by the enemy, and Great Britain, which was rocketed and isolated by the German air force and navy. And it involves the question of the logistical difficulties that plagued the United States in projecting its power on the distant European continent—the price that the United States paid for the luxury of isolation from the conflict itself.

The second question is even more basic: Why was the United States unable or unwilling to translate its vast economic and political power into a truly devastating military power in Europe, even five years after the beginning of World War II? This question, which would later be asked again in Korea and Vietnam, goes to the heart of problems such as the U.S. style of warfare, problems with infantry power, diversion of economic resources to consumer satisfaction, unwillingness to take casualties, and industrial model of army management.

In this volume we will attempt to address these questions, which have important ramifications for the development of the Cold War in particular and the entire postwar era in general. The avoidance of these subjects and particular questions has tended to skew Western interpretations, and especially U.S. interpretations, of crucial events during and after World War II.

PRELIMINARY ANSWERS

In the conclusion we will assess the postwar impact of the events discussed in this book. Here we wish to give a preview of some of the answers presented concerning the U.S. and Soviet armies in World War II. On the Soviet side, the Red Army was the single most important factor in the destruction of the German army. In the process it survived massive German blows, barbarism and devastation, and occupation of Soviet territory. With enormous heroism and sacrifice, the Soviet Union fashioned a mass popular army capable of destroying the German army, the most professional in the world. By 1945 the Red Army, an effective but primitive military machine, was on the point of exhaustion. It had suffered 7.0 million deaths and 5.5 million soldiers taken prisoner by the Germans.[34] By 1945 a devastated and prostrate Soviet Union badly needed peace, economic reconstruction, defensible frontiers, and demobilization. At the same time, the efforts of the Red Army, and the destruction of Germany and Japan (mainly by the United States), gave the Soviet Union its main claim to superpower status.

The United States, by contrast, pursued an effective benefit-cost strategy with great gains (superpower status) and minimal costs (300,000 fatalities) in the war.[35] Before June 1944 the United States (unprepared for war before 1943) evaded large-scale contact with the vaunted German army, using its strong air and naval power to harass Germany. Instead it encouraged the Soviet Union and the British Commonwealth to exhaust themselves in direct confrontation with and containment of Germany. Even in the last year of the war the United States displayed only modest land power and relied heavily on air power and the ground forces of the British Commonwealth and Soviet Union to batter the German army. By 1945 the United States emerged as the world's predominant superpower, barely harmed in war, possessing enormous economic power and the world's leading air, naval, and atomic power.

This study will suggest the need for political scientists and historians to pay more attention to wars and armies, because wars and armies, as in World War II, have been significant factors in shaping history. The rise of the Soviet Union to superpower status was largely created by military events—the military destruction and occupation of Germany and Japan and the outstanding military performance of the Red Army that stood in Berlin, Vienna, Prague, and Budapest by 1945. Indeed, the Soviet claim to superpower status in 1945, as even today, largely rests on military prowess rather than its more limited political, economic, and cultural influence.

There is also a strong need to look at military power as far more than simply a function of economic power, or else the Soviet role in the war would remain inexplicable. In the same vein, simple "bean counting" of men and weapons on each side of the battlefield is fruitless. We need to look at wars as reflecting the totality of societal capabilities, including such factors as political arrangements, economic mobilization, societal mobilization, the quality of its military organization, and morale of army and society. Only then will we see that economic capabilities are necessary, but often not sufficient, conditions to assure victory on the battlefield.

FEASIBILITY

This topic is an ideal one for a comparative historical analysis, which relies primarily on secondary sources. Comparative historical analysis, with a distinguished pedigree dating back to the work of John Stuart Mill, has been used profitably by such modern scholars as Barrington Moore and Theda Skocpol.[36] It is, as Skocpol has noted, "the mode of multivariate analysis to which one resorts when there are too many variables and not enough cases."[37] The usual problems in using this method—lack of parallel historical cases, interdependence of units of comparison, and need for some theoretical bearings to guide the study—are minimized in this case. The rise of the two nations to superpower status in the 1914–1945 period forms a nice parallel case, since Soviet–U.S. relations were largely marked by coaction rather than interaction throughout most of the period. As to some theoretical considerations, we have posed important questions to guide our study earlier in this chapter.[38]

While studies in Soviet politics are often data poor and must rely on arcane techniques to produce acceptable results, this study suffers if anything from an overabundance of data and material. The two lengthy official histories of the war, and particularly the recent twelve-volume effort (1982), are especially useful.[39] There are literally many hundreds of memoirs, documents, and studies on various aspects of World War II. There is, as well, considerable Western material on the Soviet role in the war, both in the form of a number of secondary works and in numerous official Western governmental series on the war.[40]

On the U.S. side matters are even better. The United States Army has published to date seventy-four volumes in its series on the *United States Army in World War II*.[41] Many of these volumes have valuable material with regard to the U.S. role in the last year of the war. There are a huge number of memoirs, studies, and official histories on all aspects of the war. Even to list the material would be a significant undertaking.

ORGANIZATION OF VOLUME

These voluminous materials provide a solid base for examination of the questions raised in this introductory chapter. The comparative chronological perspective adopted in the volume allows for an in-depth examination of the issues.

In this volume we begin with a detailed review of U.S. and Russian military performance in World War I. This section shows how the United States, despite minimal participation and weak military performance, emerged as a great power in 1918, at the very time that Russia, despite maximal exertion and high cost, was withdrawing from the war. The intrawar chapter demonstrates the reversion to traditional political isolationism and military weakness by the United States, further devastated by the Great Depression. By contrast, the Soviet Union, though an international pariah, made great economic progress and transformed itself into a strong military power during the 1930s. In the lengthy review of World War II, Section 3 on the early war years shows a United States relatively disengaged from the war, building up its strength, and biding its time. Its only engagements were relatively small scale and low risk before 1944 in Europe. By contrast, the Soviet Union, invaded and nearly overrun by Nazi Germany in 1941, suffered enormous losses while barely holding out in the 1941–1943 period. Only after Stalingrad and Kursk–Orel was survival certain for the Soviet regime.

In the final year of the war the United States, still relying heavily on its British and Soviet allies, launched a successful invasion of France and then Germany that brought the war to a close. It achieved great victories at low cost. By contrast, the Red Army, facing greater forces and tougher opposition, incurred enormous losses in achieving its victory. By the end of the war the very different trajectories to power of the two nations would have major consequences for the lessons they would draw from the war and the perspectives they would adopt in the ensuing Cold War. The book ends with a look at these lessons and the evolution of the Cold War, as seen from the battlefields of World War II.

The basic thrust of this volume, to paraphrase Skocpol, is "to bring the military back in" to a discussion of the origins of the Cold War.[42] This necessarily entails understanding the correlation between military success and failure on one hand and political, economic, societal, and military factors on the other. This also involves analyzing the specific military aspects of the participation of the two future superpowers in the two world wars, with specific reference to the great change in Soviet power over time. In this process, we look at the sources of and relative advantages and disadvantages of the Soviet and U.S. styles of war. And, inevitably, the political and economic context of specific military decisions becomes important. In this manner the destruction of the Third Reich in 1945 serves not only as an important event in and of itself but also as a powerful symbol of the capacity of the two emerging powers to reshape the world in their own image.

This volume uses this neglected military vantage point to analyze a number of unexamined or rarely examined Western views on the world wars and the development of the Cold War. By so doing we can gain a more balanced view of the creation of the modern international political order, now over four decades old.

NOTES

1. Keegan, *Six*, p.25.
2. Nutter, *Growth*, pp.582–593.
3. Urlanis, *Wars*, pp.209–210.
4. Michel, *Second*, p.819.
5. Urlanis, *Wars*, pp.209–210.
6. See Adelman, *Revolution*
7. Stein, *Nation*, p.87.
8. See van Creveld, *Fighting*, pp.30–31, 174.
9. For the orthodox view, see Spanier, *American* and Feis, *From*. For the revisionist view see Kolko, *Politics* and Williams, *Tragedy*. For the postrevisionist view see Yergin, *Shattered* and Gaddis, *United*.
10. For diplomatic and political works, see Feis, *Churchill* and Mastny, *Russia's*. For economic works, see Paterson, *Soviet–American* and Pollard, *Economic*
11. See Alperovitz, *Atomic*.
12. See note 10 for examples of such volumes.
13. Gabriel, *Antagonists*, p.3.
14. Brzezinski and Huntington, *Political*.
15. In recent years there has been a renewal of interest in World War II among U.S. specialists. As we will see in the later chapters, the quality and sophistication of this work and willingness to ask more challenging questions (like the lack of a second front) have markedly increased in the 1980s. Among the most interesting of recent works on U.S. military history in World War II are Weigley, *Eisenhower's;* Keegan, *Six*; Hastings, *Overlord*; and Eisenhower, *Eisenhower*.

16. See, for example, Clark, *Barbarossa*; Ziemke, *Stalingrad*; Seaton, *Russo–German*; and Erickson, *Road*.

17. See Erickson, *Road*.

18. As M. Hastings recently concluded, "Even forty years after the battle, it is astonishing how many books have been published which merely reflect comfortable chauvinistic legends, and how few which seek frankly to examine the record." See Hastings, *Overlord*, p.11.

19. Millar, "Conclusion" in Linz, editor, *Impact*.

20. Dupuy and Martell, *Great*, p.1.

21. Stein, *Nation*, p.5.

22. The concept of correlation of forces is used by Soviet scholars to reflect not simply to a narrow military relationship between two opposing sides but to a broad relationship encompassing the political, economic, social, and military forces on both sides. See Lider, *Correlation*.

23. Voznesensky, *Economy*, p.10; Vorontsov, *Voennye*, p.110; and Aldcroft, *European*, p.110.

24. For the basic comparative figures see, *Istoriya vtoroi*, v.12, p.192 and Millar, *ABCs*, p.50.

25. For the U.S. figures see Ellis and Warhurst, *Victory*, p.406. For the Soviet figures and best analysis of the later stages of the war, see *Istoriya vtoroi*, v.12.

26. In the first eighteen months of the war General George Marshall reported to the secretary of war that U.S. casualties totalled 8,800 fatalities. See *War*, p.132.

27. For German division figures, see Seaton, *Russo–German*, p.458; *War*, p.97; and *Istoriya vtoroi*, v.12, p.217.

28. See MacDonald, *Last*, p.478 and *Istoriya vtoroi*, v.12, book 1, p.613.

29. See Bialer, editor, *Stalin*, p.6.

30. For the most detailed study of the subject, see Jones, *Roads*.

31. For an earlier attempt to deal with aspects of this issue, see Adelman, *Revolution*.

32. *Ibid*.

33. Cohen, *Rethinking*, pp.14–15.

34. Urlanis, *Wars*, pp.209–210.

35. *Ibid*.

36. See Nagel, editor, *John*. Mill proposed two ways to accomplish the goal of demonstrating a clear connection between possible causes with the phenomenon under study when there were relatively few cases. These were the Method of Agreement and the Method of Disagreement. Here we utilize the Method of Disagreement. This method contrasts the case in which the phenomenon that needs to be explained and the hypothesized causes are present to another case in which the phenomenon and the hypothesized causes are absent but many other similarities abound between the two cases. In this volume we contrast the different paths to power of the two rising superpowers, the Soviet Union and the United States, while noting the many similarities between the two powers and

between the two world wars that marked their ascent. For typical modern works utilizing this approach, see Moore, *Social* and Skocpol, *States.*

37. Skocpol, *States,* p.36

38. The analysis by Skocpol gives a good recent summary of the method. As she said, "Comparative history is commonly used rather loosely to refer to any and all studies in which two or more historical trajectories of nation-states, institutional complexes or civilizations are juxtaposed." See Skocpol, *States,* p.36.

39. See *Istoriya vtoroi,* 12 volumes.

40. See, for example, Werth, *Russia* and Carell, *Scorched.*

41. See Linz, editor, *Impact* and Harrison, *Soviet*

42. The phrase was inspired by the title of Skocpol's coedited work with Evans and Rueschemeyer, *Bringing.*

Section 1
World War I

2

An Economic and Political Overview of World War I

The events of World War I, now almost three quarters of a century old, seem distant and remote. The mindless, endless slaughter on the Somme and at Passchendaele, the two spirited French defenses of Paris and on the Marne, and the humiliation and disintegration of the Russian army in the East all seem to belong to a different world. So, too, do the leaders of the major powers involved in that conflict—men such as Tsar Nicholas II, Kaiser Wilhelm, and Georges Clemenceau. The openly imperial aspirations of nearly all of the great powers, save for Wilson's United States and later Lenin's Soviet Union, seem far closer in spirit to the Congress of Vienna in 1815 than to the post-1945 modern age. Why, then, apart from pure historical interest, should we be concerned with such far-off events, and their military aspects at that, in discussing the advent of the modern age?

Three reasons present themselves. First, World War II was not an isolated event without historical antecedent. Rather, World War I and World War II cannot be easily separated, as they represented two separate rounds of the same macroconflict. Politically, in both wars the central issue in Europe was that of German predominance. Economically, all major powers in both wars were forced to develop full-scale mobilization of their resources, in which the anti-German coalition enjoyed a distinct superiority. This total mobilization of men and resources over a period of years in both world wars greatly strained domestic structures and accelerated international and domestic changes. Materially, they caused enormous human losses and physical damage on a vast scale and promoted political centralization, bureaucratic control, and incorporation of the lower classes into the polity. Militarily, the world wars ushered in an era of modern, mass technological warfare.

Second, the events of World War II can only be truly understood through comparison with World War I. Given the many similarities between the two wars, the differences attained especial importance. The most important one is the most glaring: why was there such a vast improvement in Russian/Soviet military power between the two world wars? And how could this happen in the slowly changing field of military power, especially given the far greater German military force deployed against Russia/the Soviet Union in World War II than in World War I and the heightened impact of modern technology (in which Germany enjoyed a natural superiority) in World War II? And, correspondingly, how do we assess the much more extensive U.S. military role in World War II than in World War I? And, last but not least, how do we assess the comparison of Russian/Soviet and U.S. military performance in World War II against the backdrop of World War I?

Third, World War I was important in and of itself. It marked the beginning of the modern era, with the rise of the Bolsheviks to power in Russia, the involvement of the United States in European affairs, and the liquidation of four dynastic empires. World War I denoted the beginning of the end of the classic Eurocentric balance-of-power politics that had reigned for almost three centuries since the Treaty of Westphalia in 1648. And it marked the emergence of two philosophies that would dominate the world after World War II, Wilsonian liberalism and Leninist socialism. World War I seriously weakened the old order, setting the stage for its total demolition in World War II and creation of a new international order after 1945.

SIMILARITIES AND DIFFERENCES
BETWEEN TWO WORLD WARS

There were a number of important similarities between the two world wars. In both world wars the principal front was in Europe where a powerful German-dominated coalition held sway as the single strongest force in Europe in the center of the continent. Superior German military power could be destroyed only by a heterogeneous and uneasy Allied coalition (France, England, United States, and Russia) in a prolonged four-to-six-year struggle. So strong was German power and the natural geographic and military advantages it enjoyed in the center of Europe that even at the beginning of the last year of the war (November, 1917, May, 1944) its troops were outside of Germany. Only in a series of enormous military massacres (Somme and Passchendaele in World War I, Moscow, Stalingrad, Kursk-Orel, and Berlin in World War II) could the German army finally be decimated.

In both wars the United States, the world's greatest economic power, remained militarily unprepared and eager to stay out of the conflict. It was protected by its oceans and weak neighbors. Until the last year of the war the United States relied heavily on its allies, who exhausted themselves in battling the Germans. Then, fresh while everyone else was weakened, the United States provided a decisive blow to waning German power. In this way the German coalition was finally defeated by the Allied coalition, which enjoyed a great superiority in correlation of forces in the economic, political, and demographic spheres.

There were strong similarities between the U.S. and Russian/Soviet war roles in World Wars I and II. In both wars the Russian/Soviet armies suffered severe defeats early in the war and took far more casualties (twenty to forty times more) than the U.S. armies. In World Wars I and II the Russian/Soviet economy was severely harmed by the war while the U.S. economy flourished as it went from strength to strength. And neither army performed outstandingly in the two world wars, each stressing its great national assets in place of a superior, high-quality land army. For the Americans this would be an emphasis on high-technology warfare, for the Russians a stress on overwhelming quantity of men and machines. In this way the two future great powers, though mediocre military powers in terms of their level of efficiency per unit, could utilize their huge physical sizes, geographical remoteness from the center of Europe, vast human and natural resources, and industrial powers to compensate for their problematic military powers.

The two world wars were the first genuinely modern wars, involving many millions of men and huge quantities of equipment and materiel. The technological revolution was amply reflected in and accelerated by the world wars. The most direct linkage between the two world wars is shown by the fact that by 1918 the major weapons dominant in the Second World War—including tanks, planes, and motorized transportation—had already appeared in force on the battlefield. While World War I was noted for its technical innovation, World War II was famous for its tactical innovation.

Each of the major powers applied the lessons it thought it had learned from World War I to World War II. The French, seeing the power of defense and superior German military capability in World War I, built the strong Maginot line to protect themselves from similar German offensives in the next war. The British, still reeling from the massive casualties of World War I, adopted a peripheral strategy in World War II of avoiding direct and massive confrontation with German power, until it was clearly on the wane. The United States, seeing the advantages of great gains at minimal costs through avoidance of frontal assaults on German positions until near the end of World War I, sought to repeat the strategy in World War II. The Russians, having been bloodied in pointless offensives against the superior German army in World War I, sought to act more cautiously and build up their technical capability against the Germans in World War II. And, finally, the Germans, having seen their superior military capability blunted by the trench warfare of World War I, tried in World War II to utilize fluid blitzkrieg warfare and not get bogged down.

This is *not* to say that the two world wars were fundamentally alike without significant differences. Indeed, there were some serious differences and, given the many similarities, these attain special importance. The greatest difference, and the one most relevant to our study, was the role of Russia. In World War I the Russians sacrificed a great deal (almost two million fatalities) and gained very little. They suffered repeated defeats at the hands of the Germans and finally withdrew from the war in the disastrous Treaty of Brest Litovsk in March 1918. During World War I the Western front was the decisive theater for destroying German military power. The Eastern front, while important, was only a secondary one. During the entire four-year struggle, only in 1915 did the Germans ever make a major effort in the East.

But, during World War II the Eastern front was the main theater for the destruction of German military power, with the Western front remaining peripheral until June 1944. Even after D Day, the bulk of German forces and fighting power lay in the East. At great sacrifice the Red Army ultimately earned the most credit for the destruction of the vaunted Wehrmacht. Given the usual slowness in changes in military power in most countries over time, the remarkable transformation in Russian/Soviet power, from vanquished and humiliated force in 1918 to triumphant, nascent superpower in 1945, demands attention as one of the central themes of this volume.

A second principal difference concerns the nature of warfare in the two world wars. The defense predominated in World War I, as seen in the long paralysis and slow movement of trench warfare. By contrast, the offense predominated in World War II, as seen in rapid mobile victories of the German armies in the 1939–1942 period and the Allied armies during 1943–1945. Tanks, planes, and mechanized transportation restored the mobility and fluidity so lacking in World War I and produced the decisive victories and defeats so rare in the earlier war. This heightened technological sophistication, and concomitant increased demands on generalship made it even more difficult for the peripheral powers of World War I—Russia and the United States—to gain the necessary capabilities to become the predominant powers of World War II.

The third major difference, worthy of note although of less importance to our study, concerns the impact of war on civilians. Despite German atrocity stories, World War I was relatively free from the murderous maltreatment of civilians so common in this century. World War II, however, was marked by mass genocide practiced by the Germans and Japanese. Of particular relevance were the atrocities committed by the Germans against the Jews in the Holocaust, the mass terrorism practiced by the Germans on occupied Soviet territories, and the German liquidation of several million Soviet prisoners of war. German barbarism in the East helped numb Soviet resistance in the early phase of war but later galvanized Soviet patriotism and stiffened Soviet support for the war effort. This German behavior had, by contrast, almost no effect on the U.S. war effort, which was remote from these atrocities. German barbarism in the West was often matched by Japanese barbarism in the East, especially in China. Furthermore, fluid fronts and area bombing of cities inevitably sharply accelerated civilian casualties in World War II over World War I.

Fourth, there were major differences in Russian/Soviet foreign policy between the two wars. In World War I, Tsarist Russia recklessly plunged into the war from the very start despite an abysmal lack of preparation. The result was a series of disasters, beginning with Tannenberg in August 1914. Throughout the war the Russian army, responding to urgent pleadings from beleaguered allies on the Western front, repeatedly launched ill-conceived offensives in the East that led to recurrent disasters. By contrast, Stalinist foreign policy, more realistic about Soviet military weakness, worked assiduously to keep the Soviet Union out of the war, even reaching the notorious Molotov-Ribbentrop Pact with the Germans in August 1939. The Soviets, while agreeing to a loose coordination with their Western allies, operated solely in terms of Soviet national interest and with greater awareness of their capabilities during World War II.

In addition, the contrast between the role and inter-relationship of the two powers in the two world wars is strong. In World War I the two powers were totally out of synchronization, with the United States only entering the war in April 1917, while Russia, with the 1917 February and October Revolutions, was leaving the war. By contrast, from December 1941 until May 1945, the Soviet–U.S. alliance was the central axis in the defeat of the Third Reich. In World War I, the Russians and Americans were largely peripheral to the main struggle on the Western front. Both relied heavily on British and French arms and expertise for the fighting. But, in World War II the two future superpowers projected themselves as the central figures in the war.

RUSSIAN AND U.S. PARTICIPATION IN WORLD WAR I

Let us turn to a detailed analysis of aspects of U.S. and Russian participation in World War I. Neither side remained in the war from beginning to end, with Russian participation lasting effectively for a little over two years. Most striking of all in limiting their future postwar roles was their heavy dependence on their allies, mainly England and France, in fighting the war. To this extent both Russia and the United States remained peripheral actors in the main struggle on the Western front throughout the war.

Let us now look at the extent of this dependence of the two future superpowers on England and France. A generation later England and France would be strongly dependent on the United States and the Soviet Union. Especially important was the great reliance of the U.S. army on the British and French armies in

World War I. The United States remained aloof from the conflict in 1914 and 1915 and did relatively little to prepare for war in 1916. Thus, the Americans, effectively gearing up for war by 1919, were unable to attain a truly effective or independent force. The symbols of this dependency were the constant battles over the creation of an independent U.S. army in 1918 and the ritualistic subordination of General John Pershing to French Marshal Henri Petain as head of all Allied forces in France.

The U.S. dependency ran the gamut from A to Z and began before the U.S. army even saw battle. Indeed, it started before the U.S. army reached France, for the majority (51.2 percent) of all U.S. soldiers traveled to Europe in British ships. Once there, the Allies provided significant training in the grim realities of trench warfare. The French provided nearly all the land transportation to move the U.S. troops, who used French and Italian horses. Indeed, roughly 60 percent of all U.S. supplies and equipment were purchased in Europe (10 million tons) rather than brought from the United States (7 million tons).[1]

The United States was not the arsenal of democracy in World War I. Except in small arms, the American Expeditionary Force was almost totally reliant on English and French weapons. Despite American technological capabilities, the English and French produced most of the tanks and airplanes used by the Americans in France. The commander of the American Expeditionary Force, General John "Black Jack" Pershing, has written that

> With no previous plans for their manufactures, the prospects of obtaining tanks from home by the time they should be required for operations seemed so remote that it appeared best to arrange, if possible, for their manufacture overseas.[2]

As a result, the U.S. army had no standard U.S.-made tanks (except for some light ones) and a few U.S. planes (forming only a minority of its force) even by the end of the war in November 1918.

Nowhere was this U.S. dependency so visible and evident as in the realm of artillery. Artillery was the most potent weapon of the war. Yet the reliance of the American Expeditionary Force on its allies for cannons and shells was almost total right through the armistice accord. When General Pershing complained about an "acute" problem in November 1917 when the French did not deliver artillery shells, the War Department in Washington tartly informed Pershing that "the French Government must furnish it, for there is no other way of getting it. At the present time there is not in this country any actual output of ammunition of the types mentioned. None has been expected."[3] Even by August 1918, sixteen long months after the United States' entry into the war, the American Expeditionary Force had not received a single cannon from home.

In the first major U.S. offensive of World War I, at St. Mihiel, in September 1918, not one of the 3,000 guns used in the battle was produced in the United States. Even on the last day of the war, 11 November 1918, a staggering 86 percent of the artillery pieces and 99 percent of the artillery rounds used in combat by the U.S. army in France were produced not in the United States but by U.S. allies in Europe.[4]

Table 2.1 shows the remarkable extent of U.S. dependency on foreign supplies by the end of World War I.

Thus, while the United States did manage to produce roughly two-thirds of its smaller weapons by the end of the war, it still had to rely on British and French factories for over 80 percent of its tanks, planes, and cannons. These, then, were the stark realities facing the American Expedition Force in France during World War I. As Winston Churchill wrote to the British War Cabinet in July 1918,

> During the rest of 1918 and the first half of 1919 the limiting factor on the employment of American troops will not be men or tonnage of food, but equipment of all kinds. For the time being the American munition program, particularly in guns and aeroplanes, is woefully behind their available resources in manpower. Unless we and the French are able to supplement promptly every deficiency in the American munitions program, the despatch of very large numbers of their troops may be retarded from this course. . . . The first 1,000,000 who have come have been almost entirely equipped by the British and the French. But for the fact that we were able to supply them with artillery, machine guns, rifles, trench mortars, etc., and to feed them with munitions of all kinds, no use in the present crisis could have been made of this first million.[5]

Similarly, the Russian army in World War I was also highly dependent on English and French help in fighting the German army. The sources of this dependency were somewhat different. U.S. dependency was caused primarily by the lack of military

Table 2.1 Sources of Weapons Used by the American Expeditionary Force in France in 1918

Weapon	Manufactured in United States	in Europe
caissons	70.5% (6,365)	29.5% (2,658)
automatic weapons	67.7% (83,868)	32.3% (40,484)
trench mortars	34.8% (891)	65.2% (1,664)
airplanes	19.1% (1,213)	80.9% (5,132)
tanks	12.5% (36)	87.5% (253)
artillery pieces	11.9% (502)	88.1% (3,692)

Source: 1. James Huston, *The Sinews of War: Army Logistics 1775–1953* (Washington, D.C.: Government Printing Office, 1966), pp.344–346.

preparedness before 1917, a weak military tradition, a poor plan of economic mobilization, and difficulties in shipping massive weapons across the ocean to the war zones. Once U.S. mobilization swung into full gear, the U.S. army was prepared by late 1919 to field a four-million-man army in Europe largely equipped by U.S. factories. But while Tsarist Russia suffered from many of the same maladies facing the United States at the onset of its entry into the war, it also lacked the two great U.S. advantages that would ultimately allow the United States to overcome these disadvantages: a strong economy, and a capable and effective political system. The result was a fatal reliance by Russia on foreign weapons that would endure throughout the entire course of Russia's participation in World War I.

The degree of Russian dependency on Allied weaponry to fight well in World War I was remarkable. Table 2.2 makes the point very clearly.

The Russians had to import even elementary, low-technology products—they imported one billion bullets, which was 20.4 percent of their needs. In rifles and machine guns, two critical staples of infantry fighting, the Russians had to import 43.1 percent and 60.2 percent of their needs. And in more

Table 2.2 Sources of Weapons Acquired by the Russian Army in World War I

| Weapon | Manufactured in | |
	Russia	Foreign Countries
bullets	79.6% (3.9 billion)	20.4% (1 billion)
rifles	56.9% (3.3 million)	43.1% (2.5 million)
machine guns	39.8% (28,000)	60.2% (42,000)
planes and motors	37.7% (4,900)	62.3% (8,900)

Source: 1. G. I. Shigalin, *Voennaya ekonomika v pervuyu mirovuyu voinu (1914–1918)* (Moscow: Voenizdat, 1956), pp.170–172, 174, 179.

sophisticated, higher-technology weapons like planes and tanks, the reliance on foreign imports was even greater. Such a huge reliance on Allied weapons was to contribute to the demise of the Russian army. The power of the German army would inevitably push England and France to reserve the great majority of their war production for their own hard-pressed armies and later for the U.S. army on the same Western front. At the same time, the effective German blockade of Russia forced the Allies to send convoys to ports, such as Arkhangel'sk, Murmansk, and especially Vladivostok, quite remote from the battlefield.

This heavy Russian dependency on foreign weapons hampered the Russian army and sharply limited the independence of Russian foreign policy. The effects were seen shortly after the beginning of the war in August 1914 when Russia, like the other European powers, was caught unprepared for the massive demands of a protracted war. Already by the end of 1914 it was apparent that, without large-scale foreign supplies, the Russian army would be incapable of any significant offensive action in the early months of the new year.

In 1915 after the German victories over Russia in Poland, Major General Alfred Knox, British military attaché to Russia, observed that only "if the Allies in the West were able to provide for its rearmament, the Russian army would once more take the offensive in spring 1916. The main problem of the next six to eight months seemed to be the rearmament of Russia."[6] And in July 1916 at the inter-Allied conference at the British War Office, General Beliayev, complaining that Russian equipment was still "very inferior to that of the Allies," conceded the extent of Russian dependency on the West when he pleaded that

> It [Russian equipment] must be improved at all costs, even at the price of entrenching upon the more generous equipment of the English and French armies. It is not to the interests of the Allies that the Russian offensive and possibility of future offensives should be rendered impossible.[7]

Beliayev's concerns were quite justified, as the disintegration of the Russian army in 1917 in the wake of two revolutions would demonstrate. Even the shipment of over five million tons of equipment from England to Russia during the war could not remedy the situation.[8] Not until the United States and Russia could reduce their heavy dependency on Western Europe would they be able to emerge as superpowers by the end of the next world war.

The enormous disproportion in military (and civilian) losses suffered by the two powers in World War I would later be replicated in World War II. Indeed the staggering difference between the very heavy casualties suffered by the Russian army—casualties so heavy that they helped promote the disintegration of the Russian army and February and October Revolutions of 1917—and the extremely light casualties suffered by the U.S. army was one of the significant features of the First World War. The figures tell the story in stark and somber detail: 1,500,000 Russian battle deaths, 71,000 U.S. battle deaths. Twenty-one Russian soldiers were killed in battle for every one U.S. soldier. If disease, accidents, and fatalities while in POW status are added in, the figures become even greater: 1,800,000 Russian soldier deaths, 114,000 U.S. soldier deaths in Europe and at home. Russian military losses were as appalling as they were fruitless, with Russia having the dubious honor of attaining first place among the entente powers in this area. France (1.3 million) and England (.7 million) lagged far behind. Only Germany, the sole major power to fight on both major European fronts, edged out Russia in this category with 2.0 million military losses.

The United States, by dint of its belated entry into the war, unreadiness to fight seriously until the fall of 1918 (and even then at reduced strength), and extreme distance from the major battle-fields, suffered very few casualties in the Great War. Its military losses placed it tenth in the world, after Italy (578,000), Serbia and Montenegro (278,000), Rumania (250,000), and Bulgaria (88,000). The United States incurred 1.2 percent of the 9.4 million military losses stemming from the war.

And on a per capita basis the losses were even lighter, given the great population of the United States. Calculated on the basis of military losses per 1,000 people, Serbia and Montenegro lost 57 men, France 34 men, Rumania 33 men, Russia 11 men—and the United States 1.1 men. Even in the final months of the war, when the U.S. army belatedly entered the fray in force, the U.S. losses remained disproportionately low. From July–November 1918 the 200,000 American casualties represented only 15 percent of Allied casualties while the U.S. army was holding 25 percent of the front. In short, the Americans proved as adept at avoiding casualties in World War I as the Russians were in incurring them.[9]

An interesting tangent connected to this was a strong disparity between the size of the land armies the two powers were able to field in Europe during the war. With their huge populations, both powers could have fielded the two largest armies in Europe. But Russia was severely hampered by its antiquated political structure and backward economy, while the United States was handicapped by its late entry into the war, military unpreparedness, and geographical distance from the European battlefield. Nevertheless, the historic patterns prevailed, with Russia maintaining, from geo-graphic necessity, a far larger land army in Europe than the United States. An important corollary of interest to our later study of World War II is that, despite a population more than twice the size of Germany, Russia was unable to maintain an army larger than that of Germany. Indeed, at crucial times the German army not only was qualitatively superior but even quantitatively superior to the Russian army. Table 2.3 makes this point quite strongly.

Even taking into account that the average U.S. "square" divi-sion with 22,000 men was at least twice the size of a typical Euro-pean division, the disparity between 42 U.S. divisions in November 1918 and 202 Russian divisions in September 1917 was consider-able. The gap between the two sides would have narrowed sharply only with the proposed U.S. expansion to 80 divisions in 1919, al-though this is a moot point.

Table 2.3 Number of German, Russian, and U.S. Infantry Divisions at the Front in World War I

Date	Germany	Russia	United States
August 1914	94	108	0
December 1914	117	108	0
May 1915	149	112	0
February 1916	159	136	0
August 1916	169	142	0
July 1917	232	?	0
October 1917	234	202	3
March 1918	234	0	5
July 1918	235	0	25
November 1918	210	0	42

Source: 1. Marc Ferro, *The Great War 1914–1918*, translated by Nicole Stone (London: Routledge, Kegan and Paul, 1969), p.129.

RUSSIAN AND U.S. MILITARY PERFORMANCE

As we turn to an analysis of the actual performance of the U.S. and Russian armies in the Great War, a few general comments are in order. Any overall appreciation of the role of the United States and Russia in the conflict is bound to be complex and variegated. The Russian role in World War I is especially hard to grasp. There was the long and torturous transformation from vaunted "steamroller" prematurely invading East Prussia in August 1914 to the vanquished power signing the humiliating Treaty of Brest Litovsk that took Russia out of the war in March 1918 at great price.

Several things are clear. One is that the Russians were never a decisive force against the Germans, as they suffered repeated defeats from Tannenberg in August 1914 to the German advance on Petrograd in February 1918. Not one time did the Russians ever achieve a significant victory over the German army or even seriously threaten Germany itself (after the early disastrous probes). The Allied victory over Imperial Germany was won preeminently by the English, French, and, at the end of the war,

U.S. forces on the Western front, not by the weak and oft defeated Russian army on the Eastern front.

There was, however, another side to Russian involvement against Germany in the East. In failure, the Russians were able to force the Germans to divide their forces between East and West, easing the intense pressure on the Allies in the West. It is almost a military maxim that the battle of the Marne in 1914 was won at least in part by the Russian disaster at Tannenberg and invasion of East Prussia, for this diverted German troops to ward off the menace from the East. Also, the existence of a large and untested Russian army led to modifications of the Schlieffen plan, and thus contributed to the ability of the French army to hold on and block the path to Paris in 1914. By the end of 1914 there were in the East 35 German divisions, during 1915 65 divisions, in 1916 42 to 47 divisions, and in 1917 64 to 84 divisions.[10] On average, roughly one-third of all German divisions were in the East during the war, with the figure rising to 40 percent during the German offensive in 1915. Without Russia the Allies lacked manpower superiority over the Central Powers. And even though the Russian army accounted for only 20 percent of German casualties in World War I, this also meant that Germany suffered 300,000 military fatalities in the East.[11] As Lord Balfour told Lord Nicholson at the end of December 1914, "The war cannot possibly be conclusive in our favor unless the Western Allies have Russia wholeheartedly on their side in the East."[12]

The Russian effort in the war cannot simply be measured along one dimension. The Russian involvement in the war was especially crucial in 1914 when the British Expeditionary Force remained a small force in France. In 1915 this factor diminished with the English buildup in France, but the German inability to knock Russians out of the war ensured a protracted war which would favor the Allies with their superiority in correlation of forces. In 1916 and early 1917 the Russians remained a factor until their demise with the twin revolutions of 1917.

The Russian contribution was greater on the secondary fronts. While the German army was the main force in the coalition facing the Allies, it was far from the only force. Its three main allies— Austro-Hungary, Turkey, and later Bulgaria—provided significant forces against the Allies in Eastern Europe, the Balkans, and the Middle East. What they lacked in quality they made up for in quantity. They provided roughly 40 percent of all Central Powers' divisions at the front during the war, and sometimes even more. In

December 1914, 117 German divisions were almost matched by 57 Austro–Hungarian divisions and 37 Turkish divisions. By August 1916, 169 German divisions were significantly aided by 70 Austro–Hungarian divisions, 53 Turkish divisions, and 12 Bulgarian divisions. Yet in July 1918, 109 Austro–Hungarian and Turkish divisions provided a strong supplement to 235 German divisions.[13] Only near the end of the war did these other fronts disintegrate, leaving the German army alone to face the Allied coalition.

The Russian effort on these lesser fronts was quite impressive as the Russian army bore the brunt of the Allied war effort in these theaters. In the Eastern theater, where the Germans (except in 1915) left the bulk of the fighting to its allies, the Russians proved more than a match for the hapless Austro–Hungarian troops. Twice in the war the Russians gained important victories over them and by December 1916 the Austro–Hungarian army was largely finished as an effective fighting force. Even at its nadir in June 1917, a weakened Russian army could advance against the Austro–Hungarian army. Overall, over 60 percent of all Austro–Hungarian soldiers who died in the war, or 450,000 men, perished on the Eastern front at the hands of the Russian army. Similarly, the Russians, despite bad terrain and long communication and supply lines, held the front against the Turks. The Russians inflicted 60 percent of all Turkish casualties suffered in World War I, or 150,000 Turkish fatalities.[14] The Russians played a much more significant role in the secondary theater of operations than in the primary theater.

The implications for the future were important. Even in the decrepitude of the waning years of Tsarism, Russia was capable of defeating lesser powers and exerting a significant effort against Germany. However, World War I ultimately so strained the fabric of Russia's backward economy and antiquated political system that it collapsed in the 1917 revolutions. The potential was surely there, and a new and progressive regime that could mobilize Russia's vast human and natural resources, modernize its economy, and transform the political system could produce a very different result. Only time would tell.

The U.S. role in the war was also distinctive. The contrasts with the Russian role are striking. While the Russians plunged recklessly and full scale into the war from the onset of the vast conflagration, the Americans stayed out of the war for almost three years, and then entered very slowly and reluctantly. The American buildup was so slow that the U.S. army did not become a significant factor on the Western front until September 1918, a little over two months before the armistice. The relative slowness of the U.S. mobilization reflected intrinsically both U.S. factors as well as the fact that both Germany and Russia had been building up since 1911. While Russia labored mightily (spending more of its national income on the war than any other great power) for a protracted period of time, the United States fully mobilized for only a short period.

The ultimate results were ironic, because the great Russian effort was capped by failure while the brief U.S. intervention produced success. After the events of 1917—French army mutiny, Russia's leaving the war, Italian defeat at Caporetto, and British losses in Flanders—the two million U.S. soldiers would prove important to ultimate Allied victory. And this effort, again different from the Russian effort, was focused on the main Western front, with no effort at all in secondary theaters in Italy, the Balkans, the Middle East, or Eastern Europe.

RUSSIAN AND U.S. ECONOMIC POWER IN WORLD WAR I

A brief review of economic data similarly highlights the sharp disparity between U.S. and Russian economic power during World War I. Ironically, the Russians actually had a strong advantage in manpower with a population of 171 million people, compared to only 93 million people in the United States. As a result of this, Russia could mobilize 12 million men for the war, compared to 11 million for Germany, 8 million for France, and 4.5 million for the tardy United States.[15] Tsarist Russia fought only by a major effort—one that helped push Tsarist Russia over the precipice and into the abyss of revolution below. Russian spending was markedly inferior only to that of Germany and England. Table 2.4 shows both the magnitude of the Russian effort and its limitations.

Table 2.4 also clearly demonstrates the stringent limitations on Russian power. While the Russian war effort lasted roughly three years, that of the United States endured seriously for only two years or less. Recalculating these figures on a yearly basis, U.S. military spending (64 billion marks) more than doubled Russian military spending (30 million marks). The gap yawns ever wider if

Table 2.4 Military Expenditures by the Great Powers in World War I (billions of marks)

Country	Expenditure
England	176.1
Germany	160.0
United States	128.3
France	103.2
Russia	90.3
Austro/Hungary	87.4

Source: l. *Rossiya v mirovoi voine 1914–1918 goda (v tsifrakh)* (Moscow: Central Statistical Administration, 1925) p.92.

we consider that the Russians mobilized almost three times more men for war (12 million men) than the Americans (4.5 million men). Russia maintained more than three times more men in Europe in 1917 (7 million men) than the United States had there in November 1918 (2 million men). This implied that the United States spent six times more per soldier in Europe than Tsarist Russia. Of course these figures are somewhat inflated by the far longer U.S. supply lines, greater equipment, and higher start-up costs, because the U.S. war effort geared to maximum efficiency in 1919, not 1918. Nevertheless, the United States enjoyed strong advantages in war spending over Tsarist Russia.[16]

The roots of this lay, of course, in the awesome economic power of the United States as the leading country in the international capitalist order and the woeful economic performance of Tsarist Russia despite successful reforms in the two decades before the guns of August sounded in 1914. Statistics limn the sad story of Tsarist Russia: in 1913 the national income of the United States (96.0 billion rubles) was almost five times the national income of Tsarist Russia (20.3 billion rubles). Given the larger population of Russia, the gap was even greater on a per capita level. The United States in 1913 enjoyed a per capita income equivalent to 1,033 rubles—nine times greater than the 119 rubles in Tsarist Russia at that time.

Equally important was the sad fact that despite the enormous population advantage enjoyed by Russia (171 million people) over Germany (65 million people), Germany still had a higher national income (24.3 billion rubles) than Russia (20.3 billion rubles).[17]

This vast U.S. economic superiority was strongly reflected in statistics on vital industrial products that served as the sinews of modern war. Table 2.5 shows just how far behind the United States—and for that matter, its archrival Germany—Tsarist Russia lagged in 1913, on the eve of the Great War.

Table 2.5 shows the extreme backwardness of Russia in all major areas of industrial activities related to war. The United States produced 14 times more coal, 7 times more pig iron, and over 6 times more steel than Russia. And on a per capita basis the figures were even more disheartening as the United States produced 27 times more coal, 13 times more pig iron and 12 times more steel per capita than Tsarist Russia.

The statistics made morose reading for the Russian war planners facing a German foe with 3-5 times the industrial production of steel and pig iron in absolute terms and 9 times in per capita terms. Germany and the United States belonged to a different world than Tsarist Russia, as World War I so strikingly demonstrated.

Russian war production lagged seriously behind not only U.S. war production but that of Germany, France, and England. Given the enormous disparity in population, this was humiliating for Russia—and deadly for its chances of victory in war. Since the U.S. war effort was short and would not hit full stride until 1919, any true understanding of the Russian war economy necessitates comparison with other European powers. Taking into account that the Russians were at war for roughly 80 percent of World War I, and the Americans for approximately 40 percent we also compare these two war economies for the duration of their participation in the war with the German and French war economies in Table 2.6.

Table 2.6 shows that the United States could produce war material roughly comparable to Tsarist Russia in general, and far superior to it in sophisticated weapons as tanks and planes, in half the time it took Tsarist Russia and before production hit full throttle. Particularly disturbing to Russian war planners was the marked superiority of the French war economy and overwhelming superiority of the German war economy to their efforts. Beleaguered France produced twice as many artillery pieces and over ten times as many machine guns as its far larger Eastern ally. In the more sophisticated weapons arena the gap deep-ended to a

Table 2.5 Economic Production of Russia, the United States, and Germany in 1913 (million of tons)

Country	Steel	Product Pig Iron	Coal	Grain
United States	31.8	34.7	517.0	146.1
Russia	4.9	4.6	36.1	123.0
Germany	17.6	16.8	277.3	85.4

Source: 1. Paul Gregory, *Russian National Income 1885–1913* (Cambridge: Cambridge University Press, 1982), pp.155-156.

Table 2.6 War Production of Russia, United States, Germany, and France in World War I (thousands)

Countries	Rifles	Weapons Machine Guns	Cannons	Tanks	Planes
Russia	3,300	28.0	11.7	0	3.5
U.S.A.	3,500	75.0	4.0	1.0	13.8
Germany	8,547	280.0	64.0	.1	47.3
France	2,500	312.0	23.2	5.3	52.1

Source: 1. A.A.Strokov, *Vooruzhennye sily i voennoe iskusstvo v pervoi mirovoi voine* (Moscow: Voenizdat, 1974), p.586.

chasm. France produced 52,100 planes and 5,100 tanks; Russia produced 3,500 planes and no tanks.

Germany even further outdistanced Tsarist Russia, especially in the more basic weapons as rifles and cannons. There Germany produced 2.5 times more rifles and 5.5 times more cannons. The numbers were somber, the record was clear. While the United States possessed the economic capacity to become a great military power of the first order, Tsarist Russia did not and lagged behind not only the United States and Germany but even England and France.

Both future superpowers failed to emerge as dominant forces in World War I but the root causes were markedly different. The United States had the political and economic capacity to dominate the war, if only by volume of men and machines, but chose not to do so. This occurred through political decisions that kept it out of the war until 1917, and even then it was militarily unprepared. By contrast, Tsarist Russia openly aspired to a predominant role on the European continent but lacked the political organization or advanced industrialized economy so essential to the attainment of this goal.

From the perspective of 1914, or even 1918, the future prospect of a world dominated by these two countries three decades later seemed unlikely. The United States seemed to lack the will or inclination to translate its economic power into military or political power. Even less likely as a candidate was Russia, whose dismal prospects seemed confirmed by its weak and lagging pace of economic development. Given the grave difficulties blocking future economic development and the political crisis engulfing a new and weakened radical regime then embroiled in a bitter civil war, the likelihood of major improvement in the Russian economy seemed minimal. If anything, it seemed more likely that a disintegrating Russia would fall ever further behind the vibrant and booming U.S. economy in the postwar era.

NOTES

1. DeWeerd, *President*, pp.208, 235 and Pershing, *My*, v.2, pp.3, 308.
2. Pershing, *My*, v.2, p.232.
3. *Ibid.*, p.221.
4. DeWeerd, *President*, p.206, Pershing, *My*, p.194, and Falls, *First*, v.2, p.337.
5. Churchill, *World*, v.4, pp.212–213.
6. See Adelman, *Revolution*, p.73.
7. Neilson, *Strategy*, p.200.
8. *Ibid.*, p.317.
9. Urlanis, *Wars*, pp.209-210 and Brook-Shepherd, *November*, p.389.
10. Adelman, *Revolution*, p.70.
11. Urlanis, *Wars*, pp.55–56.
12. Neilson, *Strategy*, p.61.
13. Ferro, *Great*, p.129.
14. Urlanis, *Wars*, pp.55–56.
15. Robbins, *First*, pp.82–83.
16. Gregory, *Russian*, p.155.
17. Edmonds, *Short*, pp.9–10 and Hart, *Real*, pp.47–50. These are two of the classic works on the war and remain well worth reading today.

3

Russian and U.S. Armies in Battle

Military events are important in and of themselves and are not reducible simply to economic or political factors. The events of World War II cannot be fully understood without analysis of World War I. The fate of the international political and economic order was decided on the battlefield: let us now turn to the battles themselves.

1914: PLANS AND INITIAL MOVES

The onset of war in August 1914 thrust Russia into prominence with the first round of fighting. This reflected the fundamental dilemma facing the German army in World War I (and later World War II). Ever since the unification of Germany in the 1860s, it had become, as demonstrated by the Franco–Prussian War of 1870, the single greatest power on the European continent. Germany possessed the strongest and most-advanced economy, the most powerful and best-trained army, and, save for Russia, the greatest population in Europe. Over time, it had significantly outstripped its traditional rival, France, in all the vital areas. Seemingly, then, Germany was unassailable, especially given its prime geographical position in the center of Europe.

But all was far from well in Berlin. German political ineptitude under Kaiser Wilhelm combined with rising European apprehension at the growth of German power to cement a powerful anti-German alliance of France, England, and Russia. This alliance united Europe's largest land power in Russia with Europe's premier naval power, England, and Europe's second finest land power, France. Only the political neutrality of the United States prevented this alliance from containing and crushing Germany fairly easily. Even without the United States, the Triple Entente was a formidable force composing the three other main European powers. Germany could gain allies only from the weak and crumbling Austro–Hungarian Empire and the even more desiccated Ottoman Turkish Empire.

The correlation of forces favored the Triple Entente in the long run, even more so if the United States could ultimately be enticed into joining its traditional French and English allies. The German war planners did perceive a potentially fatal flaw in the encircling anti-German alliance. This flowed from the physical separation of all three of their enemies, problems in alliance politics (Germany, by contrast, would simply dominate its weak allies), and difficulties inherent in the military organization of the three countries. The bottom line was simple: Germany, using its central position and unified command, could bring its power to bear against the Allies before they were fully mobilized and coordinated.

Each of the three members of the alliance had a serious problem. The British were traditionally a great sea power, but the application of a successful naval blockade would be a long and tedious process against German land power, now reinforced by U-boats. England was historically a weak land power, and in the fall of 1914 the British Expeditionary Force could muster a puny 6 divisions in Europe, a force equal to the Belgium contribution to the war effort. This left France with 62 divisions as the main power in the West, but France had been defeated in 1870 and now lagged markedly behind Germany in population and economic development. Finally, there was Russia, the largest land power with 114 divisions, but plagued by long distances, weak transportation, poor equipment and leadership, and very low levels of economic and political development. Here, then, was a golden opportunity for Germany to strike the Allies before the sluggish Russians could assemble and mobilize their ill-trained and only sporadically effective forces against Germany.

These facts strongly promoted the adoption of the Schlieffen Plan by the German High Command. With only 136 Central

Powers divisions arrayed against 199 Triple Entente divisions, the Germans hoped to rapidly crush France with 83 divisions before Russia could mobilize adequately against them. The Germans relied on speed, surprise, and numerical superiority to destroy France. This necessitated leaving East Prussia almost naked against a Russian invasion, with General von Prittwitz's paltry 9 divisions in the Eighth Army the sole guard against attack. Even this represented a greater force than was contemplated in the original Schlieffen Plan.

Once France had been crushed, Germany would then rapidly move its troops eastward either to destroy Russia or accept its surrender. The Russians, in turn, tried to forestall this by a premature attack on East Prussia in an attempt to relieve the relentless German pressure on their French ally.

The natural Russian desire was to concentrate its armies first against the weaker Austro–Hungarian army and deal with the more powerful and retreating German army later, after full Russian mobilization. But the French insisted on a second offensive against the Germans as well, even though the Russians were hardly ready. The Russians developed a plan to use four armies against the Austro–Hungarian forces in Galicia and two armies against the German forces in East Prussia. Under the circumstances, the Russian army was embarking on a suicidal course. For as Basil Liddell Hart, the renowned British military historian, wrote about Russian military strategy in 1914,

> Russia, whose proverbial slowness and crude organization dictated a cautious strategy, was about to break with tradition and launch out on a gamble that only an army of high mobility and organization could have hoped to bring off.[1]

On the surface the Russian generals seemed to have some grounds for optimism. After all, the majority of the German army (eighty-three divisions) was in the West, where it was absorbed in the intricate maneuvers against France dictated by the Schlieffen Plan. Only General von Prittwitz's Eighth Army in East Prussia stood in the way of a Russian invasion of Germany. Both of the two Russian armies invading East Prussia were larger than von Prittwitz's army. The Russians could immediately send twenty-one divisions against the nine German divisions. Similarly, in September 1914, by German figures, 563,000 German and Austro–Hungarian troops would face 950,000 Russian troops in the East.[2]

Second, the speed of the Russian mobilization took the Germans by surprise. By 17 August 1914, earlier than expected, the Russian troops had already crossed the frontier in force. The early Russian victories at Stalluponen on 17 August and Gumbinnen on 20 August shocked the German commanders. The relentless Russian advance and loss of 6,000 German POWs at Gumbinnen so unnerved General von Prittwitz that he requested a general retreat to the Vistula and immediate reinforcements from the West to hold his new position. For his efforts he was immediately sacked and was replaced by two German generals destined for fame and glory, General Paul von Hindenburg (commander) and General Erich von Ludendorff (chief of staff).

The early Russian successes masked deeper problems pervading the Russian army. While the Germans disposed of a strong railroad network, the Russians were seriously hampered by a weak transportation and supply system on their side of the border. General Alexander Samsonov's Second Army even lacked field bakeries. The two Russian army commanders, General Pavel Rennenkampf (First Army) and General Alexander Samsonov (Second Army), were on poor terms and failed to cooperate properly with each other. German leadership and communications were distinctly superior to their Russian counterparts. The terrain favored the Germans, as the two Russian armies were separated by a fifty-mile chain of Masurian lakes. The quality of Russian communications was so poor that the Russians even broadcast uncoded radio messages in the clear. The Germans could easily decipher Russian intentions, while poor Russian intelligence failed to unearth German plans or moves.

The most basic problem was the unreadiness of the Russian army for battle against the German army, no matter how inferior in numbers the German army was. The quality of the Russian officer corps was poor, and the bulk of the soldiers were semiliterate peasants. The premature Russian offensive was especially devastating to an army of questionable value, even when fully mobilized. It took thirty-six days to fully mobilize the army, but in the north the army moved forward without reserves and so hastily that Samsonov's "troops were tired and hungry, their transport incomplete and their supply services in chaos."[3]

The Germans saw their opportunity and took it. The new team of Hindenburg and Ludendorff, operating on interior lines and following the line already worked out by their predecessor, was soon strengthened by the arrival of two army corps from the West, where they might have played an important role on the Marne. They could now strike at will against one of the widely separated Russian armies, now 95 kilometers apart from each other. The German command chose to attack Samsonov's Second Army, which was spread out over 210 kilometers, exhausted, devoid of reserves, and isolated from Rennenkampf's First Army.

General Ludendorff put six divisions against Samsonov's left wing and then maneuvered the remainder of German forces against Samsonov's right wing. Only a cavalry screen was left against the First Army of the slow and cautious Rennenkampf. The ensuing German attack destroyed Samsonov's flanks and encircled his center. Samsonov committed suicide, 92,000 Russians were taken prisoner by the Germans, and the battle of Tannenberg became the symbol of Tsarist decay (so well depicted by Alexander Solzhenitsyn in his *August 1914*).[4] Then, at the beginning of September in the battle of the Masurian lakes, the Germans turned on Rennenkampf's First Army, which was forced to retreat from East Prussia to the Neman and Narew rivers. In three weeks 150,000 German troops had smashed the Russian invasion of East Prussia and inflicted 250,000 losses on the Russians.[5]

But the German victory had come only at the cost of weakening the drive into France. The ensuing Austro–Hungarian disaster in September 1914 forced the Germans to end their pursuit of the retreating Russians. Against the even weaker Austro–Hungarian armies the Russians had been able to score a significant victory. The fighting in the south was bitter and confused as four Russian armies collided with three Austro–Hungarian armies. The Austro–Hungarian forces under General Conrad von Hoetzendorff had dreamed of largely eliminating the dangerous Russian Polish salient by a northern advance from Galicia. A series of seesaw battles in late August and early September ended in Russian victory and occupation of Galicia as the Austro–Hungarian forces retreated towards the Carpathians. While not destroyed by the Russians, the Austro–Hungarian army never fully recovered from the loss of over 400,000 men and afterwards always needed German aid to be successful.[6]

At this point, two points were clear: the German army was markedly superior to the Russian army, which in turn was superior to the Austro–Hungarian army. Just how weak the Russian army was compared to the German army has been suggested in a recent study of four major Russo–German battles in 1914 and 1915. The study concludes that, without taking into account POWs, German effectiveness was a startling 2.8:1.0, Russia:Germany—in crude terms, this means that 10 German soldiers were of the same value as 28 Russian soldiers. When POWs are taken into account, the German effectiveness superiority soars to a phenomenal 7.9:1.0 over Russia. The average German superiority score was 5.4:1.0. What this meant has been succinctly summed up as follows:

> This suggests that—on a broad front, with plenty of room to maneuver and to employ their strategic and tactical leadership superiority—German armies could hold off Russian armies three to five times as large as their own.[7]

During the fall and winter of 1914 the fighting on the Eastern front was intense and often uneven. Both sides poured troops into the conflict. The German forces doubled in size by December 1914, and the Russian army doubled by January 1915. As a result, by German figures, in the East 1.2 million German and Austro–Hungarian troops faced 1.7 million Russian troops in December 1914. By January 1915 the Russian advantage increased, with 1.0 million German and Austro–Hungarian troops squared off against 1.8 million Russian troops.[8]

The German victories in East Prussia encouraged Berlin to launch a major offensive into Poland at the end of September 1914. During October 1914 the fifty-two mixed German and Austro–Hungarian divisions under General Mackensen advanced close toward Warsaw, only to retreat when a reinforced Russian army counterattacked and invaded Silesia. By the end of October 1914 the Russian army had regained Russian Poland and pushed the German and Austro–Hungarian armies back to their starting positions. In November, after repelling a second Russian threat to East Prussia, the mixed army of the Central Powers again thrust to Lodz and Warsaw, only to be stopped by the Russian Fifth Army. The ensuing Russian advance pushed the Germans back into East Prussia, and in the south the Russians entered Silesia and pushed the Austro–Hungarian forces towards the Carpathians. By December 1914 the fighting left the Russians and Germans close to the starting point of the war. Much smaller German forces, aided by Austro–Hungarian troops, had repelled Russian forces twice their size. Under these circumstances the German reinforcements in 1915 might have been able to turn the tide and oust Russia from the war, or at least neutralize its offensive capabilities.[9]

1915: RUSSIAN DEFEATS IN THE EAST

The events of 1915 were indecisive. Italy came in on the side of the Allies while Bulgaria joined the Central Powers. The British and French mounted costly and useless frontal attacks, gaining little ground but suffering 1.6 million casualties. In the Middle East the Allies failed in the Dardanelles. In the East the Germans scored major gains against the Russians but were unable to commit adequate forces to destroy the Russian army.

During 1915 the Germans, keeping 85 divisions in the West, maintained a strong force of 65 divisions in the East. The primacy of the Western front ensured that the German army in the East was too small to destroy the larger Russian army in the vast expanses of western Russia. And the Austro–Hungarian army, while significant in numbers, was even weaker than the Russian army. Only a stronger force, equal to the 150 to 190 German divisions thrown against the Red Army in World War II, would have had a serious chance of decisively defeating Russia.[10] Until France would be defeated in the West, this would only represent wishful thinking for German military planners, who more realistically hoped to neutralize Russian offensive power and recurrent threats to occupy East Prussia.

During the winter of 1914–1915 the Germans decided to forestall renewed Russian offensives. A February 1915 German attack ousted the Russians from East Prussia but, despite limited success at Augustów, was unable to destroy the Russian army. In March 1915 the Russians succeeded in taking the Przemyśl fortress and moved towards the Carpathians and, hence, Budapest. The Austro–Hungarian forces with some German aid did stop the Russian drive, which made small gains at an enormous price. Russian plans for 1915 were well drawn but poorly executed with limited means.

By late spring 1915 the Germans, with major Austro–Hungarian support, launched a large-scale offensive that in five months devastated the Russian army, despite the Russians' having a 35 percent numerical advantage. Only half of the 1.3 million Central Powers troops were Germans. In May 1915 the Central Powers offensive at Gorlice broke through Russian lines and forced the Russians out of Galicia. In June the Russians lost Przemyśl and Lvov; in July, Lublin; in August, Warsaw. By September Russian Poland was lost to the Germans, who had now reached Riga and Vilna. At this point the Tsar removed the Grand

Duke Nicholas as commander-in-chief of the Russian army and personally took command. By the end of September 1915 the exhausted Germans ended large-scale operations in the east on a line stretching from Riga in the north to Czernowitz in the south.

This massive defeat had seriously weakened Russia and removed it as a direct threat to Germany. Russia was in such disarray that, in June 1915 at the Chantilly conference, General Joffre warned that a Western offensive was needed to save Russia.[11] This unprecedented disaster lost Lithuania, Poland, and Galicia. The Russian front was repeatedly broken, and almost 50 percent of the Russian army was destroyed. The Russians lost a staggering 1,700,000 men, including 151,000 men killed, 683,000 men wounded and a huge 895,000 POWs lost to the Germans.[12]

1916: RUSSIA STRETCHED TO THE LIMIT

During 1916 the Russians were unable to launch a successful offensive against the German army. The massive German attack at Verdun and on the Somme in 1916 led to strong Allied pressure for a premature Russian campaign to save them from the German onslaught. But after the disaster of 1915, the Russian army was ill-prepared and hardly eager to take on the German army so soon again. In the spring of 1916, 130 Russian divisions lacked superiority (because they were so poorly equipped) over 46 German divisions and 40 Austro–Hungarian divisions, and the sudden German attack at Verdun robbed the Russian army of the time so vital for adequate preparation for battle.

In March 1916 General Alexis Kuropatkin's North Army Group of eighteen divisions attacked the German Tenth Army east of Vilna at Lake Naroch. In extremely heavy fighting Kuropatkin's troops made minor gains at prohibitive costs. The massive 5:2 Russian numerical advantage over the Germans availed the Russians little in the face of overwhelming German qualitative superiority. Everything went wrong for the Russians: the ice began to break up, the Russian artillery assault went poorly, the German troops were on alert, and the Russians could advance only a few hundred yards against strong German defense lines. The extent of the disaster was reflected in the appalling statistics: 100,000 Russian casualties, 20,000 German casualties, with a further 10,000 Russian POWs taken by the Germans.[13]

This marked the last significant Russian offensive of the war against Germany. Only twenty months after the beginning of World War I in August 1914 and fully thirty-two months before its conclusion in November 1918, the Russian army was reduced to impotence before a vastly numerically inferior German enemy. Not even half-way into the war the Russian army had lost all offensive fighting power against Germany, the main enemy of the Triple Entente. Now it could be deployed only against Germany's two disintegrating allies, the Austro–Hungarian Empire and the Ottoman Empire.

Given the desperate fighting in the West, the Russian army felt compelled to take action somewhere to show Russia's value as an ally. The logic pointed to the Austro–Hungarian front. General Brusilov prepared the offensive in a different from usual manner. Rather than the customary laborious preparation that alerted the enemy, Brusilov developed plans for a quick campaign emphasizing speed and surprise. He ensured surprise by preparing to attack at 20 points on a 300-mile front and dispersing his reserves. With 40 Russian divisions facing 38 largely Austro–Hungarian divisions, Brusilov turned a probing action in June 1916 into an outstanding success. Within two weeks he had torn a huge gap in enemy lines and taken 200,000 Austro-Hungarian POWs. In a five-month stop-and-go campaign that lasted until October 1916, the Brusilov offensive captured Bukovina and much of east Galicia, 25,000 square kilometers in all, and captured over 400,000 POWs. It forced Germany to transfer 16 divisions to the East, saved Italy, and prompted Romanian intervention (later suppressed by German moves into Bucharest).

Yet the costs of success, even if limited and achieved against a weak foe, were enormous. Russia suffered more than one million casualties, a huge figure. This final display of Russian military power, this last gasp of a decaying giant, completely exhausted the Tsarist army. The morale of the men, who had fought so hard and so long for so little, sank to new depths.[14]

Thus, even Russian successes against Austro–Hungary and Turkey (in Armenia) in 1916 could not restore a deteriorating situation. Although by January 1917 the army had accumulated good stocks of arms and ammunition, it faced manpower, transport, and agricultural crises in civil society and deterioration in the army's morale and overall effectiveness. A December 1916 conference at Stavka (army headquarters) rejected any winter initiatives, preferring to wait for spring. The Allies began to lose faith in the Russian army, cutting aid one-third by January 1917 from 1916 levels, with total cutoff in April 1917. In January 1917 the Petrograd conference rejected large Russian demands for equipment, while the Russians refused to attack concurrently with the Nivelle offensive despite French pressure.[15]

1917: TWIN RUSSIAN REVOLUTIONS AND PASSIVITY IN WAR

The repeated Russian failures in war were a powerful prod to the February Revolution, which overthrew Tsarism and brought the provisional government to power. The army refused to march on Petrograd to save the Tsar, and all the army commanders supported Tsarist abdication. The mutiny of the Petrograd garrison propelled the revolution forward, and not one organized army unit intervened to protect the Tsar. However, at this time, most Russians still supported the war. Even the majority of soldiers, though desirous of peace, opposed an immediate peace if it meant humiliation for Russia. The new foreign minister, Professor Milyukov, supported a continuation of the war. In the words of Marc Ferro,

> Finally of war, the Russian people were ready nevertheless, to bear the vicissitudes of a new campaign if it were clear that the new regime would do everything possible to conclude a just peace. If the enemy refused, he would be fought until he consented.[16]

The new government was not able either to reform or rally the army for a new campaign. The Petrograd Soviet Order Number 1 in March harmed discipline in the army. At the same time, revolutionary defensism was the order of the day. When Lenin in his April Theses denounced the war, he was widely unpopular among a population that opposed a separate peace. But most Russians also rejected Milyukov's desire to carry on the war to a decisive victory, and he was soon forced out of the government. The new war minister, Aleksandr Kerensky, in May 1917, tried to whip up a war frenzy and prepare the army for a new offensive. At that time the Russian government declared its support for a general peace without annexations or indemnities and opposition to a separate peace with Germany. As the new, more socialist, government declared in May 1917,

> Convinced that the defeat of Russia and her allies would not only be a calamity for the Russian people but would also have the effect of making world peace founded on the above principle impossible, the Provisional Government firmly believes that the revolutionary army will not allow the German troops to defeat our Western allies and then throw all their might against us. The reinforcement of democratic principles in the Army and the development of its military might, both offensive and defensive, will be the most important task of the Provisional Government.[17]

A fatal gap thus opened up between the government and army. The Provisional Government believed that only through a successful offensive would the Allies, now dismissing Russia as militarily impotent, regain faith in their eastern ally and take its political program seriously. Even the Russian socialists, unable to get the international socialist community to meet and move towards peace, thought a successful offensive would restore their position. And the conservatives hoped a military success would strengthen the military against the left.

There was only one problem: the army was disintegrating and demoralized and showed no inclination to fight. Kerensky's stirring appeal of June 1917, "Warriors, our country is in danger," fell on deaf ears. In 1916, 1.5 million men deserted the army; in 1917 this number was to increase further.[18] As early as March 1917 a staff conference had rejected any possible spring offensive. An official army document that spring of 1917 found the Russian army "an exhausted mass of undernourished men in rags, full of bitterness and united only in their resentment and thirst for peace."[19] Perhaps the harshest words came in an April 1917 report by General Mikhail Alekseyev. He found that the authority of officers had "collapsed," desertions were increasing, discipline was falling apart, and a strong defeatist and pacifist mood was pervading the ranks. In short, "the situation in the army grows worse every day, information coming in from all sides indicates that the army is systematically falling apart."[20]

Under these conditions the offensive planned by the new commander-in-chief, Aleksei Brusilov, was doomed to failure. Intended to aid the third Ypres offensive in Flanders, the attack was aimed at Austro–Hungarian positions near Brody in July 1917.

The initial Russian attack with thirty-one divisions in the north was soon supplemented by a second attack of thirteen divisions under General Lavr Kornilov on the Dniester and in the Carpathian foothills. Initial Russian gains were soon negated by a German counterattack which rapidly wiped out all Russian advances. By August the Russian army had been driven from Galicia and Bukovina.[21]

The disaster of the Brusilov offensive in July and August 1917 soon begot one more disaster at Riga in September 1917. There General von Hutier threw his eight German divisions into attack, aided by new techniques of hurricane artillery bombardment without registration and small unit infiltration. The Russian defenses collapsed as the Russian army fled eastward without a fight. The rout was total and the message was clear: the Russian army as an effective fighting force was finished.[22]

These military events greatly affected the political arena. The failure of the Brusilov offensive helped provoke the leftist upsurge of the "July Days." The leftist failure led to General Lavr Kornilov being made supreme commander of the army. With the support of the Allies, the top front commanders, and general staff, Kornilov made an abortive bid for power. It was beaten back by Kerensky, the left, and the soldiers. In the aftermath, the power of the antiwar sentiment grew mightily, the Bolsheviks gained power in the Moscow and Petrograd Soviets and in the army, and the army further disintegrated. The mounting economic chaos led to growing food and supply shortages in the army. By the time of the October Revolution the last Provisional Government war minister, General Verkhovsky, was already calling for immediate peace talks with the Germans, since "general disintegration has gained momentum, particularly under the influence of the Kornilov affair. . . . We can no longer wage war."[23] Not one Petrograd regiment rose to protect Kerensky from the Bolshevik insurrection in October 1917.

1918: SOVIET UNION LEAVES THE WAR

The denouement followed closely on the heels of these fresh military disasters. The Bolsheviks, responding to mass antiwar sentiment in the civilian population and the daily decay in the army, signed an armistice with Germany and opened peace talks in December 1917. Harsh German demands and Russian propaganda and stalling tactics protracted the negotiations. In February 1918 the German army advanced 150 miles in five days, demonstrating that the Russian army could neither fight nor retreat properly. After this shock, even the new head of the Russian army (Krylenko) admitted that, properly speaking, the Russian army no longer existed. At this point, the Bolsheviks finally acceded to the German terms.

In March 1918 the Russians signed the Treaty of Brest Litovsk with Germany. In it, the Russians lost the Baltics, Finland, Kurland, much of Belorussia and Ukraine to Germany, and Kars, Ardahum, and Batum to Turkey. Fully 32 percent of the land, 34 percent of the population, 54 percent of industry, and 89 percent of the coal mines in Tsarist Russia were now lost, seemingly forever. Russian frontiers were rolled back to the sixteenth century. The price of military impotence was devastatingly clear, and only the Allied victory over Germany with U.S. help in November 1918 could erase the shame of Brest Litovsk.[24]

Even here the Russian/U.S. nexus was striking. The Western allies were probably unable to defeat Germany by themselves, now that Russia was gone, without large-scale U.S. aid. The departure of Russia from the Allied coalition, informally in 1917 and formally in early 1918, strongly altered the correlation of forces much more favorably in the direction of Germany. It ended the nightmare of a two front war and halted the significant drain of German resources to the East. With the large-scale redeployment of German troops from East to West and German unrestricted submarine warfare against Allied shipping, Germany could now go on the offensive.

For the first time since 1914 Germany would possess a numerical advantage on the Western front and a real possibility of victory given German qualitative superiority, now supplemented by quantitative superiority. From November 1917 to March 1918 the German army moved 40 divisions from the East to West and 10 more divisions in the following two months. As a result, the German army now had 192 divisions in the West in March and 204 divisions there in May, compared to 53 divisions and 38 divisions left in the East. This gave the German army numerical superiority over roughly 170 Allied divisions.[25]

The German army, now free on the Eastern front (at the cost of 11,300 killed and missing there during 1917–1918) launched five great offensives on the Western front from March to July 1918.[26]

The goal was simple—to drive the four armies of the British Expeditionary Force into the sea and then drive across the Marne and seize Paris. The U.S. role here was crucial because all this had to be accomplished during the Allied "window of vulnerability" before the U.S. army was prepared for large-scale intervention in the fall and winter of 1918. Yet only seven months later, in October 1918, Imperial Germany, seemingly on the brink of victory in March, was actively seeking peace. And the man they sought it from was not the premier of England or France (let alone Russia), their main antagonists for four years, but the president of the United States, which had actively joined the fighting only the month before. Equally remarkable, only one month later, Imperial Germany signed an armistice ending the war and admitting defeat at a time when its troops were everywhere on foreign soil, and Russia, its main eastern nemesis, was crushed, humiliated, and driven from the field of battle.

What did this say about the role of Russia and the United States in World War I? First, it shows that Russian power was on the whole modest and declining during the war. Not only could Germany knock Russia out of the war, but the withdrawal of Russia was inadequate to give Germany victory. Second, it demands an answer to the question of how the United States could play a much greater role than Tsarist Russia, even a possibly decisive one, when its military role was so relatively slight? It is to attempt to answer this question that we turn from the Russian role to the U.S. role in World War I.

UNITED STATES UNPREPAREDNESS FOR WAR, 1914–1918

The United States, trying to stay out of World War I and not directly threatened by the war in Europe, was poorly prepared for war at the time of its entry into the fray in April 1917. This directly reflected the 1916 campaign promise of President Wilson to keep the country out of war, U.S. hostility to participation in the war, and its tradition of noninvolvement in European affairs. As a consequence the U.S. army played a minimal role in the war until September 1918, and even somewhat afterwards. Therefore, we need both to understand the nature of the U.S. military role in the war and the seemingly paradoxical relationship between its very weak military involvement and powerful political role.

The lack of U.S. involvement or war preparation before its dramatic entry into World War I was deeply rooted in American history, politics, and geography. In the almost half a century elapsing since the end of the American Civil War, the United States had avoided participation in any major war, save for a brief and spectacularly successful encounter with the decaying Spanish empire in 1898. Blessed by vast oceans on either side of the continent and weak neighbors on its north and south, the United States, so unlike Tsarist Russia, was invulnerable to invasion and could afford the luxury of standing apart from European conflicts. Unlike Tsarist Russia, the United States had nothing to fear from any potential enemy.

In 1914 the United States, with over 90 million people, could safely afford to maintain a miniscule army of 87,000 men, less even than the 1902 congressional authorization of 100,000 men. While all the major European powers developed multimillion-man armies, the United States remained in luxurious isolation with the seventeenth-largest army in the world. This army could do no more than protect the borders or suppress riots. The army was in the U.S. military tradition of a weak constabulary force, scattered in dozens of isolated outposts in small units across the United States. The army was designed to fight militarily impotent and technologically primitive Mexicans and Indians. Truly, in Russell Weigley's phrase, this was the American way of war.[27]

President Wilson's proclamation of neutrality in thought and deed in August 1914 was widely popular at home. Most Americans, especially those in the rural South, West, and isolationist Midwest, opposed the war or any preparation for it. Only in the East were voices raised for war preparation by distinguished men like Theodore Roosevelt, Elihu Root, and Henry Stimson, but even in the East, most people supported neutrality. Wilson's 1915 declaration that the United States was "too proud to fight" reflected not only public opinion but even elite opposition to war preparation. General James Harbord, General John Pershing's chief-of-staff, later commented that in 1914 baseball aroused greater passions in the United States than the assassination of the Austrian Archduke Ferdinand and at that time,

Not half a dozen of our statesmen could see any probability of the United States being involved in the War. A few silent soldiers who had studied the development of the German Army after 1870 had opinions but they did not offer them and they were not sought.[28]

From 1914 to 1916 the United States was largely isolated from the titanic struggle for world domination being waged in Europe. Trade with the Allies quadrupled to 3.2 billion dollars by 1916 while that with the Central Powers dwindled to insignificance. Almost 2 billion dollars in loans were floated to the Allies. The United States, protected by oceans and the British navy, saw war orders push its balance-of-trade surplus from a mere 0.76 billion dollars in 1913 to 3.0 billion dollars in 1916.[29]

The Wilson government, hampered by pacifism, public isolationism, and a weak army and government, did very little to prepare the country for war. The national sentiment for the Allies, as reflected in the trade figures, geographical imperatives, and power considerations, was strong. It was reinforced by German submarine warfare, German aggression against Belgium, the German attack on Russia and France, and traditional Anglo–U.S. ties. But during 1914 to 1916 the main American action was a punitive expedition into Mexico against Pancho Villa led by General Pershing with 15,000 men.

President Wilson and the bulk of the U.S. public resolutely opposed U.S. intervention in a distant, unnecessary war being fought out by decadent European powers. Newton Baker, who served as secretary of war in World War I, later observed to Frederick Palmer that almost until the very date of the entry of the United States into the war in April 1917, "the President gave me the idea...that to him the function of the United States was to be the peacemaker, and that the idea of intervening in the war was the last thought he had in the world."[30] Under these circumstances, Newton Baker went on,

> Preparation for intervening with guns and munitions would have been regarded as madness. Suggestions from the War Department that we increase the appropriations with a view to putting the American Army on a better footing in case of hostilities would have been regarded as provocative.[31]

Only in June 1916, almost two full years after the beginning of World War I, were any significant attempts undertaken to prepare for war. These efforts enjoyed some success but were only a first step on the long road to war preparedness. That month Congress passed the National Defense Act that edged the United States slightly away from total military impotence. Congress more than doubled the defense budget, federalized the National Guard, created the Reserve Officer Training Corps, empowered the secretary of war to conduct a survey of war and munitions industries, and gave powers of industrial and war mobilization and control to the president. Over five years the act doubled the size of the army to 235,000 officers and men and the National Guard to 457,000 officers and men. In August, President Wilson mobilized industrialists, trade union leaders, and six Cabinet officers in a Council of National Defense and in September 1916 formed a shipping board to regulate sea traffic.[32]

But these measures were of relatively minimal value. They were instituted by a president who won reelection that fall of 1916 on the slogan "He Kept Us Out of War." The major U.S. preparedness had come, ironically, more in the civilian sector where 2.1 billion dollars of war materiel had been shipped to the Allies by April 1917 and prompted a limited industrial war preparation.[33] In the military sector, as Marshal Petain would caustically note a year later, "In April of 1917, at the moment of their entrance into the war, the United States did not have, properly speaking, an army."[34] Perhaps General John Pershing, commander of the American Expeditionary Force in France, put the matter best,

> The World War found us absorbed in pursuit of peace and quite unconscious of probable threats to our security. We would listen to no warnings of danger. We had made small preparation for defense and none for aggression. . . . Little more than a gesture was made to get ready for eventualities; in fact, practically nothing was done in the way of increasing our military strength or providing equipment.[35]

The state of the U.S. military was deplorable in April 1917. Not one complete division existed in an army with only 127,600 regular army officers and men and 80,500 national guardsmen on federal service. The armed forces had 9,000 officers in all; it would need 200,000 officers for a modern multimillion-man army. Of these 9,000 officers, only 6,000 were regular army, the rest being from the National Guard. And even those 9,000 officers had no modern battle experience, having seen combat only against the Sioux Indians (1890–1891), Spanish army (1898), Filipino rebels (1900+), and Mexican marauders (1914–1916). Since 1898, the U.S. army in almost two decades had seen only minor actions involving less than a division in Mexico and the Philippines. The bulk of the officers had not even had this minimal experience.[36]

The equipment of the U.S. army was equally pathetic. In April

1917 the army had 285,000 Springfield rifles (1903 design), 1,500 machine guns (from 4 designs), and 550 antiquated artillery pieces. In each vital area the United States would need at least ten times more weapons. The existing weapons were either outdated or unstandardized. The Springfield rifles would be replaced by British rifles, the old field guns would be discarded for more modern guns, and the Browning automatic weapon would be adopted only in May 1917. Similarly, in the air force there were exactly 55 airplanes (51 of them obsolete) and only 35 officers (5 with significant flying experience) to fly them. The army could place neither a single division in the field nor a single squadron in the air—this at a time when not 1 but 300 squadrons with 5,400 modern planes would be needed for a massive U.S. army planned for Europe.[37]

Here, then, was a tiny U.S. army, without an air force, tank force, chemical warfare unit, or motorized transportation. Nor was there any strong general staff ready to transform this skeleton force into a modern army. Created only after the Spanish–American War at the urging of Secretary of War Elihu Root, the general staff was restricted by law to 190 officers in Washington, compared to many hundreds in European armies. The general staff even in April 1917 had not a single contingency plan for intervention in Europe. The existing war plans all dealt with hemispheric or continental defense. There was no serious attempt to study the war in Europe; one study even went so far as to say it had no relevant lessons for the U.S. army. As a result, in the words of General John "Black Jack" Pershing, "When the Acting Chief-of-Staff went to look at secret files where plans to meet the situation that confronted us should have been found, the pigeon hole was empty."[38]

Under these conditions, the U.S. military role in Europe was minimal to nonexistent in 1917. Since the United States lacked the preexisting peacetime military base that allowed for quick mobilization and buildup of European powers, it had to make up even more ground than the already fully mobilized warring powers. Not until October 1917 was there one U.S. division in Europe. It wasn't until November 1917 that the first U.S. casualty occurred in Europe. Even by January 1918 there were only 4 American divisions (only 1 of which was truly ready) and 200,000 men in France. This was at a time when the German army had 239 divisions and the Austro–Hungarian army 76 divisions on various fronts![39]

The outcome of the war was basically decided by the five great offensives launched between March and July 1918 by a German army eager to act while the Russian army was out of the war and before the U.S. army could enter in force. With a numerical advantage and 192 war-weary and lower-quality divisions at their disposal, the German high command sought to destroy the British army and then seize Paris. At the cost of almost 1 million casualties, the German army made great progress and advanced to within forty miles of Paris before being repelled by an Allied counterattack. On 8 August 1918 a French and British counterattack with 450 tanks at Amiens smashed through German lines and pushed the German army back to the Siegfried line. That day, the "black day of the war," led Kaiser Wilhelm and General Ludendorff the next day to consider the war lost.[40]

And where was the U.S. army while the fate of the world was being decided? It was very little in evidence as the burden of repelling the German army fell on the French and British armies. This was not for lack of U.S. military manpower, which rose dramatically from 434,100 men in France in April 1918 to 1,473,200 men there in August 1918. Yet, the U.S. role at the front grew more slowly from only 6 percent of the front in April 1918 to 17 percent in August 1918. This figure exaggerates the role of the U.S. army, which did not participate in large-scale operations until the fate of the war had been decided, in September 1918.[41]

The role of the U.S. army during the five great German offensives and Allied counterattack was tangible but small, as the Allies fought "with minimal American participation" on their side.[42] Not until the end of May 1918, more than two months after the massive German thrust started, was the first division of the United States Army sent to the front and ready for an offensive thrust against Germany. Before then the hundreds of thousands of U.S. soldiers in France were relatively useless except for a handful of units. At the end of May a U.S. division made the first real U.S. offensive of the war with a successful attack against a weak German unit at the Cantigny salient. In June 1918 two U.S. divisions helped stop the German advance on Paris near Chateau–Thierry. Then, in a harsh twenty-day battle, a U.S. marine brigade and army infantry division suffered 5,200 casualties in seizing the Belleau Wood from two weak German divisions.

By July 1918 the American First Army, with nineteen divisions, was formed with 150,000 men in or near the front lines. That month two U.S. divisions, under French direction and using 360

French tanks, advanced successfully at Soissons. On 8 August 1918, "the black day of the war" for Germany, fifteen Allied divisions successfully broke through German lines. The United States deployed exactly one American division that fateful day. During the second battle of the Marne in August 1918 the Allies suffered 300,000 casualties: the Americans accounted for only 50,000 of them. On balance, then, the role of the U.S. army was minimal until August and then accelerated to a modest level in August 1918.[43]

UNITED STATES INTERVENTION IN THE WAR, SEPTEMBER–NOVEMBER 1918

Only during the last two-and-one-half months of the war did the U.S. army play a significant role. This came at a time when the German army, after four years of intensive fighting, was exhausted and its allies were leaving the war. A survey undertaken by British intelligence found that only fifty-one German divisions were considered fit for combat. With morale plummeting, starvation haunting the homeland, and all reserves drained from the army, General Ludendorff by the end of September 1918 formally called for an armistice at a Council of War meeting.[44] At this time the new German government of Prince Max actively embarked on peace negotiations with the Allies. The United States Army entered the fray in force precisely at the moment when the German army was on the verge of disintegration after more than four years of devastation and the failure of its five offensives in the spring and summer of 1918.

Even under these extremely promising circumstances, the U.S. army still did not play a decisive role. This was not for lack of manpower, since by November 1918 the two million U.S. troops in France equalled the size of the vaunted British Expeditionary Force. In the last several months of the war U.S. troops faced roughly 25 percent of German divisions on the Western front and formed 17 percent to 19 percent of the Allied divisions on the front. Yet the British army, though opposed by the majority of the German army in the West, advanced further and faster than any other army. During the final two months of the war the United States took only 21 percent of German guns and 11 percent of German POWs captured by the Allies, compared to much higher percentages for the British and French.[45]

During September and early October the Allies resumed their offensive and pierced the Hindenburg line. In these operations the British army took 200,000 casualties, the U.S. army 6,000 casualties. The U.S. role was thereby relatively minimal, as in this case role and cost (unlike with Russia) were highly correlated. However, the United States did achieve its first real victory of the war. This came at the St. Mihiel salient, a 15-mile German bulge in Allied lines between the Meuse and Moselle rivers.[46] In this action in the middle of September 1918, the United States First Army used 7 American divisions, 3,000 guns, 1,400 planes, and 267 tanks to liberate a 200-square-mile bulge of French territory. In only 36 hours, at the cost of 7,000 U.S. casualties, the U.S. army took 16,000 prisoners and 450 German guns. Unquestionably, the United States Army had come a long way under the leadership of General Pershing.[47]

However, there was considerably less to this victory than would meet the eye. First, all 3,000 guns, all 267 tanks, and the bulk of the 1,400 planes were borrowed from the British and the French. Even 40 percent of the gun crews were not American. Second, this operation represented massive overkill with 3.3 million artillery shells being fired at relatively weak German positions in five days. This was followed by an all-out assault by nine U.S. divisions (equal in size to 18 European divisions) and four French divisions. Third, in this quiet sector that had not seen action since early 1915, the bulk of the nine German and Austro–Hungarian divisions on the line were quite poor. Six of them were rated second class, two of them third class, and only one of them first class— and that one had been mauled on the Marne. The quality of German troops had strongly deteriorated since 1914 and even since March 1918. Fourth, the level of resistance was quite low, even "halfhearted." The reason for this was that the entire German army had begun retreating four days before the attack, leaving only covering forces in the forward trenches. Some heavy guns had been removed and others were out of their emplacements at the time of attack. This eliminated the obvious German advantages of possessing the high grounds with wooded heights. Finally, the U.S. army, despite light resistance, suffered three times more casualties (7,000) than the enemy (2,300) and failed to adequately pursue and trap the retreating German army. Overall, St. Mihiel was a victory, but a very limited one for the fledgling U.S. army.[48]

The final, and largest, U.S. operation in World War I spanned the last forty-seven days of the war and took place in the rugged

Meuse–Argonne region. The operation was part of four vast converging attacks conducted at the same time against the Hindenburg line. The overall role of the United States Army can be gauged by the following data: on the left wing 40 British divisions and 2 U.S. divisions faced 57 German divisions, while in the Meuse–Argonne sector 31 French divisions and 11 U.S. divisions opposed 20 German divisions. The Meuse–Argonne operation was beset by a number of difficulties. The Allies were plagued by transportation problems and hampered by three poor roads in the area. The Germans had developed three major defense lines to take advantage of the rugged terrain. The Allies had to rapidly move 400,000 troops out of the St. Mihiel salient into the starting point for the Meuse-Argonne operation. This was the first real battle for the majority of the 1.2 million U.S. soldiers involved in the fighting; training of the majority was weak or incomplete.[49]

The Meuse-Argonne offensive, involving 1.2 million U.S. troops, represented the first and last major, large-scale action by the U.S. army in the war. The objective was the main German communication line running from Metz–Sedan–Mezeries. In four years the Germans had built a powerful defense system 13 miles in depth to complement the naturally rugged terrain. During the battle the Germans kept shuttling in new divisions (albeit undermanned ones), raising the number from 20 German divisions on 25 September to 38 divisions on 11 November. On a front 24–90 miles wide, the U.S. army, at a cost of 120,000 casualties, drove the Germans back 32 miles in the north and 14 miles in the northeast in tough terrain. In the process the U.S. First Army took 16,100 German soldiers prisoner and captured 458 guns and 2,860 machine guns.

Nevertheless, the Meuse–Argonne campaign represented, at best, only a modest success for the new United States First Army. The first four days of the offensive, from 25–28 September 1918, went so badly that General Pershing had to halt the offensive. Despite an 8:1 numerical superiority (12 large U.S. divisions against 8 emaciated German divisions), the U.S. army suffered roughly 40,000 casualties in the first four days of attacks and failed on the fourth day to reach the objectives set for the afternoon of the first day. The French were so upset by this performance that they urged President Wilson either to relieve General Pershing of command or place most U.S. troops back under their command.[50]

Even though more progress was made in October and early November, the rate was very slow and the cost exceedingly high. In forty-seven days of fighting using over one million men, the U.S. army achieved only one-third of its objective. In the first month it advanced an average of ten miles. The bulk of the fighting came after 29 September, the date on which the Germans sought an armistice, at a time when German troop morale was sinking and the German army disintegrating. The German army, after over four years of battle was but a skeleton of its former self. Nevertheless, the Germans still managed to inflict more casualties (117,000) on the Americans than they suffered themselves (100,000). The number of German POWs (16,100) was extremely small under the circumstances.[51] Only the ultimate breakthrough of German lines in early November, combined with German skill at war and strong defense lines, allow the Meuse- Argonne operation to be considered a modest success. The judgment of Daniel Beaver on the final campaign of the war is sound,

> The fighting on the Meuse–Argonne front had been indecisive, for the Germans had managed to hold the American army and inflict great casualties in exchange for small gains. If an armistice had been granted at any time before November 5th, the main American military effort in France could have been labelled a failure.[52]

NOVEMBER 1918: SOVIET UNION AND UNITED STATES AT END OF THE WAR

When Germany signed the armistice agreement on 11 November 1918, it was extremely symbolic that the signing took place in Marshal Foch's railroad car in the presence of French and British officers. In sharp contrast to World War II, no U.S. or Russian officers were present, nor was it thought necessary to invite them. This was hardly cavalier on the part of the British and the French. The Russians, having made the greatest sacrifice for the war on the Allied side, were now at peace with Germany, having signed the ignominious Treaty of Brest Litovsk at Lenin's urging in March 1918. In 1917 and 1918 their role had been entirely passive, confined to holding some remaining German troops in the East.

As for the Americans, they had made the least sacrifice for the war on the Allied side, incurring perhaps 1 percent of Allied casualties. Only in the last two months of the war, and then only marginally, had the U.S. army actually made a real military contribution. Thus, the two future superpowers, performing as militarily mediocre powers in World War I, were not even present at Germany's final surrender in November 1918.

Yet, both future superpowers gained greatly from Germany's final defeat. For the Soviet Union it nullified the humiliation of the Treaty of Brest Litovsk and ousted a powerful German enemy from the economically and strategically vital Ukraine, Belorussia, Baltics, and Poland. The Allied victory in 1918 thereby promoted a Soviet victory in the Russian civil war. It also aided the Bolsheviks, as it ended the prospect of further Allied intervention in the civil war on the side of the Whites. It promoted a relatively peaceful intrawar period in which, free from any immediate German threat, the Soviet Union could peacefully reconstruct from war and civil war in the 1920s and then massively transform the society and economy in the 1930s. These benefits flowed to the Soviet Union despite its military weakness and as an heir to the February and October Revolutions that had followed, in significant part, from Russia's military humiliation and disintegration in the war.

The U.S. role in and after November 1918 was even more complex. Despite its minimal direct military role and general mediocrity on the battlefield even in 1918, the United States played a relatively decisive role in the events in and after November 1918 off the battlefield. The negotiations to end the war in October and November 1918 were conducted largely between the German and U.S. governments. The basis of negotiation was not British or French proposals but President Woodrow Wilson's Fourteen Points. During 1919 the dominant figure at the Versailles peace conference was again the U.S. president. Many historians have seen this era, with the Versailles peace conference and formation of the Comintern, as foreshadowing an ultimate collision between Russian socialism under Lenin and U.S. liberalism propagated by Wilson.

This powerful U.S. role, all out of proportion to its actual military performance, flowed from a series of factors. On the Allied side the exhaustion of France and England from a massive war effort, coupled with the withdrawal of Russia, left a vacuum which the United States could fill. This was reinforced by the growing Allied economic dependency on the United States, which enjoyed an economy with a GNP four times that of England or

France. The British and French economies were strained to the limit by the war, and the northern part of France was devastated by the war. England and France suffered millions of casualties. By contrast, the United States avoided any war devastation and suffered far fewer casualties than its allies. The war prompted an economic boom in the United States that almost doubled the level of consumption (33.4 billion dollars in 1914 to 60.6 billion dollars in 1919) and more than tripled exports (2.5 billion dollars in 1914 to 8.5 billion dollars in 1919).[53]

In this environment the dependency of the French and especially the British on the United States grew apace. The figures were enormous for that era. The United States lent the Allies 12 billion dollars to finance the war effort, of which 2.3 billion dollars were lent even before April 1917. By 1916, even before U.S. intervention in the war, 40 percent of all British war expenditures were spent in the United States. Overall, from 1915–1918 Great Britain ordered 18 billion dollars of weapons and supplies in the United States. By the end of the war the British dominance as the world's strongest financial power was rapidly ebbing as Great Britain sold off many overseas assets and ran up over 5 billion dollars in debt in the United States. While the U.S. economy boomed from war demand and emerged in 1919 as "rich, confident and nearly unharmed," "Europe emerged from the war in a seriously weakened state and with a residue of problems that were to plague it and the international economy for much of the interwar period."[54]

Second, it was not the weak military performance of the U.S. army in 1917 and 1918 that impressed the Allied power and frightened Germany but rather the *potential* U.S. military power in 1919 and 1920. While all the armies, on both sides of the front, would be totally exhausted and facing the specter of the Russian collapse, the U.S. army would be fresh and eager for combat. This was particularly frightening to the German leaders only too aware of the massive disintegration of both the army and homefront in the fall of 1918. The prospect of 80 American divisions (equal to 160 European divisions) with over 3 million men in France by the summer of 1919 struck terror in the hearts of Generals Ludendorff and Hindenburg.[55] So too did the prospect of the powerful U.S. economy at full throttle pouring out a cornucopia of vast numbers of weapons in 1919 and 1920.

Third, the end of World War I brought a political vacuum which the United States rushed to fill. The enormous and seemingly pointless conflagration that in over four years killed 10 million soldiers and inflicted 20 million casualties, as well as an economic crisis and flu pandemic that swept Europe in 1919, brought Europe to a grave crisis by the end of the war and its immediate aftermath. This political crisis saw the disintegration of four dynastic empires and the rise of the world's first socialist state after the October Revolution. At the same time it sparked a wave of incipient, but ultimately failed, radical attempts to seize power in Germany, Hungary, and Austria. In the disintegration of the old decadent European order, only the United States, apart from the European balance-of-power system, could offer a liberal view of a new international order with great popular appeal. President Woodrow Wilson's progressive foreign policy, embodied in the Fourteen Points, envisioned a world without conquest, annexation, or secret covenants, a new era of open diplomacy, free trade, decolonization, League of Nations, self-determination, and arms control.

The purely military aspects of the war were to have important implications for the future. The poor Russian military performance and the physical disintegration of the Russian army in 1917 and early 1918 were to exert a powerful hold on the Western image of Russian/Soviet power right up to 1941. Later events, such as the massive transformation of the Red Army and Soviet economy in the 1930s, would be heavily discounted as a result. Rather, the West would largely focus on negative factors, such as the Great Purges and poor Red Army performance in the Winter War against Finland. These Western images of Russia would enhance the reluctance of the Anglo–French allies to seriously seek a military alliance with the Soviet Union against Germany in the 1930s. And they would help entice Hitler into believing that the Soviet Union, like France, could be easily destroyed in a short, lightning campaign.

In this context the Soviet recovery from the massive defeats of 1941 and 1942 and the historic victories from 1943 to 1945 seemed almost inexplicable. In the coming chapters we will be looking at how Stalin was able to transform a backward and oft-beaten country into a powerful one by 1945. This is one of the leitmotivs of the volume.

For the United States the war seemed to confirm that it could emerge as a great power without a strong and prepared army or good military performance. Its economic and political power, coupled with the blessings of geography, would suffice in this regard. The lessons of World War I would promote a return to a small and weak army in the interwar period. During World War II these historical memories would undergird the Rooseveltian concept of the United States as an "arsenal of democracy" that need not seriously engage the German enemy until it was on its last legs.

NOTES

1. Hart, *Real*, p.53.
2. Ferro, *Great*, p.62.
3. Hart, *Real*, p.106.
4. Solzhenitsyn, *August*.
5. There are many useful sources on the East Prussian campaign. Apart from such standard sources as Edmonds, Hart, and Fall there are some other interesting sources such as Denikin, *Career*, pp.232–242.
6. *Ibid.*; Edmonds, *Short*, pp.52–58; and Falls, *First*, p.40.
7. Dupuy, *Genius*, p.178.
8. Ferro, *Great*, p.62.
9. Hart, *Real*, p.72; Falls, *First*, pp.55–56; Edmonds, *Short*, pp.65–66; and Denikin, *Career*, pp.243-244.
10. Adelman, *Revolution*, pp.70–71.
11. Neilson, *Strategy*, p.86.
12. Ferro, *Great*, p.61.
13. Hart, *Real*, pp.202–226 and Falls, *First*, pp.190–197.
14. *Ibid.*; Ferro, *Great*, p.78; DeWeerd, *President*, p.163; and Robbins, *First*, pp.57–59.
15. Neilson, *Strategy*, pp.232–241 and Ferro, *Russian*, p.242.
16. Ferro, *Russian*, p.159.
17. *Ibid.*, pp.367–368.
18. McCauley, editor, *Russian*, p.31 and Mints, *Istoriya*, v.1, p.361.
19. Liebman, *Russian*, p.152.
20. Wildman, *End*, pp.335–336.
21. DeWeerd, *President*, pp.176–177; Falls, *First*, pp.265–266; and Edmonds, *Short*, pp.261–263.
22. Edmonds, *Short*, p.264 and Barrett, *Swordbearers*, p.255.
23. Liebman, *Russian*, pp.217–218.
24. *Ibid.*, pp.301–312 and Ulam, *Expansion*, pp.52–73. Interestingly, one of the causes of the German defeat was that they still left significant forces in the East throughout 1918, a time when Germany faced no threat there and badly needed such forces in the West. Clearly, though, the German high command felt it only prudent to do so at this time in view of the Russian role in the war. In addition, such troops, numbering over one

million men, were needed to administer and protect the new vast German conquests in the East mandated by the Treaty of Brest Litovsk.

25. Lutz, *Causes*, pp.53–54 and Edmonds, *Short*, pp.273–276.

26. Urlanis, *Wars*, p.55.

27. For an excellent description of the U.S. style of warfare, see Weigley, *American*.

28. One of the best works on World War I is by the former chief- of-staff for General Pershing and the commander of the Services of Supply. See Harbord, *American*, p.7.

29. *Ibid.*, p.6 and Waitley, *America*, p.49.

30. Beaver, *Newton*, p.13.

31. *Ibid.*, p.12.

32. One of the finer works on the subject is that by Coffman. See Coffman, *War*, p.16. Also see the comprehensive work by Matloff, editor, *American*, pp.364–368.

33. Huston, *Sinews*, p.310.

34. Pershing, *My*, v.2, p.68.

35. *Ibid.*, v.1, p.xv.

36. Harbord, *American*, p.28.

37. Pershing, *My*, v.1, pp.27–28, 87-108, and 131 and DeWeerd, *President*, p.206.

38. Pershing, *My*, v.1, p.78; Coffman, *War*, p.21; Matloff, editor, *American*, p.372; and Huston, *Sinews*, pp.310–312.

39. Pershing, *My*, v.1, p.235, v.2, p.84.

40. Brook-Shepherd, *November*, pp.58–73.

41. DeWeerd, *President*, p.393 and Pershing, *My*, v.2, p.84.

42. Millett and Maslowski, *For*, p.350.

43. Matloff, editor, *American*, p.393; Harbord, *American*, pp.280–285, 343, and 405; Pershing, *My*, v.2, pp.60, 89–90, 160, and 389; Barrett, *Swordbearers*, p.349; and Coffman, *War*, pp.153–156, 221, and 235.

44. Edmonds, *Short*, p.410.

45. *Ibid.*, p.425; DeWeerd, *President*, pp.216, 380, and 393; and Pershing, *My*, v.2, p.84.

46. Churchill, *World*, v.4, pp.266–267.

47. Palmer, *Newton*, v.2, p.341 and Pershing, *My*, v.2, p.267.

48. Brook-Shepherd, *November*, pp.105–111; Coffman, *War*, pp.273–283 and Pershing, *My*, v.2, p.224.

49. Hart, *Real*, pp.380, 462–463.

50. DeWeerd, *President*, pp.361–362; Coffman, *War*, pp.303–313; Waitley, *America*, pp.97–104; and Beaver, *Newton*, pp.190–197.

51. Pershing, *My*, v.2, pp.388–389; Hart, *Real*, p.460; and Freidel, *Over*, pp.237–256.

52. Beaver, *Newton*, p.208.

53. *Statistical*, pp.179, 537.

54. Aldcroft, *European*, p.13; Dreisziger, *Mobilization*, pp.20; 25, Baruch, *Public*, p.73; and Gaddis, *Russia*, p.52. The decline of Europe in

the period during and after the war was striking. In 1913 Europe accounted for 43 percent of the world's GNP and a startling 59 percent of all trade. By 1923 these figures had dropped to 34 percent of the GNP and 50 percent of the trade. The main beneficiaries of this decline were the United States and Japan. For this and other interesting data, see a very useful work by Pollard, *Peaceful*, p.281.

55. Harbord, *American*, p.534.

4

Russian and U.S.
Institutions in Wartime

This final chapter on World War I is a review of the functioning of the Russian and U.S. governments, economies and armies. Why did the tremendous Russian war effort come to naught while the fledgling and belated U.S. effort bore such magnificent fruit? How did the relative U.S. and Russian institutional capabilities compare and what was their respective impact on the battlefield performance?

We will suggest that world wars, by forcing the total mobilization of a country's economic, political, and military resources, test the overall effectiveness of a nation (size, of course, being held constant). Wars relentlessly expose all of the weaknesses of a state and its social structure that are usually hidden from view. At the same time wars also reveal the strength of rising states in the international order. World War I demonstrated and accelerated the terminal weakness and disintegration of Tsarist Russia and the rising power of the United States. In short, the war demonstrated just how fatally far behind the other major powers Tsarist Russia lagged and what great latent power resided in the United States.

RUSSIAN AND U.S. GOVERNMENTS

There existed a major gap between the two countries in all three areas with regard to effectiveness and capabilities. The political capacity of the two governments was markedly different. Both Tsarist Russia and the United States did share some common attributes. Neither prepared adequately for a long war that almost no one foresaw. Both governments were able to mobilize and to enjoy widespread popular support at the beginning of the war.

In spite of these similarities the political capabilities and effectiveness of the U.S. government under President Woodrow Wilson far exceeded that of the Russian government under Tsar Nicholas II. For the United States, despite certain maladies deeply rooted in U.S. history, still enjoyed a relatively modern and effective political system. Despite problems with the rights and status of women, blacks, and ethnic minorities, there was no question that the majority of the population deeply believed in the values and legitimacy of the political system. A further testament to this was the relatively minor influence of radical parties (even though then at the height of their influence) on the U.S. system. There was a well-defined and open, shared bond between the leaders and the citizens on the role of government in society and on the proper norms and values for the political system. Western democratic ideals and notions of a liberal capitalist order were widely shared in U.S. society.

In the 140 years since its founding the United States had developed flexible and nicely integrated political institutions, often with a long tradition of adaptation to change. These institutions took many forms. The two main political parties, having just survived challenges from several other parties, were well-oiled political machines. They were accustomed to alternating in power. The official democratic ethos of the society encouraged mass participation in politics through membership in the parties and active participation in the electoral process at all levels. A vocal, combative, and competitive press actively promoted this process. The system had long-established and widely accepted procedures for political succession and limiting and controlling political violence and conflict. A small and weak standing army openly acknowledged civilian control of the military and never challenged it. This reflected the geographic reality that the United States, safe behind its oceans, could even afford total defeat abroad and still retreat safely to its borders as long as the British navy was intact. Over time, and especially during the Wilson era, the role of the government in the economy and in regulation of society greatly expanded.[1]

Due to historical and political circumstances unique to the

United States, the strength and effectiveness of the government bureaucracy was limited. In 1916, the last full prewar year, the U.S. government budget was all of 700 million dollars, a miniscule sum.[2] But the seeds of a far more expanded and effective government bureaucracy were present.

The U.S. government unquestionably enjoyed the freely given loyalty of the majority of its citizens. It thereby could easily exercise all of the authority traditionally ceded to government: to tax the people and business, to mobilize all human and natural resources for war, and to efficiently create and carry out policies. The government had the will, capacity, and legitimacy to execute its policies.[3]

During its short entry into the war, the Wilson administration was able to effectively use the levers of government to mobilize the U.S. people, industry, and labor for the war. The size of the government bureaucracy soared as U.S. government spending leaped from 0.7 billion dollars in 1916 to 1.96 billion dollars in 1917 and 12.66 billion dollars in 1918.[4] The Selective Service System classified 24.2 million men for the draft, examined 3.8 million men, and inducted 2.8 million men.[5] George Creel's Committee on Public Information, formed in April 1917, helped persuade a reluctant public of the need for the war. On the coercive side the Espionage Act and Sedition Act served to deter opposition to the war by active use of governmental power.[6] Thus, the state demonstrated strong capabilities in the political mobilization of the U.S. populace for war.

In striking contrast, Tsarist Russia, both before and even more so during the war, was an enfeebled and decaying political system. Like other traditional dynastic empires, the fate of the entire system rested heavily on the qualities of the man occupying the throne not by talent, experience, or election but by the accident of birth. Much like the French monarchy on the eve of the French Revolution, the Russian monarchy during World War I was particularly ill served by the last of the Romanov line which had ruled Russia for three centuries.

A weak-willed autocrat of the old school who believed in his own divine authority, Nicholas II seemed an anachronism in early twentieth-century European politics. Devoid of serious political skills and talents, he was indolent and preferred sports and his family to the seemingly boring and endless task of running a vast empire. Suffering from political myopia and narrow political views, Nicholas openly espoused reactionary views with a taste for the anti-Semitic "Black Hundreds" and a passion for medieval Muscovy.

Bored by his Cabinet ministers, whom he dismissed at will, Nicholas surrounded himself with mediocrity and routinely fired those men who displayed any talent for governing. Contemptuous of mass public opinion, the Duma, and the private associations that sprang up to support the war effort, the poorly educated Nicholas increasingly isolated himself and his family circle from the Russian people, and by the end of his life, this self-imposed isolation was almost complete.

When Tsar Nicholas II in the fall of 1915 abandoned Moscow for Mogilev to assume the position of commander-in-chief of the armed forces, even more sinister forces rushed to fill the power vacuum at the top of the Russian government. These took the form most notably of the personages of the Tsarina Alexandra and Grigory Rasputin, the illiterate Siberian monk.

With the departure of her husband to the front, the Tsarina rapidly moved to expand her influence. An ardent devotee of the obscurantist "Black Hundreds," the Tsarina was a naive, ignorant, and reactionary mystic in poor mental and physical health. Yet she wielded considerable power in the protracted absence of her husband from Moscow. Her adviser and confidant, Grigory Rasputin, was a narrow-minded, archconservative, unprincipled adventurer. His only saving grace was that he had warned that war would destroy the monarchy. That he could actually be highly influential at the court until his murder in December 1916 by outraged aristocrats speaks volumes about the depths to which the Russian government sank during the war.[7]

If mentioning President Wilson and Colonel House in the same breath as Tsar Nicholas II, Tsarina Alexandra, and Grigory Rasputin seems patently absurd and insulting to the Americans, the same would be true of a comparison of the top civilian leaders in the two countries. While the United States has rarely been blessed with brilliant leaders, the overall level of competence has usually been good and at times even excellent. World War I was no exception. President Wilson could count not only on men like Newton Baker as secretary of war but also on men like Bernard Baruch, whom he recruited from private industry to head the War Industries Board.

By marked contrast, the "best and the brightest" were rarely found in the Tsar's Cabinet, where mediocrity flourished. This was, to use the Russian phrase, "no accident," for mediocrity was openly rewarded, given the threatening nature of competent, more modern leaders. Apart from a brief liberal phase in 1915, the Cabinet was dominated by numerous reactionaries whose main talent was pleasing the court. From the beginning of the war in August 1914 until the February Revolution in 1917, the cabinet was in perpetual chaos with three foreign ministers, four prime ministers, and six ministers of the interior.

Take the four prime ministers. The first, Ivan Goremykin, was an enfeebled, exhausted, incompetent, and even senile seventy-eight-year-old courtier of the most reactionary persuasion. His successor, Boris Sturmer, was even worse, hated by the Duma, universally regarded as weak, incompetent, reactionary, and dishonest. Politically, he was an intimate of the Tsarina and Rasputin, who were attracted by his extreme reactionary views and association with the secret police. After the brief interlude of the moderate Alexander Trepov, the final prime minister was Prince Nikolai Golitsyn. His sole previous governmental experience consisted of serving as head of the Committee to Aid Russian POWs. He vainly pleaded ill health and ignorance in trying to avoid the assignment.

Other Cabinet ministers were equally wretched. The final minister of the interior, Aleksandr Protopopov, was widely thought to be a mentally unbalanced, bombastic ultrareactionary friend of Rasputin. And the first war minister, General Vladimir Sukhomlinov, was a rigid officer of antiquarian views who later became the scapegoat for Russian defeats.[8]

Under these conditions, and given the ponderous and corrupt nature of the government bureaucracy, the Russian political system was premodern and ineffective. The Tsarist polity, apart from the early giddy days of the Russian entry into World War I in August 1914, did not enjoy the most basic attribute vital to a viable political system—the voluntary and uncoerced belief of the majority of its citizens in the values and legitimacy of the system. There is little doubt that the majority of the population was alienated from the system. The extreme emphasis of the regime on Great Russian nationalism and active attempts to Russify non-Russian profoundly repelled the half of the population that was not Russian, especially the Poles and Ukrainians. Similarly, the enshrinement of the Russian Orthodox church as the official state church deeply offended the half of the empire that were not believers. And the vile and medieval pogroms encouraged by the state against the Jews and Armenians embittered their view of the state and enraged enlightened public opinion. The nominal rigid stratification of society into legal estates estranged the bulk of the population.

The same was true for the relationship between the Tsar and the political institutions in his empire. A devout medievalist believer in divine right and absolute monarchy, Nicholas detested all political institutions and any attempts to mobilize public opinions as deleterious to his own power and authority. On becoming Tsar in 1895, he denounced the rural *zemstvo*, made up of his most likely supporters among the gentry, as representing "senseless dreams" of popular participation in government. Forced to accede to the creation of a Duma, or popular assembly, in 1905, the Tsar dissolved it three times in ten years, severely limited its franchise and authority, and repeatedly manifested his distrust and disrespect for the institution. Finally, when during the war the public created a series of institutions to aid the war effort, he disdained their effort.

In yet a third area, that of classes, did the Tsar remove himself and his system from the affection of his constituents. Even his most likely supporters in the aristocracy and bourgeoisie were disaffected by his refusal to give them a meaningful political role in the regime. The industrial working class, living under terrible conditions and not allowed to unionize, was especially estranged from the state. The sullen mass of 100 million peasants, living in dire poverty with minimal political consciousness, was remote from the system. Peasant faith in the "Little Father" had been shattered by the Russo–Japanese War and the 1905 Revolution. If by 1914 the governmental system in George Kennan's words was in "an advanced stage of political disintegration," the failures in World War I would lead to the final destruction of a decaying polity.[9]

The lack of legitimacy of the regime was accompanied by another serious failure—the lack of an effective, flexible bureaucratic structure. The huge and ponderous government bureaucracy, backed up by a large army and strong secret police, could help maintain tsarism in peacetime. But in wartime the weaknesses of the bureaucracy became manifest and contributed to economic disintegration at home and military defeats abroad. Increasingly corrupt and venal over time, the passive bureaucracy could not cope with the increased burdens of wartime. Its total identification with the autocracy and derivation of powers only from the autocrat left it rigid and inflexible in a rapidly changing environment. The bureaucracy isolated itself from all the new social forces and pushed them onto a revolutionary path.[10]

The political capabilities of Tsarist Russia were low and declining as the country moved inexorably towards decay and regeneration in revolution. The government thereby lacked a popular consensus on the system's legitimacy and societal traditions and values. It had no strong modern and flexible integrated political institutions. There was no effective bureaucracy, well-organized political party, popular participation in the government, or effective manner for controlling political conflict. The Tsarist government, in marked contrast to the U.S. government, was a weak and declining neo-traditional force.

RUSSIAN AND UNITED STATES WAR ECONOMIES

The gap, if anything, was even greater in the economic realm than the political realm. The United States was the world's economic colossus, with a GNP equal to that of Germany, France, England, Japan, and Italy combined. In 1913 its GNP was at least three times that of Russia, the world's fifth largest industrial power. In the industrial arena the gap was far wider. In industrial production, in 1914 the United States produced 38.2 percent of the world's output, Russia 2.6 percent! The United States produced 31.8 million tons of steel, Russia a paltry 4.8 million tons in 1913. In machine building the United States produced 50 percent of the world output, Russia an even more meager 3.5 percent.[11]

A vast gulf separated the two powers. If the respective populations are taken into account, the situation became more embarrassing for Russia. In 1913 the United States had a per capita income ten times larger than that of Russia, whose level was that of Romania and Bulgaria.[12] As Marc Ferro asserted, the Russian economy, despite strong progress, still lagged so badly that in 1914, "not only was she half a century behind France and the United States, but no one saw she could catch up."[13]

During the war neither the United States nor Tsarist Russia developed a superior war economy. We have already seen the inadequacies of Russian and U.S. war production. The heavy dependency on foreign supplies was symptomatic of their problems which persisted throughout the war for both powers. From the onset of the war the unprepared Tsarist Russian economy experienced a severe munitions crisis in 1914 and early 1915. This was ameliorated only by a supreme mobilization of the Russian economy and major foreign imports. But by 1916 foreign imports fell off sharply (to 36 percent of the 1914 level) in the wake of severe Russian defeats that destroyed Allied confidence in Russian war ability.[14] And the Russian economy faltered badly under the strain of the massive war efforts. The 1916 attempt to make Boris Sturmer a military dictator was an abysmal failure. By 1917 the transportation network was disintegrating, food shortages were common in the cities, strikes were mounting among an industrial work force that had declined 40 percent during the war, and prices in 1917 were almost seven times higher than in 1913. The Allies lent 4.0 billion dollars to the faltering Russian economy, whose ruble lost 41.9 percent of its value in London from August 1914 to 1917. By the Petrograd conference in February 1917, Lord Alfred Milner, deeply worried by the disintegration of the Russian war economy, feared "not so much deliberate revolution as chaos resulting from the confusion into which a badly organized administrative system has been thrown by the strain of war."[15]

Ironically, the weak performance of the Russian war economy did not reflect a lack of effort by the government. Tsarist Russia's massive war effort placed great strain on an inefficient and technically backward economy. The mobilization of 16 million able-bodied men in the army and 80 percent of the factories for the war effort were too much for the frail and backward economy.[16]

By contrast, the U.S. leaders also made serious errors—but with a vastly stronger economy, they had far greater degrees of freedom. While output was inadequate in 1917 and 1918, the prospects for 1919 and even more so 1920 were very bright. By November 1918 the United States had produced exactly 76 tanks—but had 22,400 on order for 1919. From April 1917 to November 1918 the United States had turned out only 3,500 cannon—but by the end of the war it was producing at an annual rate of over 10,000 a year. Similarly, in all the other key areas, from machine guns to shells to rifles, after a slow start the United States was producing all these weapons in the last several months of the war at a rate two to three times faster than either England or France. Had the war but lasted another year or two, the predominance of the United States would have become manifest.[17]

The U.S. failures in World War I, then, were not economic but largely political in nature. Even in April 1917, over two and one-half years after the start of the war, the United States was woefully unprepared for war. The governmental bureaucracy was small and ill suited by temperament, tradition, and organization to direct such a vast effort. The nineteenth-century liberalism of President Wilson, which opposed a growing state coordination and direction of the economy, pervaded Washington and left it unprepared for modern bureaucratized warfare. Not until one year after the entry into the war, with the appointment of Bernard Baruch as chairman of the War Industries Board (March 1918) and passage of the Overman Act (May 1918), did the U.S. war effort finally take shape. Until then the center lacked adequate authority to move the U.S. economy in the necessary direction by fixing wages and prices, commandeering resources, and making needed personnel changes. Until the spring of 1918, in Bernard Baruch's words, there was "confusion and little progress."[18]

However, the fault did not entirely lie with the politicians. In 1917 public hostility to the war remained sufficiently widespread that many, if not most, Americans, felt that there would be no need to send a large army to Europe. This attitude later pervaded the government as well. The U.S. military was also clearly responsible for the delays in industrial mobilization. In April 1917 the War Department lacked any real plans for this critical task and was poorly organized to develop one. As a result, "the first six months of the manufacturing program were largely futile, wasted and abortive."[19]

Some progress was made in 1917. A number of new organizations were formed, vast sums of money were appropriated for the war, and millions of men were mobilized into the army. But even by January 1918 there were all of four divisions in France and "very little production of military equipment had taken place."[20] During 1918 production improved markedly but shortages persisted until the armistice. What carried the U.S. Army through the war were the inherent strengths of the U.S. economy and weaknesses of the enemy. The United States, after all, was the world's leading industrial power, blessed with large quantities of raw materials, a superb internal transportation network, a skilled and educated population, and strong engineering and mechanical capabilities. The great size and skills of the U.S. population allowed a major manpower mobilization into the army without undue harm to the economy. A strong navy, capable allies, slow but improving industrial performance, and mediocre army were more than adequate to contribute to the defeat of Imperial Germany, exhausted after four years of gruesome conflict.

NATURE OF RUSSIAN AND UNITED STATES ARMIES

Finally, a few words about the two armed forces, neither of which performed very well in combat. The lack of preparation of the Russian army for the war was so pronounced that further description seems useless. But, less known and equally important, was the remarkable weakness of the two branches of the U.S. military generally considered of superior quality, the navy and the air force. With the third largest fleet in the world in 1917 and over 533,000 men and 2,000 ships, by November 1918, the U.S. navy was quantitatively impressive. Nevertheless, it was the British Royal Navy that dominated the Atlantic Ocean, not the U.S. navy. During the last year and a half of the war, the British navy provided 70 percent of the escort ships for the Atlantic convoys, compared to a meager 27 percent provided by the U.S. navy. Far more striking were the respective roles in destroying the German U-boat menace in 1917 and 1918. The British navy eliminated 175 German submarines, the U.S. navy exactly 2 German subs—the same number as the Russian navy. Under these circumstances it was scarcely remarkable that the five U.S. battleships in the Atlantic functioned as a unit of the British navy under Admiral Sir David Beatty. The U.S. naval operation in Europe was run by Vice Admiral Sims out of a London hotel as a junior partner to the main effort of the British navy, which truly ruled the waves.[21]

Even more phenomenal was the abysmal state of U.S. air power in the war. After all, it was two U.S. brothers that had invented the airplane in 1903. So uninterested was the United States in general and the U.S. military in particular that in 1914 the United States was fourteenth in the world in spending on airplanes. In 1917 the tiny U.S. air service, having minimal funds and ignoring the war experience, lacked a single plane fit for the Western front. During the first year of U.S. participation in the war, the air service had six commanders. The U.S. air service lagged far behind the British Royal Air Force. In 1918 the RAF had 3,300 frontline planes, the U.S. air service, 740 planes. In short, the fledgling U.S. air force found itself far behind its British and French counterparts.[22]

A comparison of the quality of the officers and men in the two armies is interesting, for as we have shown elsewhere, armies are a faithful microcosm of society, and the effectiveness of armies tells a great deal about societal capabilities.[23] Nowhere was this truer than in the Russian officer corps, which dutifully reflected all the deficiencies of Tsarist society. The majority of Tsarist society was systematically excluded from consideration for the officers. In 1912 no less than 87.5 percent of the generals and over 50 percent of the senior officers came from the hereditary nobility, which represented less than 1 percent of the population. Similarly, non-Russians had virtually no hope for admission to the officer corps, which was overwhelmingly Russian (86 percent) and German (7 percent) in origin. Talent and hard work counted for little because promotion was based on seniority, family ties and personal influence.[24]

A remote general staff paid little attention to the selection and preparation of the command staff. Such a system, in words of a Duma committee report to Tsar Nicholas II during the war, "is fatal to our cause."[25] The result was unmitigated disaster. Even Tsar Nicholas II was appalled at what his rule had wrought, even if he didn't really understand it. In letters the Tsar wrote to the Tsarina in March and June 1916 this despair was evident:

> Many generals are making serious blunders. The worst of it is that we have so few good generals...many of our commanding generals are silly idiots, who, even after two years of warfare, have not been able to learn the first and simplest ABC of the military art. I cannot tell you how angry I am with them. . . .[26]

The U.S. officer corps also suffered from some serious maladies. Like the Russian army, the U.S. army promoted largely on seniority, creating, in the words of General James Harbord "a somnolent inefficiency."[27] The situation was even worse in the National Guard where political influence and seniority prevailed over talent. Under these circumstances any reforms, as those implemented by Elihu Root after the Spanish–American War, had limited impact. Most officers above the rank of captain had entered the army before the Spanish–American War at a time when Civil War veterans were dominant. So lethargic was the army and so uninterested in foreign military developments or technological change that Secretary of War Stimson in 1911 called it "a profoundly peaceful army."[28]

The biggest problem of the U.S. army lay, however, not in the admittedly mediocre quality of the officer corps but in its size and experience. The United States Army did have some excellent officers such as George Marshall and John Pershing and a group of officers who had gone through the Fort Leavenworth Staff College. Yet in 1917 there were only 6,000 regular army officers and 55 general staff officers to lead an ultimately multimillion man army.[29] During World War I the weak training and inexperience of the officers led to serious problems, as seen in General Pershing's cable to Washington in December 1917,

> Officers from colonels down and including some general officers are found ignorant of handling units in open warfare, including principles of reconnaissance, outposts, advance guards, solution of practical problems and formation of attack; . . . many officers of high rank are hopelessly ignorant of what this training consists.[30]

There was a significant problem in both armies, but especially in the Tsarist army, with the quality of soldiers. Perhaps nowhere else was the backwardness of Tsarist Russia, and its dramatic lag behind the West, so evident. The soldiers mostly came from peasant families with very primitive standards of culture and living. The soldiers, being illiterate or semiliterate, were passive and unable to perform anything more than very simple tasks. Maltreated and abused by their officers and only vaguely aware of the cause for which they were fighting, the peasants fought with courage and physical endurance but without understanding. Truly, the army reflected the society.

The U.S. army, by contrast, could draw on a far better educated and mechanically adept population. The United States' role as the world's leading economic power created an excellent base for the army. The only drawback was their complete lack of military experience and weak military training, which retarded the formation of the U.S. army in Europe until 1918.

World War I in many ways foreshadowed World War II. While a powerful Germany would ultimately be beaten by a loose and heterogeneous coalition in both wars, the constellation of victorious forces would change between the wars with dramatic consequences for the international political order after 1945. The most dramatic and pitiable actor in World War I was Tsarist Russia. Beaten and beaten again by the German army, the Tsarist Empire finally collapsed amid the 1917 February Revolution, soon followed by the October Revolution and self-abasement of the

Treaty of Brest Litovsk in March 1918. Under these pitiful circumstances only a valiant French defense and British naval blockade kept the Allies in the war before the belated U.S. entry into the war in force in the fall of 1918.

These events graphically demonstrated the extreme weakness in Russian government, economy, and military. Only a powerful transformation in the Russian polity and economy, with concomitant improvements in the military, would be able to alter this dismal situation. The prognosis, then, in 1918 was very poor, unless the Bolsheviks and the Russian revolution could make profound changes in Russian capabilities to compete in the modern world.

The contrast with the United States was stark. The U.S. government and economy was strong and vibrant. Its geographic position allowed it the benefit of being able to make choices and act while Russia, by dint of its geography, was often caught up in the immediate threat and reacting to it. A relatively weak and small army was a luxury that the United States, but not Russia, could afford, especially as long as the U.S. and British navies ruled the Atlantic. The future, then, for the United States seemed as bright as it seemed dark for the new rulers of the Soviet Union. The likelihood that the leaders of the fledgling Soviet state, barely holding out against Denikin and Yudenich thrusting towards Moscow and Petrograd in the fall of 1919, might only three decades later be considered in the same superpower class as the leaders of the United States, seemed very remote in the aftermath of World War I.

NOTES

1. See Skowronek, *Building*.
2. *Statistical*, p.720.
3. See Huntington's classic work, *Political*, p.1.
4. *Statistical*, p.720.
5. *Ibid.*, p.735.
6. DeWeerd, *President*, p.243.
7. The letters of the Tsar to the Tsarina and her letters to him are fascinating in showing the degeneration of tsarism in World War I and demonstrating their unfitness for the mantle of leadership. See both *The Letters of the Tsar to the Tsaritsa 1914–1917*, translated by Hynes and *The Letters of the Tsaritsa to the Tsar 1914–1916*, translated by Hynes.

8. *Ibid.* See also Pearson, *Russian,* pp.100–107, 124–127 and Liebman, *Russian,* p.77.

9. See the well-known essay by Kennan, "Breakdown" in Pipes, editor, *Revolutionary,* p.14.

10. For an interesting Soviet view of the Tsarist bureaucracy, see Eroshkin, *Istoriya.*

11. Gregory, *Russian,* pp.158, 194; Munting, *Economic,* p.33; and Blackwell, editor, *Russian,* p.356, Appendix I. The Blackwell book is a particularly interesting compendium placing Stalinism in its Russian context.

12. *Ibid.*

13. Ferro, *Russian,* p.320.

14. *Ibid.,* pp.19–22 and Neilson, *Strategy* , p.236.

15. Many Soviet specialists are fond of denigrating Soviet accomplishments by asserting that Tsarist Russia was already well on its way to becoming a modern, industrialized state before 1914 and that only the outbreak of war nipped in the bud these promising developments. Of course, Tsarist Russia did make significant progress in the half-century before the February Revolution. But the important points are, first, that Tsarist Russia was still extremely backward in 1914 and, second, that its rate of growth was inadequate to keep it from slipping ever further behind all of the major Western powers. The comparison with the United States is especially telling. Despite the economic advantages of backwardness, Tsarist Russia had an annual growth rate of only 2.5 percent in the 1860–1913 period, compared to a much stronger 4.3 percent annual growth rate for the United States in the 1870–1913 period. The story was even worse when population was taken into account. During these same periods, the Russian annual growth rate per capita was 1.0 percent while the U.S. rate was more than twice as high, at 2.2 percent. Finally, it is well to remember that while a Tsarist Russia that survived the war (in itself, an unlikely proposition considering the demise of three other empires in the war) might have done reasonably well in the 1920s, it would certainly have suffered severely from the Great Depression of the 1930s, leaving it little better off in 1940 than 1914. For the best analysis of the economic growth issues see Stanley Cohn, "The Soviet Economy: Performance and Growth," in Blackwell, editor, *Russian,* p.324. See also Neilson, *Strategy,* p.243. This book is exceptionally useful for this period.

16. This point is important since it was not for lack of mobilization of manpower or resources that Tsarist Russia did so poorly in the war. Rather it was precisely that such a mobilization strained a weak and inefficient political system and economy to the breaking point. See Skocpol, *States.*

17. Randall, *Stalin's,* p.324 and Crowell and Wilson, *Armies,* pp.34, 36, 50.

18. Pershing, *My,* v.1, p.388.

19. Crowell and Wilson, *Armies,* pp.xv, xvii, xxii.

20. DeWeerd, *President.* p.223.

21. Coffman, *War,* pp.101–102, Freidel, *Over,* pp.34, 65 and Churchill, *World,* v.4, p.76.

22. Harbord, *American,* p.501; Edmonds, *Short,* p.298; Crowell and Wilson, *Armies,* pp.325-326, 332, 346; and Coffman, *War,* pp.195, 210.

23. See Adelman, *Revolution* for a more detailed treatment of this subject.

24. For a good Soviet treatment of the topic see Strokov, *Vooruzhennye,* p.23.

25. Liebman, *Russian,* p.76.

26. See some interesting aspects of this in *Letters of the Tsa,* pp.157, 216.

27. Harbord, *American,* p.46.

28. Coffman, *War,* p.18.

29. DeWeerd, *President,* pp.11, 236.

30. Pershing, *My,* v.1, p.266.

Section 2
The Interwar Years
1919–1939

5

The Interwar Years

The interwar years were crucial to the ultimate outcome of the second great international conflict, which would erupt in 1939 and consume much of the world for six years. These interwar years formed a bridge between the two components of one macroconflict. Certain aspects of the interwar years were to prove vital to the early German successes and later failures, belated U.S. intervention in the war, and initial Russian catastrophes and later successes. The strong progress made by the Soviet Union in the 1930s, compared to the Great Depression wracking the United States at the same time, helped create a Soviet/U.S. relationship radically different in 1945 from that in 1918. It also helped to set the stage for the Cold War that ensued almost concurrently with the creation of a new international order after 1945.

OVERVIEW OF SOVIET AND U.S. POLITICAL AND ECONOMIC DEVELOPMENTS

At the end of World War I the contrast between the positions of the United States and Russia in the international order could hardly have been greater or starker. Fortune itself seemed to be smiling on the New World. Untouched by the ravages of war and having escaped with minimal war casualties, the United States in 1919 seemed to be a rising new superpower, fresh and awesome.

By contrast, all of the European powers seemed old, worn down by war, and decadent.

Economically, the United States towered over war-devastated Europe. While its exports more than quadrupled from 1914 to 1919, its stock of gold almost doubled. From being a debtor nation in 1913, the United States became a strong creditor nation in 1919. Even more dramatically, the American balance-of-payments surplus soared from 56.0 million dollars in 1914 to a phenomenal 4.9 billion dollars in 1919.

All this reflected a massive war-fueled economic boom that saw a strong gain of 41 percent in U.S. GNP between 1914 and 1919. The size of this increased output alone was greater than the GNP of any European power in 1919 and almost equal to the GNP of Germany in 1914. And it was even more impressive since, apart from Japan, this major expansion took place at a time of major economic decline for all other great powers, including victorious England (–15 percent) as well as humiliated Germany (–34 percent). One single fact tells a simple story: by 1919 the GNP of the United States actually exceeded the total economic output of the world's seven other great powers *combined*—and by a comfortable margin.[1]

The German–U.S. peace negotiations in October 1918, the enthusiastic reception accorded President Wilson in Europe in 1919, and the prominent U.S. role at Versailles all reflected this newfound U.S. role. The economic preeminence provided a strong base for the attractiveness of Wilsonian political liberalism. And it was the U.S. military potential for 1919 and 1920, rather than actual battlefield activity in 1917 and 1918, that hastened the German call for an armistice that ended the war. On balance, then, the United States emerged from World War I as a potential superpower in all critical areas. If in the aftermath of the 1920 League of Nations debate this role was never exercised, this was due mainly to U.S. domestic politics and the unrealistic romanticism of the Wilsonian vision than to any deficiencies in its power position.

If the United States after World War I had vast power but refused to use it, Russia after the armistice found itself in exactly the opposite position. The international power and prestige of Russia, already at a low ebb after the disintegration of the army in 1917 and humiliation of the Treaty of Brest Litovsk in 1918, sank to nearly zero in 1919—Soviet Russia under Lenin found itself embroiled in a civil war that lasted from May 1918 to November 1920. Several times, most notably in the summer of 1918 and fall of 1919, much of the country was under White or foreign rule, and the Bolsheviks seemed on the verge of collapse.

The extreme weakness of the Red Army, as I have discussed elsewhere at length, was repeatedly evident throughout the civil war period. The major problem was that the Bolsheviks, lacking any military cadres in their ranks or broad support from Tsarist officers, had to create virtually a new army from the wreckage of the old Tsarist army in 1918. Further hampered by weak political support from the peasant soldiers in the ranks, the inevitable chaos of a revolutionary situation, war weariness of the Russian population, and serious internal clashes over the nature of such an army, the Bolsheviks were able to create at best a minimally effective Red Army by 1920. It was plagued by almost three million desertions in the ranks in 1918 and 1919 and hundreds, if not thousands, of cases of treasons among a predominantly Tsarist officer element in the elite of the army. In every major campaign of the civil war—from Kolchak to Yudenich to Denikin—the Red Army suffered initially disastrous defeats before rallying. In the end, the Bolsheviks eked out victory through a combination of factors ranging from good political leadership, internal lines of control, and inheritance of Tsarist war stocks to White political ineptitude and divisions, minimally adequate Red Army, and capable secret police.

Two Leninist statements at the end of the civil war clarified both the extreme weakness of the Red Army and the debt the Bolsheviks felt towards the Whites for being even weaker. Lenin felt that the Red Army was far below the level of European armies. In December 1920 he bluntly asserted that, "we do not possess one hundredth of the forces of the combined imperialist states," and in October 1921 he speculated that "perhaps they [the Whites] might have crushed us had any of the capitalist states that were fighting us mobilized a few army corps in time."[2]

As a consequence, the Bolsheviks faced a serious long-term problem of building up a new Red Army that could adequately compete with European armies and avoid the degradation inflicted on Russia in World War I. In the 1920s, though, with a perceived stabilization of the international political situation and serious domestic problems of reconstruction and economic development at home, the Red Army remained a weak force and low priority for the regime. Only in the 1930s, with the rise of the German and Japanese threats, would the transformation of the Red

Army into a modern and powerful force become the highest priority of the Stalinist regime.

The price of victory in the civil war was exceedingly high. The military weakness of the new regime caused the Bolsheviks to lose a significant part of the Tsarist patrimony. Poland, Finland and the Baltics all became independent; western Ukraine and western Belorussia were lost to Poland; and Bessarabia was lost to Romania. Three centuries of Russian expansion westward were rolled back in the course of a few years. By 1921 the Soviet Union, despite successful campaigns in 1920 and 1921 in the Ukraine, Belorussia, and the Transcaucasus, still represented but a truncated form of the Tsarist Empire of only four years earlier.

Politically, the new radical regime was an international pariah, excluded from European conferences until Genoa in 1922. Like other successor regimes to dissolved imperial dynasties in Germany, Austria, and Turkey, it found its power and influence sharply diminished from that of the preceding regime. Reduced to futile calls for international revolution and the creation of the Comintern in 1919, Soviet Russia perceived a sharply hostile world in which no less than twenty-six nations intervened, albeit on a small scale and ineffectually, to support the White armies in destroying it in the civil war.

The civil war accelerated the disintegration of the Russian economy. By late 1920 over 10 million people had died, mainly from the pandemic sweeping Europe, industrial production sank over 80 percent, and even agricultural production declined over 50 percent. Overall, by the end of the civil war Russian GNP had collapsed an incredible 60 percent from the 1913 level.[3]

Thus, by 1919 the gap between the United States and Russia, always large, had widened to a huge chasm. The great potential U.S. military power was answered only by Russian military impotence that could not even fight off such traditionally weak powers as Romania or Poland or easily crush weak and dispersed White forces. Politically the United States stood at the apex of its influence, the Soviet Union at its nadir. And, economically, the U.S. economic surge and Russian economic collapse left the United States in 1919 with an economy that had a GNP a tremendous twelve times the size of that of the Russian economy.[4]

A simple, even obvious, question then presents itself—given the enormity of the distance between the United States and Soviet Union after World War I, the undeniable power of the enemies of the Soviet Union in the interwar period, and the poverty of the

Soviet inheritance from its Tsarist ancestors, how was it possible that World War II would spawn not just one superpower but two superpowers? And how did the Soviet Union manage to become that second superpower only a quarter of a century later? To at least partially answer these questions we will turn our attention to a brief review of the principal military, economic, and political trends of the interwar period.

1920s

Certainly, the 1920s did little to improve the Soviet position as the gap between the two countries widened even further in absolute terms by 1929. For the United States the 1920s were a period of economic boom and prosperity, of political normalcy and isolation. The Roaring Twenties witnessed strong growth in the U.S. economy. With this sterling performance the U.S. economy by the end of the 1920s still surpassed the aggregate production of the five largest European economies.

By sharp contrast, the Soviet economic recovery staged during the New Economic Plan (NEP) in the 1920s did promote a major improvement over 1919 and 1920. But by the late 1920s NEP had run out of steam, and the devastation of the world war and civil war were so great that by 1929 the Soviet economy showed an anemic 16 percent gain over 1913. Given Soviet population increase, this actually represented a negative growth rate per capita over the past sixteen years.[5]

But what was really appalling was the realization of the enormity of the gap with the West after more than a decade of socialist rule. In 1928 the Soviet Union had over 70 percent of the labor force in agriculture, similar to such underdeveloped countries today as India and China. Soviet per capita income of roughly $200 put the Soviet Union on a par with the United States in the 1870s, the decade after the American Civil War. In 1928 the economic statistics were very stark for Soviet planners: 4.3 million tons of steel, 5.0 billion kilowatts of electricity, 2,000 machine tools, and 800 cars. In 1928 U.S. GNP was fully 5 times greater than Soviet GNP and 7 times greater on a per capita basis, despite Soviet improvement since 1919.[6]

The situation seemed hopeless. By the late 1920s the Soviet Union, despite NEP, was largely an underdeveloped country. While it had taken a decade to recover to the low Tsarist levels of 1913, the Western economies had surged further ahead. The sad record of development of less developed countries (LDCs) in this century underscores the sense of desperation that permeated the Soviet economic debates in the 1920s.[7] Only a handful of more than 100 LDCs have successfully become more developed countries (MDCs)—and nearly all were special cases, mainly trade-driven smaller authoritarian Asian countries closely tied to the West (Taiwan, South Korea, Singapore, and Hong Kong) or unique countries like Israel. Not a single country had characteristics remotely resembling those of the Soviet Union in 1928.

Despite some progress in normalizing relations with the West, Moscow was politically isolated. International revolution seemed a distant prospect after so many failures (Hungary, Germany, China, etc.). The Red Army was still weak, with only 200 tanks and armored cars, 1,000 old planes, and 560,000 men.[8] It lacked any indigenous tank- or ship-building industry and, after some improvement, could perhaps at best have repelled a Polish or Romanian thrust. The German military connection in the 1920s was undoubtedly a major aid to the Red Army but was sharply limited by the poor material conditions extant during that decade. Throughout the 1920s "the defences of the Soviet Union were extremely weak....Soviet Russia was in no condition to fight a war against any but the weakest enemy until about the early 1930s."[9]

The position of the Soviet Union, then, was perilous. Unless the Soviet Union could somehow close part of the enormous gap between itself and the United States and overtake Germany, the next war would likely be fatal to the Soviet Union. Surprisingly, the Soviet Union was able to meet the challenge, due to the positive accomplishments of the Stalinist transformation of Russia in the "third revolution" in the 1930s and the negative impact of the Great Depression that swept the West in the 1930s.

1930s

Any comparison of the Soviet Union and United States in the 1930s is bound to be complex and controversial. Despite the indubitable importance of the era, Western political scientists and historians have generally ignored or downplayed it. The reasons for this are manifold. The main reason, though, is simple: any serious comparison is bound to be more favorable to Moscow than Washington. Economically, the West languished in the Great Depression that for an entire decade seemed to call into question the entire viability of Western capitalism. The Soviet Union, by contrast, though slowed by the Great Purges at the end of the 1930s, made massive economic gains.

Politically, the West failed to do anything to halt the rising tide of fascism, even appeasing Nazi Germany at the Munich conference in 1938 and ignoring strong anti-fascist appeals for help in the Spanish civil war. The Western nations did not perceive the development of a new, imperialist, and dynamic form in fascism and its attendant threat to themselves. This tendency was accentuated by memories of the great losses in World War I, fear and loathing of the Soviet Union, and absorption in domestic difficulties caused by the Great Depression.

In sharp contrast the Soviet Union, under the energetic direction of the cosmopolitan Foreign Commissar Maksim Litvinov, strongly lobbied for a Western anti-fascist alliance. Only by 1939 was the futility of such a quest evident, and Litvinov was fired as foreign commissar. In the aftermath Stalin moved towards accommodation with Nazi Germany, when he reached the Molotov-Ribbentrop Nonaggression Pact in August 1939.

Militarily, the tortoise pace of Western rearmament, coupled with traditional German superiority (as seen in World War I) in leadership and organization, allowed Nazi Germany to gain a temporary military advantage over its industrially and numerically superior Western enemies in the late 1930s and early 1940s. At the time the relatively slow pace of Western rearmament seemed logical, both in terms of political perception and economic realities of the Great Depression era.

Militarily, all the major Western powers felt relatively secure. Great Britain felt little urgency in this area, given its continuing naval superiority over Germany and confidence in a powerful French army, now reinforced with the Maginot line, that had triumphed in the previous war. France, as the previous victor, felt the same way. As to the United States, its geographic removal from any putative battlefield and its confidence in the British navy and French army and in its own strong navy and economy, reinforced the natural domestic tendencies of isolationism from European affairs. This was especially true given the disenchantment with U.S. involvement in the previous war, domestic attention focused on the Great Depression, and its own antimilitarist sentiment. Surely before September 1939 almost no one foresaw the enormity of the collapse of French and British power by 1941—and hence there was little urgency to rearm before that time. And, should that become necessary, then, as in World War I, the U.S. economy could always form the base for victory, shielded by U.S. and British naval power. Under the circumstances, then, there seemed little cause for major U.S. rearmament, and especially not that of the army, for the navy and then the air force seemed likely to carry the day.

By contrast, the Soviet Union, facing imminent danger to its existence from the rise of Japanese militarism and German fascism in the 1930s, made a large-scale and ultimately successful effort to lay the basis for a strong defense industry and powerful Red Army. Hitler's rise to power, his virulent anti-Communism and openly imperialistic ambitions for *lebensraum* in the East, naturally frightened Moscow. This was especially true since it was coupled with the rebuilding of a war machine on the powerful German economic and military base already so well demonstrated in World War I. Moscow was also worried about the growing threat from the East with the concurrent rise of an openly hostile Imperial Japan. Japanese power and antagonism had already been demonstrated in its victory over Russia in the Russo–Japanese War (1904–1905) and in clashes between the two sides in Lake Khasan and Khalkin-Gol in 1938 and 1939. These developments, coupled with the lack of any large geographic buffer zone between the Soviet Union and Japan and Germany, historical memories of prior invasions, Marxist perceptions of ineradicable capitalist hostility to Communist states, and Soviet isolation in the international arena, prompted Stalin to push hard for building up a strong military base in the 1930s.

While Stalin was largely successful in this aim, he also made serious mistakes in this regard. The Great Purges (1937–1940) were by far the greatest blunder. The liquidation of the bulk of the top officers, the paralyzing of initiative in an officer corps ravaged by loss of 10–20 thousand officers, and the promotion of relatively incompetent and aged officers on the mold of the Horse Marshals (who still believed in the cavalry mystique) were serious mistakes. So too was the failure of the army to adequately assimilate the new technology and doctrines of modern warfare, and learning the wrong lessons from the Spanish Civil War and Finnish Winter War. All this was worsened by the elimination of the important Russo-German military collaboration after Hitler's rise to power in 1939. And the Great Purges seriously slowed Soviet economic growth in the late 1930s at the time it most urgently needed to be growing to counter German military mobilization. Although these developments were to have a deleterious impact on the performance of the Red Army in the first two years of the war, the broader gains from the 1930s, as we shall see, outweighed these deficiencies.

SOVIET ECONOMIC TRANSFORMATION OF THE 1930S

Let us focus on the economic front, the most important one for protracted war. The Great Depression ravaged the United States, as it did the West in general. Even by 1938 and 1939, American national income and industrial production were still significantly below the 1929 level and GNP only slightly higher. Meanwhile, Soviet GNP roughly doubled in the 1930s while Soviet industrial production more than quadrupled. By 1937 the Soviet Union was first in Europe in machine building production, second in Europe in electrical production, and third in Europe in coal production.[10] Table 5.1 shows the dramatic Soviet accomplishments in the period of the first several five year plans:

The table illustrates the remarkable Soviet progress, especially in the heavy industrial area so vital to a war effort. Steel and coal production grew by more than fourfold, electricity production by more than ninefold, and machine tools by an astounding twenty-ninefold. Combined with the Great Depression in the West, this allowed the Soviet Union to narrow the gap between Moscow and Washington.

By 1940 U.S. GNP was less than 3 times of that of the Soviet Union, compared to 5 times in 1928. And even more importantly Russian/Soviet industrial production, only 10 percent of the U.S. level in 1913 and even less in 1928, had now climbed to roughly 30 percent of the U.S. level in 1940. The Soviet Union still lagged far behind the United States. In 1940 fifteen Soviet industries lagged an average of twenty-one years behind the United States. But the gap was smaller and Moscow could now compete in certain areas with Washington, and especially with Berlin.[11]

We saw in the previous chapter the fatal consequences for Tsarist Russia of its great lag behind Germany, as well as behind the United States. Table 5.2 shows how Stalinist Russia dramatically caught up with Germany and even improved its position markedly vis-à-vis the United States.

Table 5.1 Soviet Industrial Production, 1928-1940

Producta	Output	
	1928	1940
steel	4.3	18.3
coal	35.3	165.9
electricity	5.0	48.3
metal-cutting machine tools	2.0	58.4

*Steel and coal figures are expressed in millions of tons, electricity in billions of kilowatts, and metal-cutting machine tools in thousands.

Source: 1. Mark Harrison, *Soviet Planning in Peace and War 1938–1945* (Cambridge: Cambridge University Press, 1985), p.6.

Table 5.2 Soviet, U.S. and German Industrial Production, 1938

Producta	United States	Soviet Union	Germany
steel	28.8	18.1	23.2
pig iron	19.5	14.8	18.6
electricity	115.9	36.4	55.2
coal	352.3	132.9	186.2

Source: 1. *Statistical Yearbook of the League of Nations 1938/9* (Geneva, 1939), pp.132, 133, 135, 141, 146, 147.

* All figures are in millions of tons except for electricity, which is expressed in billions of kilowatts.

By 1938, Germany no longer produced three to four times more industrial goods than the Soviet Union, as it had in 1913. The Soviet Union had closed most of the gap separating it from Germany. Even compared to the United States, the Soviet Union was a viable competitor in such key areas as steel and pig iron. The United States still remained more powerful, as seen in its great lead in electricity and coal, in a merchant vessel fleet 9 times larger and exports 120 times greater than the Soviet Union, in a

GNP almost 3 times greater.[12] But the Soviet Union could now match Germany and compete with the United States in some areas. This was an economic feat of crucial relevance to the coming war.

The Stalinist transformation of the Soviet Union in the 1930s, in a word, worked—and very effectively. This simple truth has been most unpalatable to the bulk of Western specialists on the Soviet Union, and for a number of reasons. First, the hardline Cold War anti-Communism of the 1950s, 1960s, and now 1980s has made it extremely difficult for Western scholars to openly acknowledge positive accomplishments of the Soviet Union. Second, the glaring defects of Stalinism in the 1930s—mass repression of kulaks, forced collectivization, staged show trials, forced labor camps, Great Purges, arbitrary rule, mass public adulation of Stalin—have deeply troubled scholars and overshadowed the great accomplishments of the regime. Third, the great waste inherent in the Stalinist economy obscured its accomplishments. The high accomplishments were matched by high costs. Finally, the fact that Soviet events in the 1930s were soon overtaken by the much greater events of World War II have led scholars to downplay or ignore these changes.

The key to Soviet success lay in the October Revolution and the subsequent creation of a powerful party and strong state bureaucracy to direct change. This new party-state complex radically and directly mobilized all human and natural resources in a collectivist and authoritarian manner first seen during the civil war. Employing administrative rationalism, it could build on the Tsarist legacy and on strong untapped natural and human resources.

The autarchical model insulated Russia from the Great Depression. Moscow could use its power to ruthlessly exploit peasants and workers, thereby limiting consumption and maximizing investment, largely in heavy industry. Massive labor and capital inputs fueled the economic growth as tens of millions of peasants moved to the city, doubling the urban population in a decade. Freed from usual political constraints, the regime could institute sharply inegalitarian and hierarchical systems of control and reward to promote progress. Mass coercion was always available to suppress dissent.

On the more positive side, the Stalinist system invested massively in education and staged large-scale campaigns to eliminate illiteracy. By 1940 over 812,000 students were enrolled in universities, and the number of engineers and scientific workers, had septupled since 1926. The talents of women, ethnic minorities, workers and peasants, previously suppressed under Tsarism, were now mobilized and encouraged on a vast scale. By 1939, for example, women became 47 percent of the labor force. Rapid social mobility became the order of the day.[13]

Perhaps Abram Bergson and Simon Kuznets best captured the complex nature of the Stalinist economic model in the 1930s:

> It is a case of high rates of growth, with large inputs of resources and heavy human cost; of rapid shifts in the industrial structure, away from agriculture and with emphasis on the industrial sector—both in terms of shares and relative product per worker—that differed in its speed and concentration from other countries; of limiting consumption and maximizing capital investment, achieved in combination with relatively moderate capital-output ratios to permit rapid aggregate growth; and of deliberate isolation from the rest of the world so that the selective borrowing of production devices and the very limited exposure to the example of high and free consumption levels in other countries could be assured . . . the 1928-40 period [was characterized by] . . . violent internal shifts, tremendous input of resources, low and falling consumption and low rates of growth per unit of output.[14]

1930S: SOVIET AND U.S. MILITARY PREPARATION

The Soviet Union poured far greater resources into defense spending and defense-related activities during the 1930s than any other country except Germany. During the 1933–1938 period Germany (2.9 billion English pounds) just edged out the Soviet Union (2.8 billion English pounds), vastly outspending either the United States (1.2 billion English pounds) or the United Kingdom (1.1 billion English pounds).[15] Table 5.3 shows that this trend continued even after the war began in September 1939.

The Soviet Union then spent four to six times as much on defense as the United States in the 1938–1940 period, and almost twice as much in 1941. Given the economic disparity between the two sides, this represented a tremendous effort on the Soviet side and minimal exertion on the U.S. side.

The massive Soviet military investment in the 1930s paid

Table 5.3   Soviet, U.S. and British Defense Expenditures, 1938-1941 (billions of English pounds)

Year	Soviet Union	United States	Great Britain
1938	4.4	1.0	1.4
1939	6.6	1.1	3.2
1940	9.2	1.5	10.4
1941	11.4	6.0	14.9

Source: 1. V. I. Lan, *SShA v voennye i poslevoennye gody* (Moscow: Nauka, 1978), p.138.
2. A. J. Brown, *Applied Economics: Aspects of the World Economy in War and Peace* (London: George Allen and Unwin, 1947), p.30.

handsome dividends. The entire economy in the 1930s was organized essentially on the lines of a war economy in peacetime. The Stalinist policy of armament emphasized not only the building up of a strong stockpile of weapons but also stress on arms industries and related civilian industries. The whole economic structure was built around massive investments in the heavy industrial base so crucial to a war economy. Factories were built with a dual capacity able to convert easily to wartime production.

Stalinism had radically altered Soviet military capacity on the eve of war. In 1914 Tsarist Russia was strikingly negligent in this area, and even by 1929 the Soviet Union had only some weak artillery and ammunition factories, and largely prerevolutionary weapons. It had no tank- or ship-building industries. By contrast, by 1940 Stalinist Russia had created a powerful defense industry on an excellent military-technical base. Table 5.4 shows the remarkable quantitative progress made by the Soviet defense industry. Quantity was not sacrificed for quality. Russian artillery, T-34 medium tanks, KV heavy tanks, and Katyusha rockets were all as good as or even better than comparable German weapons.

Not all was perfect with the Soviet defense industry, as one might expect given its youth and inexperience. Too many weapons and plants were kept near the vulnerable Western frontier, the Great Purges seriously retarded further progress, and the Soviet aircraft industry lagged behind the international standard. Overall, though, Stalinist war preparation was thorough.

Table 5.4 Soviet Weapons Production, 1930-1940

Weapons	1930	1940
tanks	170	2,794
planes	899	10,565
cannons	952	15,300
rifles/carbines	126,000	1,461,000

Source: 1. Mark Harrison, *Soviet Planning in Peace and War 1938–1945* (Cambridge: Cambridge University Press, 1985), p.8.

As Mark Harrison observed in a recent fine study of the Soviet war economy,

> Considered in this light, the scale of Soviet rearmament was not only impressive in itself but it also revealed a more thorough and longterm character than the rearmament of any other great power, including Germany.[16]

The contrast with the very weak state of U.S. military preparation in the 1930s was clear. Protected by a fine navy and vast ocean distances, the United States did little to prepare for war. As suggested earlier, the Great Depression, antimilitarist and isolationist sentiments, disenchantment with the results of World War I, and the lack of any immediate threat to the United States seemed to justify minimal American war preparation. This was especially true when the U.S. and British navies and French army, already in existence, seemed, on the basis of the previous war, to be more than adequate to handle any existing threat. As late as 1939 even a perspicacious President Roosevelt was unable to stir an isolationist Congress or public, determined to stay out of the coming war, to support minimal war preparation. The World War I experience seemed to many Americans to validate the concept that the United States would need to mobilize seriously for war only after it entered a war, if that should ever occur.

During the entire two decades up to 1939 the War Department received an average appropriation of a miniscule 252 million dollars a year. Tanks were to be the decisive new land weapon of the coming war. Yet in July 1940, when General Chaffee was given command of the new armored corps, he inherited less than 1,000 tanks, all outdated and most of World War I vintage. With doctrine stressing light tanks, the U.S. military was not even developing heavy tanks to combat the German Tigers and Panthers.

Similarly, while the air force was promoting an excellent long-range bomber, the total production of military planes in 1939 was only 2,555. And the P-39 Aircobra was no match for the Japanese Zero or German Messerschmidt. In 1939 Italy had a better air force on paper. Even in artillery, the production lines were relatively silent because the 1940 army relied mainly on 5,000 French guns from World War I.[17] Overall, then, the United States was as unprepared for war in 1940 as the Soviet Union was ready for war.

Only after World War II actually began in September 1939 did U.S. war preparation start in earnest, and even then slowly. President Roosevelt was reluctant to order mobilization until the May 1940 German conquest of France and the Low Countries stirred U.S. opinion. After that shock, the United States did begin to rearm more seriously, but the lack of any central control remained a serious problem until the formation of the Office of Production Management in 1941. War mobilization proceeded so slowly that even though 36 billion dollars was appropriated by December 1941, only 6–7 billion dollars was actually spent. Only by the fall of 1941 did the defense industry begin to go into high gear, producing 2 billion dollars of weapons a month.[18]

The serious U.S. lag behind Soviet and German war production would retard U.S. participation in the war. The results were highly visible in the army. In the depressing Louisiana maneuvers in the summer of 1941, iron pipes substituted for cannon, communication trucks for tanks, and light sports planes for bombers.[19] Even in the period of heightened mobilization from July 1940 until December 1941 the production statistics of the fledgling U.S. defense industry remained anemic, far below the demands of the world war and the production of the Soviet Union, Germany, and even Great Britain. Table 5.5 makes this point very clearly.

The same contrast between Soviet preparedness and U.S. unpreparedness was also evident not only in the defense industries and nascent war economies but in the care paid to the armed forces themselves. Stalin may have had many faults but one of them was not neglect of the Red Army. Indeed, during the 1930s he lavished attention and money on the military, which was the main beneficiary of the massive societal transformation of the

Table 5.5 U.S. Weapons Production, July 1940-December 1941

Weapon	Monthly rate
heavy field guns	4
light field guns/ anti tank guns	261
tank guns/ howitzers	377
mortars	528
light tanks	233

Source: l. John Millett, *The Organization and Role of the Army Service Forces* (Washington, D.C.: Government Printing Office, 1954), p. 185.

1930s. Under Stalin's careful tutelage, the weak and outmoded Red Army of 1930, which could barely repel a Romanian assault, by 1939 could decisively beat strong Japanese forces at Khalkin Gol. The contrast between the care lavished on the Red Army and the neglect of the U.S. army is starkly reflected in Table 5.6.

Thus, while Stalin massively built up the size of the Red Army to an impressive 3 million men in 1939, the United States kept a puny force of less than 300,000 men under arms. As a result, even when both sides went to war in 1941, the Soviet Union retained a 3:1 numerical superiority throughout the mutual buildup against the Axis that year. This was to be important in the first two years of struggle against Nazi Germany.

Stalin showed his solicitude for the army in many other ways than men and material. The officer corps became a lionized prop of the new Stalinist order. Very high pay and social status, servants, rapid promotion, and even French ballroom dance instruction followed in close order. Recruitment and promotion were especially quick for talented soldiers from the lower classes.

As for the soldiers, the massive modernization program wiped out illiteracy and promoted education and mechanical aptitude among the recruits. The elimination of Tsarist discrimination against ethnic minorities and the official socialist promotion of workers and peasants as the leading strata in the state boosted the morale of the soldiers. Stalinist industrialization in the 1930s

Table 5.6 Size of the Armed Forces of the Soviet Union and the United States, 1931–1941 (millions of men)

Date	Soviet Union	United States
1931	0.6	0.3
1933	0.6	0.3
1935	0.9	0.3
1937	1.4	0.3
1939	3.0	0.3
June 1941	4.2	1.5
December 1941	6.5	2.1

Source: 1. *The War Reports of General of Army George C. Marshall, General of Army H.H. Arnold and Fleet Admiral, Ernest King* (Philadelphia & New York: J.B. Lippincott, 1947), p.18.
2. Maurice Matloff, editor, *American Military History* (Washington, D.C.: Government Printing Office, 1969), pp. 412, 419.
3. *Istoriya vtoroi mirovoi voina 1939–1945* (Moscow: Voenizdat, 1982), Vol.4, pp.270–271.

greatly increased the size of the urban working class among the soldiers at the expense of the more backward peasant class. The political commissars worked hard to instill a more sophisticated political outlook in the soldiers.

The Red Army in the 1930s was also rapidly evolving toward the next war. As early as 1936 Marshal Tukhachevsky held major war games in which Nazi Germany was identified as the aggressor. Under Tukhachevsky's leadership, the Red Army was highly innovative and creative, holding the world's first large-scale combined arms exercises. The Red Army consistently emphasized the need for large-scale procurement of the most modern weapons. Overall, operational concepts were progressive before 1937 and again after 1939 (after the purges).

Not all was roses for the Red Army. The very weak Tsarist inheritance, further degraded by the ravages of World War I and the civil war, provided a thin base for building a new, powerful Red Army in the 1930s. Stalin himself made several key blunders. Collectivization and dekulakization in the early 1930s seriously alienated many peasant soldiers from the regime. The Great Purges slowed economic growth and decimated a large portion of the most talented and creative commanders, led by Tukhachevsky, Yakir, and Blyukher. It also paralyzed initiative by army officers and promoted the dominance of the small and backward-looking Stalinist commanders, such as Kliment Voroshilov and Semyon Budenny, in the 1937–1941 period. Progressive military thought withered on the vine during the Great Purges and would revive only as the great successes of German blitzkrieg warfare in 1939 and 1940 vindicated its views. Hastily in 1940 and 1941 the Red Army would scramble to reorganize its armored units and once again prepare for modern warfare in the wake of a weak performance in the Winter War against Finland in 1939–1940.

Despite Stalin's serious errors, the overall Stalinist military record was strong in the 1930s. The army expanded greatly in quality and quantity throughout the 1930s. Operational plans focused clearly on the Axis powers. The scale of military spending rose logarithmically, from 1.6 million rubles in 1929 to 56.7 billion rubles in 1940. As the *milost'* (darling) of Stalin and the party, the Red Army received the kind of enthusiastic support and aid that by 1941 foreshadowed its powerful role in World War II.[20]

While the Red Army basked in the center of attention in the Soviet Union, the U.S. army was being neglected in the New World. Protected by vast oceans and a strong navy, warmed by thoughts of strong potential allies and a long-range bomber force in the making, the United States luxuriated in its isolationism and let its army rot. This neglect continued throughout the 1930s— in September 1939 the U.S. army consisted of a mere 190,000 men.

At the onset of World War II the United States had the 15th largest army in the world, ranking just after Portugal.[21] The army had only 3 organized infantry divisions (all at less than 50 percent strength), inadequate transport for field maneuvers and armor for one mechanized cavalry brigade (at 50 percent strength). Backed up by a poorly trained 200,000 man National Guard, the army was scattered in skeleton units over 130 posts, camps, and stations. Two of the most knowledgeable army commanders were also the most caustic. General Dwight Eisenhower later wrote in *Crusade in Europe* that the United States in 1939 represented a state of "almost complete military weakness . . . as close to zero as a great power could conceivably allow itself to sink."[22] Chief of Staff General George Marshall later called the U.S. army in 1939 "absurdly small and ill-equipped" and observed that in September 1939, "As sick as any (nation) was the United States of America. We had no field army . . . we were, in terms of available strength, not even a third-rate military power."[23]

Only in 1940 and 1941 did the United States begin to repair this neglect, but it was too little and too late. President Franklin Roosevelt declared a limited national emergency in September 1939 and unlimited national emergency in May 1941. Despite massive appropriations, a peacetime draft and call up of the Reserve and National Guard, the United States remained markedly unprepared for war even by December 1941. The 5 divisions and 1 mechanized brigade of the United States Army in January 1940 had multiplied to 30 divisions and 5 armored divisions by December 1941. However, by the time of Pearl Harbor only 17 divisions were considered combat-ready, and even they seriously lacked adequate training, support units, and key weapons.

It would be many months before any serious U.S. offensive abroad could be entertained—and this at a time when over 300 German and Soviet divisions were locked in mortal combat in Europe. A U.S. War Department intelligence-branch conference in May 1941 estimated that if Germany defeated Great Britain, it would be at least eighteen months (after November 1942) before the United States could train, equip, and ship an expeditionary force of 430,000 men abroad. Such a force, even if gathered, would have been unlikely to make much of an impact in Europe where the Soviet and German armies had over 11 million men in their infantry forces by the end of 1941.[24]

The U.S. deficiencies penetrated every aspect of the armed forces. In an environment that stressed avoidance of war and no entanglement in European affairs, it was hardly surprising that military plans were unrealistic and incomplete. Even in the 1930s these plans focused almost solely on the defense of the United States and ignored international realities. Until 1937 the RAINBOW war plans focused on Great Britain and Japan, but not Germany. Only in 1939 did the RAINBOW series finally contemplate an alliance with France and England against the Axis. Even then the thrust of U. S. planning changed only from guarding the United States in 1939 to hemispheric defense in 1940.[25]

The operational concepts of the U.S. army were equally antiquated. While the navy and air force had at least kept *au courant* with international developments, the army remained firmly rooted in its historical role as a small constabulary force chasing troublesome Mexicans or Indians. The frontier created a

U.S. army geared to fluid small-scale campaigns over huge areas against ill-trained and poorly armed enemies.

In this army the horse mystique, and therefore the cavalry, remained as powerful in the United States as among the much derided Horse Marshals of Stalin's Red Army. The U.S. tank corps had disappeared after 1920, and for two decades tank warfare was completely neglected. As late as 1939 Colonel George Patton, then in his fifties, was still conducting elaborate horse shows at Fort Myer. Only the great German blitzkrieg victories would force the creation of an armored force with two divisions in 1940 and mercilessly reveal how antiquated U.S. military thinking had become by 1940. General Omar Bradley later graphically recalled the U.S. reaction to the early German victories:

> Militarily the Nazi forces had operated with awesome efficiency. The coordination between air and ground, tanks and motorized infantry, exceeded anything we had ever dreamed of in the U.S. Army. We were amazed, shocked, dumbfounded, shaking our heads in disbelief. Here was modern open warfare—war of maneuver—brought to the ultimate. To match such a performance, let alone exceed it, the U.S. Army had years of catching up and little time in which to do it.[26]

Nowhere did two decades of neglect take a heavier toll than in the officer corps of the army and air force. The size of the officer corps of the regular army (12,000) and number of trained pilots (7,000) was absurdly low. The bulk of the National Guard officers were aging, minimally competent, or political appointees. The quality of the regular army officers was often poor. Small congressional appropriations for twenty years, drab life on isolated army outposts, promotion solely by seniority, and widespread public antimilitary sentiment led many good officers to leave the service. Many who stayed in became cut off from any real challenge and vegetated; the results were predictable. In the 1940 Louisiana maneuvers General Omar Bradley noted "the undistinguished and unimaginative leadership displayed by generals conducting maneuvers."[27] And an official government sponsored study of the war has reported that,

> The unfitness for combat leadership of many officers of all components was a fact well known to the War Department. In the early part of 1941 General McNair frequently expressed the

opinion that many officers neither had nor deserved the confidence of their men.[28]

Finally, most of these problems pervaded the ranks as well. The low status and neglect of the army and poor living conditions repelled most potential soldiers. The very low pay was a strong disincentive. The tasks of the army, mainly drilling, were mundane. Combat training was rare to nonexistent, and, when it was conducted, occurred with poor equipment under inexperienced officers.

1930S: SOVIET AND U.S. POLICIES TOWARD WAR PREPAREDNESS

Before concluding, we need to briefly review the politics that helped produce these respective Soviet and U.S. defense policies. During the 1930s Stalin and the Soviet elite consistently showed great concern for war preparation. Many factors accounted for this awareness of the external danger so evident in Stalin's 1931 speech declaring that if the Soviet Union did not close the gap with the West in a decade it might cease to exist. Geographically, the Soviet Union, as a great Eurasian land power, could hardly ignore the rising twin menace of Nazi Germany and Imperial Japan near its borders. Historically, all Soviet leaders were well aware of the geographical vulnerability of the Russian western frontiers to such invasions as those of Napoleon in 1812 and Germany in 1915.

Politically, as Bolsheviks, they feared the ineradicable hostility of powerful Western capitalist countries as seen by large-scale Western intervention in the Russian civil war. The rise of violently anti-Communist Nazi Germany and Imperial Japan in the 1930s, coupled with the appeasement of the Fascists by the West, raised great alarm in the Kremlin. The large economic gap between the Soviet Union and the West, especially Germany, in the late 1920s prodded the Soviet leaders to action. Finally, searing images of the revolutionary consequences of military defeats at the hands of Japan in the Russo–Japanese War and Germany in World War I helped focus the attention of Stalin on the Red Army in the 1930s.

Many of these factors helped push the Soviet population toward strong support for rearmament in the 1930s. Moreover, the highly authoritarian Stalinist system enjoyed great advantages in this area over the Western democracies. The Soviet regime could strongly influence public opinion through propaganda and newspapers, as well as the promotion of organizations like OSOAVIAKHIM, which prepared the Soviet air force for war. Furthermore, on an issue as critical as rearmament, it could ignore significant opposition to its policies or even label opponents of its policies as agents of Western imperialism. Coercion and terror were always viable options. The Soviet Union for many years manifested a high concern for its security. And even during the period of the Russo–German Nonaggression Pact the Red Army proceeded to rearm at a feverish pace.

The contrast between the United States and the Soviet Union in the political arena in the interwar period, and especially in the 1930s, could not have been greater. From 1920 until September 1939 isolationist sentiment among the public and Congress was so powerful that even President Roosevelt, awakened to the danger in the late 1930s, could do little. Already by the early 1920s the majority of the U.S. public saw intervention in World War I as a mistake never to be repeated. Even the rise of Nazi Germany and Imperial Japan failed to shake the U.S. elite and public consensus in the 1930s, especially as the Great Depression focused all attention on domestic concerns.

From 1934 to 1936 Congress passed a series of neutrality laws to prevent U.S. export of arms, ammunition, and war goods to any belligerent nation. While at the same time the Nye Committee held protracted hearings blaming U.S. involvement in World War I on bankers and munitions makers, the 1934 Johnson Act prohibited U.S. loans even to allies who defaulted on their World War I loans. Although President Roosevelt by 1938 had decided that war seemed inevitable, isolationist views remained popular and he was set back in the congressional elections that year. As late as June 1939 the isolationists passed a congressional act restoring an arms embargo on all belligerents.

The period between the onset of World War II in September 1939 and U.S. entry into the war in December 1941 saw a marked shift to internationalism. Yet the isolationists remained a powerful minority hindering full war preparation. Only after the fall of France in May 1940 could Congress approve a peacetime draft and pass Lend Lease legislation (by one vote), in August 1940 and early in 1941, respectively. In 1941 the America First Committee, under General Robert Wood, General Hugh Johnson, Charles

Lindbergh, and Eddie Rickenbacker, and isolationist allies like Gerald Nye and Robert McCormick, remained influential. As late as August 1941 Congress approved the extension of selective service for one year by a vote of 203–202—this was the last hurrah for the isolationism the Japanese Imperial Navy would destroy by bombing Pearl Harbor. But the isolationists, even in retreat, had further retarded the full-scale mobilization of U.S. resources for war.[29]

In this light it is far from surprising that Soviet–U.S. relations were poor and had no impact on the war or preparations for the war. Until 1933 the United States refused to recognize the regime that had come to power in 1917. Even after U.S. recognition of the Soviet Union, relations remained cool throughout the decade. In 1933 the United States remained concerned about the Comintern, disposition of Tsarist property, and the dictatorial nature of the Stalinist regime. During the mid-1930s, coinciding with a moderate phase in Soviet politics, relations improved somewhat, and in 1936 the United States signed a trade agreement with the Soviet Union. But relations soon deteriorated with the onset of the Great Purges and the U.S. refusal to cooperate with the Soviet Union to stop German expansionism. Trade remained minimal and relations hit bottom in 1939 with the Molotov–Ribbentrop Pact, Russo–German division of Poland, and the Soviet Winter War with Finland. In December 1939, after the Soviet attack against Finland, President Roosevelt proclaimed a moral embargo of material goods to the Soviet Union. Relations stayed chilly during the twenty-two months of the Russo–German neutrality pact and especially with the signing of the April 1941 Russo–Japanese Non-Aggression Pact.

Only with the German invasion of the Soviet Union in June 1941, adding the Soviet Union to Great Britain as Germany's main enemies, did Soviet–U.S. relations greatly improve. By August that year Harry Hopkins, President Roosevelt's alter ego, was on his way to Moscow. In November 1941 President Roosevelt ordered Lend Lease aid to the Soviet Union. After the Japanese attack at Pearl Harbor and the German declaration of war on the United States, the Soviet Union and the United States, in December 1941, became allies in the struggle against Germany. By the end of 1941, forty-one million dollars worth of U.S. arms and war material had been shipped to the Soviet Union for cash and a little over half a million dollars of Lend Lease supplies had reached the Soviet Union.[30]

The interwar years, and especially the 1930s, are crucial for understanding how the Soviet Union began to close the vast gap that separated it from the United States in 1918 or even more so in 1929. Stalin did make serious mistakes in the 1930s—the ultraleftist foreign policy of the early 1930s and Great Purges of the late 1930s being the most spectacular. But, overall, the thrust of Soviet policies in the 1930s was extremely positive. Militarily, the Red Army was greatly modernized, expanded vastly in size, and professionalized. Economically, the regime created a powerful heavy industrial base that provided a large stream of modern weapons for the new Red Army. Socially, the vast modernization program provided a far larger stratum of literate, mechanical-minded, and educated soldiers for the army. Politically, the regime mobilized considerable popular support for its rearmament program in the 1930s. By 1940 the Soviet Union, despite the Great Purges, was vastly better prepared to fight a major war than in 1930.

Alas, the same could hardly be said for the United States. The United States casually wasted the entire decade and began a modest rearmament program, prodded in part by foreign war orders, only in 1939. The great political power of the isolationists and economic devastation wrought by the Great Depression seriously retarded any U.S. reaction to European events. The U.S. political system was so structured that, unlike in the Soviet Union, a vocal minority could stop, or at least seriously slow, rearmament. The U.S. opposition to active cooperation with the Soviet Union—or even France and England—against Nazi Germany crippled U.S. power. By 1940 U.S. military power was only marginally better than the antiquated and backward state it had been in 1930. The United States would be seriously affected by its lack of war preparation in the early years of the coming war.

NOTES

1. *Rossiya*, p.7, *Statistical History*, pp.564, 649 and Aldcroft, *European*, p.75.

2. See Adelman, *Revolutionary* for a fuller treatment of the subject, and p.64 for the quotes from Lenin.

3. *Rossiya*, p.93; Nutter, *Growth* p.3; and Avrich, *Kronstadt*.

4. *Ibid.*

5. Cohn, "Soviet Economic Performance and Growth" in Blackwell,

editor, *Russian*, pp.328, 356, and Maddison, *Economic*, p.155.

6. Cohn, "Soviet Economic Performance and Growth" in Blackwell, editor, *Russian* pp.326–327; Bergson, *Productivity*, p.117; and Harrison, *Soviet*, p.5.

7. On the topic of the Soviet economic debates, see Lewin, *Political* and Erlich, *Soviet*.

8. *Istoriya velikoi*, v.1, p.90.

9. Vigor, *Soviet*, pp.201–202.

10. Aldcroft, *European* p.81, *Statistical Yearbook*, p.181, Maddison, *Economic* p.155, Blackwell, editor, *Russian*, p.356 and *Istoriya vtoroi*, v. 12, p. 183.

11. Scherer, editor, *USSR*, V.1, p.129, Brown, *Applied* p.28, Nutter, *Growth* pp.237, 25, 273, 279, 282; Blackwell, editor, *Russian*, p.356 and Jasny, *Soviet*, p.34.

12. *Statistical Yearbook*, pp.199, 218–219.

13. Ulam, *Expansion*, pp.226–233; Cohn, "Soviet Economic Performance and Growth" in Blackwell, editor, *Russian*, p.342; Voznesensky, *Economy* p.15; Scherer, editor, *USSR* V.1, p.212; and Bergson and Kuznets, editors, *Economic*, p.84.

14. Bergson and Kuznets, editors, *Economic*, pp.367–368.

15. Milward, *War*, p.25; Brown, *Applied*, p.30 and Joint Economic Committee, *Soviet*, p.127.

16. Harrison, *Soviet*, p.48 and Holloway, *Soviet*, p.7.

17. Blumenson, *Patton*, p.9; Huston, *Sinews*, p.481; and Perrett, *Days*, p.194.

18. Huston, *Sinews*, p.412 and Perrett, *Days*, pp.174–175.

19. MacDonald, *Mighty*, p.24.

20. See Adelman, *Revolution*.

21. Keegan, *Six*, p.25.

22. Eisenhower, *Crusade*. p.2.

23. *War Reports*, pp.17, 290 and Bradley, *General's*, p.86.

24. Greenfield, Palmer, and Wiley, *Organization*, p.116; *War Reports*, p.18; Matloff, editor, *American*, p.435; and *Istoriya vtoroi*, v.4, pp.270–271.

25. Verrier, *Bomber*, p.53; Huston, *Sinews*; and Matloff, editor, *American*, p.414.

26. Bradley, *General's*, pp. 88–89, 97–98 and *War Reports*, pp.36–37.

27. Bradley, *General's*, p.89 and *War Reports*, p.137.

28. Greenfield, Palmer, and Wiley, *Organization*, p.48.

29. Perrett, *Days*, pp.55–64, 193; Porter, *Seventy-Sixth*, back cover; Ellis and Warhurst, *Victory*, v.2; *Defeat of Germany* p.11; and Ulam, *Expansion*, pp.9, 18.

30. Gaddis, *United*, p.4; Sivachev and Yakovlev, *Russia*, p.165; and Williams, *American–Russian*, pp.231–255.

Section 3
Prelude to Goetterdaemmerung
June 1941—June 1944

6

A Military and
Political Overview

This chapter is a military–political overview of events from June 1941, the date of the German invasion of Russia, to June 1944, the date of the Anglo–U.S. invasion of Normandy. Especially to the older generation, the names of the battles against Nazi Germany have a familiar ring: Moscow, Stalingrad, Kursk-Orel, El Alamein, North Africa, Sicily, Italy. Traditional U.S. analyses of these events, stressing U.S. actions and perspectives, are well known; in this chapter we will provide a different interpretation, with stress on the diverse roles played in Allied operations by the U.S., British, and Soviet armed forces.

GERMAN LOGIC

The year 1941 was to prove decisive both in determining the outcome of World War II and deciding the ultimate shape of the new postwar order. The arbiter of the fate of the world, strangely enough, was to be Adolf Hitler and the Third Reich. By his twin decisions to invade the Soviet Union in June 1941 in Operation Barbarossa and to declare war on the United States in the wake of the Japanese attack at Pearl Harbor in December 1941 he sealed the fate of the old order and of German predominance in Europe.

From our safe historical vantage point the decision to unilaterally invade one future superpower and declare war gratuitously on the other, even stronger, future superpower seems like the height of madness. And surely the actual record of the Second World War would seem to bear out such a judgment. This notion of the insanity of German foreign policy would seem to be further supported by the stated rationale for such policies: that defeating the Soviet Union, governed by a "Jewish-Bolshevik conspiracy" of *untermenschen*, would be "child's play" and that the Americans were "too soft" to fight.[1]

Yet, what is also striking is that from the perspective of 1941— and this is perhaps a testimonial to the limits of theories of rational decision making—there was a powerful logic to the German invasion of the Soviet Union and a lesser one to the declaration of war on the United States. In May 1941 the power of the Third Reich was undisputed in continental Europe. Only two European powers—The Soviet Union and Great Britain—stood in the way of Hitler's Wagnerian dreams of world domination, or at least total domination of Europe, which at that time seemed the same thing.

One of those powers, Great Britain, was not only a so-called "Aryan country" but, more important, the leading naval and air power in Europe. Historically, Germany was the most powerful land power in Europe but, like Napoleonic France, weak at sea against the Royal Navy. Without air or sea protection the German army, unprepared and inexperienced in amphibious landings, would have had grave difficulty in conquering England. The 1940 battle of Britain had convinced Hitler of the futility of renewing Operation Sea Lion in 1941. But something more was at stake here, something that today is hard to recall. To Hitler, as to Stalin and many other leaders of the time, Great Britain remained the leading power of the day, a financial superpower, an outstanding naval power, and the world's greatest colonial power. Given the innate military difficulties of launching an invasion of England, why attempt such a feat?

By contrast, an invasion of the Soviet Union would remove the only significant land power left on the European continent to contest Nazi hegemony. Hitler had needed the Molotov–Ribbentrop Pact to avoid the nightmare of repeating the classic World War I German error of dissipating its strength on two fronts. Now that the powerful French army was disposed of, Hitler could turn against the Soviet Union. Hitler's basic denigration of Soviet power was shared by most other Western leaders, who similarly ignored the great improvements in Soviet military and economic power in the 1930s. To the extent that they were aware that the Soviet Union was striving to build up effective military power, they felt that there was a great difference between building an effective force and achieving it. As British Prime Minister Neville Chamberlain confided to his diary in March 1939, "I must confess to the most profound distrust of Russia. I have no belief whatsoever in her ability to maintain an effective offensive, even if she wanted to."[2]

The almost unanimous consensus was that the Soviet Union was a weak, unstable, and illegitimate regime, scarcely able to cope with overwhelming German military power that had crushed a far stronger French army in a matter of weeks the preceding year. This image of unremitting weakness was further shaped by the poor, even abominable, performance of the Red Army in the early months of the Winter War against Finland. The massive Great Purges and the execution of the majority of top military commanders (including the flamboyant and renowned Marshal Tukhachevsky) and up to 15,000 officers in the 1937–1941 period drastically reduced confidence in the Red Army. All of these images were reinforced by the historical memories of Russian military impotence in the Russo–Japanese War and World War I, let alone the miserable record of the Red Army in the Russian civil war. If the German army in World War I, deeply involved in the West, could smash in the Russian army and drive it from the field with only a fraction of its forces, then what could a far more powerful German army devoting all its effort do to a feeble and embattled Red Army in World War II?

The German logic in declaring war on the United States in December 1941 was far weaker, and even specious in part, but nevertheless retained a kernel of sanity. It was based on several considerations. The most important one was that the United States, enraged by the Japanese attack on Pearl Harbor and already deeply involved in the Pacific Ocean, would devote most of its resources to the war in Asia rather than Europe. Second, the United States was, as we have already seen, ill prepared to take an active part in the war in Europe for at least two more years. By then, even if the United States were to be successful to some degree in the Pacific, Germany expected to have defeated the Soviet Union and forced a beleaguered Great Britain to come to terms. Third, the record of U.S. military power was weak and uninspiring, especially compared to that of German military power, ever since the 1860s. The brief U.S. war record in World

War I, and the much longer history as a weak and dispersed constabulary force fighting mainly Indians and Mexicans, provoked overweening self-confidence in the commanders of the Wehrmacht and Luftwaffe. After all, had they not easily occupied all of Europe in stunning blitzkrieg warfare? Finally, Hitler counted on winning the battle of the Atlantic with his U-boats, which in 1942 would sink more shipping than the Allies could build. With the putative surrender of Great Britain and control of the vast Atlantic in German hands and the Pacific in Japanese hands, what was there to fear from the United States? Surely there seemed little to fear, especially given the enormous distances needed before a U.S. army could ever be brought to bear on the European continent.

All of these more "rational" motives were reinforced by the complex of pseudoracial and bogus psychological views so dear to Hitler. In the wake of initial German successes and after purges of the German military, even the German military assessments in 1941 came to resemble those of Hitler. As Michael Geyer has written in Ernest May's fine new study of intelligence assessments before the two world wars,

> While the military developed their own general assessment, it dovetailed by and large with Hitler's own. Assuming that the United States and the Soviet Union were vastly different from France and Britain, the working level of "Foreign Armies" based judgments less on military than on economic and political factors. In the case of the United States, economic estimates were shaped by a single person whose assumptions were plausible but wrong. In the case of the Soviet Union, right-radical anti-Bolshevik groups produced equally plausible, but equally wrong political estimates. Since the military were not very adroit in economic, social and ideological matters, they took these judgments at face values.[3]

If these twin German decisions would ultimately push the United States and Soviet Union to superpower status by the end of the war, this was far from apparent in 1941. These German moves also, inevitably, provoked very different responses from the two powers. For the Soviet Union the German decision to launch an invasion forced on them a pitiless struggle in which the very survival of the regime and the nation was at stake. Although the Soviet Union had made great progress in the 1930s, it still lagged a considerable distance behind Nazi Germany, especially now that all the resources of Europe were at the disposal of the Fascists. The Red Army was still in the process of recovering from the ravages of the purges. It needed time to assimilate its new weapons and the lessons of the radically new warfare unleashed by the German army in the past two years. As a result, the first four months of the war would be catastrophic for the Red Army and only eighteen months later, after the historic battle of Stalingrad, would the survival of the regime seem to be secure.

If the German invasion of the Soviet Union provoked a life-or-death struggle for the Soviets, the same could hardly be said of the German declaration of war on the United States that same year. For the Americans the war in Europe, even after the German declaration of war, seemed remote and almost unreal. The United States had the luxury, totally lacking to the Soviets or even the British, of deciding when, how, and where to fight the Germans. As long as the British and U.S. navies controlled the Atlantic Ocean against an inferior German navy and German land power was safely absorbed in the invasion of the Soviet Union, the United States, given the technology of the day, had nothing to fear. It even could decide whether to mobilize first against Japan or Germany, or both at the same time.

ROLE OF THE SOVIET UNION AND GREAT BRITAIN

The fundamental U.S. decision for the two and one-half years that elapsed from December 1941 after Pearl Harbor until the Normandy landings on D Day in June 1944 was to place primary reliance on its Allies to fight the Germans and to take for itself only a secondary role. This hardly meant abstinence from the brutal struggle in Europe. The United States would serve as a true "arsenal of democracy," providing a large stream of weapons to its allies under the Lend Lease program. The U.S. navy would patrol the Atlantic Ocean, the U.S. air force would protect England and fly bombing raids on German-occupied Europe, and the U.S. army would build up its forces in England for an ultimate cross-channel invasion of France. Indeed, the U.S. army would even engage in small-scale assaults against peripheral German and Axis defenses in North Africa, Sicily, and Italy.

Always, though, the main burden of destroying the greatest military power in this century (and perhaps in history) was borne by the Soviet Union and Great Britain. Of this there can be no doubt. No less a personage than United States Army Chief-of-Staff General George Marshall in his report on the war to the secretary of war in September 1945 could soberly recall,

> In good conscience this Nation can take little credit for its part in staving off disaster in those critical days. It is certain that the refusal of the British and Russian peoples to accept what appeared to be inevitable defeat was the great factor in salvage of our civilization. Of almost equal importance was the failure of the enemy to make the most of the situation. . . . The crisis had come and passed at Stalingrad and El Alamein before this Nation was able to gather sufficient resources to participate in the fight in a determining manner.[4]

The preponderant role of the Soviet Union and Great Britain in the war effort against Germany until June 1944 can be easily demonstrated by a few simple statistics. Until D Day the great bulk of the land fighting against Nazi Germany was carried out by the Red Army. As late as January 1944 the Red Army was actively fighting over 200 German divisions in the Soviet Union while the U.S. army was actively engaging perhaps 20 German divisions elsewhere.[5] According to German statistics, from June 1941 to June 1944, the German armed forces suffered the enormous total of 4,193,200 men dead, wounded, or missing in the East and 329,000 men dead, wounded, or missing everywhere else.[6] In simple terms this meant that the Soviets in this three-year period inflicted 93 percent of all battle losses suffered by the German army.

Similarly, Great Britain and its Commonwealth allies bore the brunt of the fighting on the fronts other than in the East. From September 1939 until June 1941 Great Britain fought against the Third Reich without the active support of either of the two future superpowers. This role had been especially lonely and important after the fall of France in June 1940 and the start of the battle of Britain. For one year Great Britain stood alone against the entire power of Nazi-dominated Europe until the Germans decided to provide it with allies. Even after June and December 1941 the role of Great Britain remained very strong, until 1944.

The British Commonwealth role in the major campaigns on the periphery of Europe, from North Africa to the Middle East and Italy, was powerful and even dominant. As late as January 1944, according to official British statistics on the war, more British Empire divisions (24) were in contact with the German army than U.S. divisions (16). In June 1944 there were still twice as many British Commonwealth troops in Italy and three times as many British Commonwealth troops in the Mediterranean as U.S. soldiers. The role of the British navy, British air force, and British commanders in Allied operations tended to be strong and decisive.[7]

A more in-depth look at the basic role of these two great powers in this period is definitely in order. The Red Army could easily claim the mantle of the greatest role in defeating the German army in this period because the Eastern front became the main front of the war. Here the war was at its bitterest and most intense. The large-scale Soviet victories in the East, from Stalingrad to Kursk-Orel to Leningrad, destroyed the basic fighting power of the Wehrmacht and firmly turned the initiative over to the Allies.

By 1944 the possibility of any strong German thrust in the West to counter an Allied invasion of France was gone, because Germany was forced on the strategic defensive. At a cost of enormous losses that surpassed 5 million Soviet soldiers taken prisoner by the Germans and almost 6 million Soviet soldiers killed, the German bid for world supremacy was finally brought to a halt in the East by the Red Army. German losses in men and material were awesome on the Eastern front. By June 1944 the German army had lost over 2 million men who were dead, missing, or discharged from the service for illness and wounds. Further German data indicates that while 1,250,000 German soldiers were killed on the Eastern front in this period, only 150,000 German soldiers died on all other fronts.[8] In the words of one observer of World War II, by June 1944,

> Nazi Germany had already been defeated by the Red Army in the East. . . . There was to be much hard fighting ahead on both the eastern and western fronts before the remnants of the once-proud Wehrmacht were at last subdued, but the European war was already winding down to its inevitable denouement by the time Eisenhower launched his crusade.[9]

The predominant role of the Red Army in these three critical years of the war was reflected in the disposition of German troops on the various fronts of the war. In World War I the bulk of German troops were on the Western front in France, and a fraction of the German forces were in the East. Only in 1915 was there a strong German effort in the East and, even then, the majority of the forces were in the West. The opposite was true in World War II, where the bulk of the German army remained in the East through the entire period, locked in combat with the Red Army. Table 6.1 starkly shows the grim realities facing the Red Army from June 1941 until June 1944, when the Allies finally created an effective second front in Europe.

Table 6.1 shows that most of German land power was deployed in the East until the threat, and finally the reality, of an Allied invasion of France in 1944 drew off significant power to the West. For the entire three-year period, despite huge losses, the Wehrmacht maintained 153–190 German divisions in the East. These were supplemented by several dozen allied divisions, many of which saw serious and sustained fighting. The Romanians, for example, suffered 250,000 soldiers killed over these three years.

In addition, the large majority of the vaunted Panzer legions were found in the East throughout this entire period. In July 1943, during the battle for Kursk-Orel, the largest tank battle in history was fought between the German and Soviet armies. At the time there were 3,800 German tanks and self-propelled artillery pieces in the East, 1,300 in France and Italy.[10] Still in January 1944 there were 24 Panzer divisions in the East, only 8 in the West.[11] The Luftwaffe largely stayed at home in the West to fight off a threatened invasion and to protect Germany from Allied bombing raids. During the entire three-year period only 30–40 percent of German combat planes were in the East.[12]

The quality of German soldiers in the West was lower than those in the East. This was only natural, as the German command used the Western front for rest and recuperation of men and units battered in the East and created numerous low-quality static units to fill in the Atlantic Wall in the West. This meant that from 1941 until 1944 the Red Army faced the cream of the German army and many of its best commanders. The relative inactivity on the Western front meant that the German army could constantly shuffle in numerous new divisions and refit old divisions to replace divisions battered by the Red Army in such battles as Stalingrad and Kursk-Orel. Thus, even many of the divisions listed as being on other fronts actually formed a reserve for the Eastern front, at least until 1944.

A more detailed breakdown of the other fronts shows that several of these fronts were in the ultimate zone of combat of the Red Army rather than its Allies. Let us look at U.S. intelligence estimates cited by Captain Harry Butcher, General Eisenhower's

Table 6.1 German Troop Disposition, June 1941–June 1944
(number of divisions)

Year	Eastern Front	Other Fronts
June 1941	153	64
December 1941	156	64
September 1942	190	50
July 1943	162	58
January 1944	179	125
June 1944	165	129

Source: 1. Earl Ziemke, *Stalingrad to Berlin: The German Defeat in the East* (Washington, D.C.: Government Printing Office, 1968), pp.8–9.
2. Trevor Dupuy and Paul Martell, *Great Battles on the Eastern Front* (Indianapolis: Bobbs-Merrill, 1982), p.26.
3. John Keegan, *Six Armies in Normandy* (New York: Viking Press, 1982), p.44.
4. Walter Dunn, Jr., *Second Front Now 1943* (University, Alabama: University of Alabama Press, 1980), p.259.
5. Fred Majdalany, *The Fall of Fortress Europe* (Garden City, New Jersey: Doubleday and Company, 1968), p.305.
6. Max Hastings, *Overlord-D-Day and the Battle for Normandy* (New York: Simon and Schuster, 1984), p.60.

aide, for German troop disposition in April 1944, only two months before the landings at Normandy. On the surface there were 199 German divisions then at the Eastern front and 137 divisions at other fronts. A deeper analysis shows, however, that no less than 36 of the divisions on other fronts were situated in such zones of future Red Army activity in the next few months as Finland (7 German divisions), Poland (3 German divisions), Hungary (5 German divisions), and southeast Europe (21 German divisions). Moreover, the intelligence estimate found 10 German divisions in Germany and uncertain locations, thereby unallocated for either front. When all these considerations are taken into account, there were 235 German divisions in or near the Eastern front, 91 German divisions in Scandinavia, Western Europe, and Italy in the U.S. and British zone of activity, and 10 indeterminate divisions. Thus, on the eve of the Normandy invasion, roughly 70 percent of all German divisions were found in the East.[13]

If the Soviet army drew the assignment of holding and destroying the bulk of German land forces in the East in this period, the British army and navy drew the equally unenviable task of containing and pushing back German expansion on the European periphery. Given the initial dynamism of German expansionism, this was a formidable task. Fortunately for the fate of the world, the British Commonwealth met the challenge, not only in the 1941–1944 period, but in the preceding two years as well.

Despite its vast inferiority in human and natural resources and economic wealth to the United States, Great Britain enjoyed a number of advantages that allowed it to play such a powerful role for the last time in its history. Facing physical annihilation at the hands of Nazi Germany, Great Britain, like the Soviet Union, moved rapidly to a full mobilization of all its resources. Drawn into the war at the outset, it enjoyed a two and one-half year lead in full-scale mobilization of its economy and armed forces. Table 6.2 makes clear the dramatic difference between the rate of British (and Soviet) wartime mobilization and that of the United States.

Table 6.2 demonstrates the great advantage Great Britain enjoyed over the United States. First, by dint of its early and strong mobilization from an initially weak start, Great Britain was able not only to outproduce the United States in war material from 1939 to 1941 but, even more important, to outproduce a more powerful, but slow to mobilize, German economy in such vital weapons as tanks, planes, and self-propelled artillery pieces from 1940–1942.[14] Equally important was the impact of the rapid and efficient total mobilization of British manpower. As early as December 1939 Great Britain already had more than 1.5 million men under arms, and this number rapidly escalated to 3.8 million men by June 1941 and 4.5 million men by June 1942. As a consequence, in June 1941 the British had over 2 million men more in uniform than the Americans and even as late as June 1942 had over 800,000 more in the army than the United States.[15]

Second, even after being ousted from the European continent in 1940, the British still held a number of vital overseas bases of great strategic importance, especially in the Far East, Middle East, and Africa. While they lost their bases in the Far East to Japan in 1942, their bases in the Middle East and Africa were of great importance to the United States. By June 1941 there were over 530,000 British soldiers (including 130,000 African soldiers) in the Middle East. In 1942 General Bernard Montgomery held the region for the Allies against a determined German offensive led

Table 6.2 The Share of British, U.S., and Soviet National Income Spent on Defense in World War II

Date	Great Britain	United States	Soviet Union
1939	15%	2%	22%
1940	39%	3%	26%
1941	49%	12%	35%
1942	53%	33%	45%
1943	53%	45%	47%
1944	54%	45%	45%

Source: 1. W. K. Hancock and M. M. Gowing, *British War Economy* (London: His Majesty's Stationery Office, 1949), p.369.

by General Rommel. This victory was of inestimable value to the Allied cause, not only in containing German expansionism but in holding onto Middle East oil supplies and keeping Vichy France and Spain neutral in the conflict.[16]

Third, there is no gainsaying the importance of the Royal Navy and the Royal Air Force in those dark days. From 1939 until 1941 German submarines seemed to be winning the battle of the Atlantic as they sunk more shipping tonnage than the United States and Great Britain could build. Only late in 1942 and early in 1943 was the battle of the Atlantic finally won by the Allies, with a powerful role reserved for the British navy. As late as March 1942 there were 383 British escort vessels and only 122 U.S. escort vessels for the convoys making the perilous voyage across the Atlantic. The strong British naval presence in the Mediterranean and key role in the Atlantic freed the U.S. navy for duty elsewhere.[17]

In the early days of the war the Royal Air Force (RAF) played a powerful role, first in winning the crucial battle of Britain in 1940 and then later in attacking Germany and protecting the Allied buildup in Great Britain. Given the slow U.S. buildup, not until 1944 would the U.S. air force take pride of place over the RAF in assaulting the German heartland. Until December 1943 Great Britain dropped eight times more bombs on Germany than the United States dropped.[18]

Fourth, Great Britain in those trying days could count on

significant support from its Commonwealth allies. Canada and Australia provided over 1.2 million first-rate troops for the war effort and India furnished over 2.1 million troops of some value in a defensive role. Moreover, the British Commonwealth also provided the Allies a significant 9.5 billion dollars in war material, a sum equal to almost half the entire massive U.S. Lend Lease infusion of help (21.0 billion dollars) to Great Britain. This assistance from its Commonwealth allies was an important factor in enabling Great Britain to maintain an offensive posture against Nazi Germany.[19]

Finally, the British role as an advanced forward base against the Third Reich was vital to the ultimate success of the Allied cause. On one hand, Great Britain's proximity to the Continent left it extremely vulnerable to the threat of invasion or incessant Luftwaffe air attacks. These attacks destroyed considerable valuable property, forced the dispersal of production units, interfered with the transportation system, and promoted worker exhaustion from enforced factory blackout conditions and night duty in the Home Guard and civil defense. The island needed defensive weapons to protect itself from any possible attack while the Allies needed offensive weapons to push back the German onslaught.

On balance, though, the advantages of Great Britain as a forward base greatly outweighed these negative features. It could deploy its men and war materiel much more quickly and efficiently into the theaters of battle than the United States. A U.S. buildup for an offensive against the Continent could also protect Great Britain from attack. Without such a close and powerful support base, the United States would probably have found it well nigh impossible to invade France in 1944.

The British ability to maintain troops fighting against Germany was much stronger than that of the United States, given its much shorter lines of transportation and communication. The British could maintain a force rising from seventeen divisions in January 1942 to thirty-one divisions in January 1944 in the Mediterranean and Africa with far less difficulty than the United States. Under these circumstances it was not surprising that as late as January 1944 the British played a great role in the war effort. In the words of the U.S. military historian Russell Weigley, "In the European war the United States was dependent on Britain as a base and until late 1944 the British military contribution which in 1942 surpassed and then long equalled America's own."[20]

ROLE OF THE UNITED STATES

The most important question for us is to understand why the United States, soon to be the world's first and strongest superpower, was unable or unwilling to take any decisive role in the war until almost five years after it started in September 1939. A number of reasons suggest themselves. First, and most important, is the simple fact that the United States was unprepared for war in December 1941. The United States lacked any strong military tradition or significant army. The full-scale mobilization of the nation's human and material resources would take until 1943. Until that time, necessity, reinforced by the difficulties of building up strong forces to be transported enormous distances for a difficult amphibious assault in Europe, dictated heavy reliance on U.S. allies.

Second, the reliance on Great Britain and the Soviet Union also represented over time a growing awareness that these two powers were able at the least to contain and even to push back German power while the United States was mobilizing its vast resources. This conviction was not widespread in 1940 or 1941, in the wake of repeated British and Soviet defeats. By 1942 the survival of the Soviet Union and Great Britain bred new confidence in United States' allies. In June 1942 President Roosevelt could confide to Henry Morgenthau that "the whole question of whether we win or lose the war depends upon the Russians. If the Russians can hold on this summer and keep three and a half million Germans engaged in war, we can definitely win."[21] The great Soviet and British victories that fall and winter over Germany at Stalingrad and El Alamein would finally destroy the myth of the invincible German war machine and greatly reassure U.S. military planners.

This reflected both the strong British and Soviet military performance and the correlation of forces between the two sides. Even without the United States the Soviet Union and Great Britain (especially with the Commonwealth) could contest with Germany on a relatively even basis. This mirrored mainly the great economic progress made by the Soviet Union in the 1930s and the ongoing power of the British Commonwealth. It also reflected the critical error made by Hitler in only fully mobilizing the powerful German economy belatedly in 1943 and 1944 rather than in 1941 and 1942.

Even if we take all three Axis powers into account, the Soviet

Union and the British Commonwealth had 21.0 million men under arms at their peak, compared to 20.6 million men for Germany, Japan, and Italy.[22] In terms of their economic power, the Soviet Union and Great Britain at the start of the war accounted for roughly 19 percent of the world's GNP, almost identical to that of Germany and Japan.[23] In terms of such vital industrial indicators as steel and pig iron, the Soviet Union and Great Britain had achieved parity with the Axis powers. Their inferiority in coal was compensated by a superiority in oil.[24] Finally, as the world's leading naval power and the world's largest land power, they complemented each other well.

Third, there was no coherent grand thrust to U.S. policy in the early years of U.S. involvement in the war. Rather, the Roosevelt administration, in itself an untidy decision-making unit, operated against a background of inadequate resources (only really resolved late in 1943), serious logistical problems in power projection, intraservice, and international rivalries. Under these conditions the United States stressed building a large pool of multipurpose resources with only the grossest ranking of priorities. The United States, facing numerous emergencies caused by Axis advances and possessing limited resources, was unable to concentrate adequate resources for a main thrust against Germany except in peripheral arenas. For as Robert Coakley and Richard Leighton concluded in their excellent study of logistics in World War II,

> Emergencies dictated deployment in 1942 far more effectively than did long-range plans. Before the end of the year the decisions to invade North Africa and to undertake limited offensives in the Pacific produced a multifront pattern of strategy for waging the war in 1943 rather than a strategy of concentration.[25]

It is precisely these factors that undermine the recent revisionist claim, put forth nicely by authors such as John Grigg and Walter Dunn, that the Allies should have launched a second front in Europe in 1943. In retrospect, of course, this would have been a great event had it occurred and succeeded. And some of their arguments—weaker Atlantic Wall, fewer and lower quality German divisions, greater separation of German forces, and adequate Allied resources in 1943 as compared to 1944—have surface plausibility.[26]

But these arguments imply a perfect foresight and smooth

alliance functioning that never did, and never could, exist in reality. Any such invasion would have had to be approved in the summer of 1942, leading to the elimination of Operation TORCH (invasion of North Africa) and the halting of all operations in the Pacific. At a time of German advances in the Soviet Union and Japanese advances in the Pacific, it would have been very unlikely that any leaders would have voted to husband all their resources for a counterblow in one difficult sector rather than trying to strengthen endangered sectors or finding a weak spot to attack. This was even more unlikely given the predominant role at this time of Winston Churchill, with his traditionally British stress on indirect and peripheral attack and desire to safeguard the Mediterranean lifeline to the British Empire.

Furthermore, within the United States there were sharp interservice rivalries with only the army (under men such as Dwight Eisenhower and George Marshall) favoring such an assault. The navy, under Admiral Ernest King, naturally favored a war in the Pacific in which it would enjoy a predominant role. The army air force, under General Hap Arnold, favored strategic bombing of Nazi-occupied Europe. Finally, President Roosevelt's urgent desire to "do something" in 1942 to show the Soviets and the U.S. public that the United States was really in the war ended any notion of an invasion of France in 1943.

Military considerations also were highly negative. In 1942 there was no prospect that the battle of the Atlantic would be won in time. That year the Germans sank six million tons of shipping, more than the Allies built. The battle would not be finally won until the fall of 1943, yet without firm control of the Atlantic no U.S. buildup in Great Britain was possible.[27] The German army remained very powerful in 1943 and the Allies could not have mounted as strong an offensive in 1943 as they could the following year. U.S. troops were inexperienced and unbloodied, as the battle of the Kasserine Pass would show early in the coming year. Both the U.S. and British administrative machines had not yet built up to the peak of excellence they would demonstrate in 1944. And merchant shipping would have been a severe problem in supporting the buildup and offensive, even if the U-boat menace could have been contained earlier. Under these conditions the 1943 postponement of ROUNDUP (invasion of France) until 1944, when it became OVERLORD, made sense, not simply because the extension of Operation TORCH had already made the issue largely moot.[28]

Fourth, there was a passionate debate within U.S. policy circles throughout the war on the proper priority to be assigned to the war in Europe versus the war in the Pacific. Theoretically, this debate was resolved in 1942 by the victory of the advocates of a Europe First strategy. Yet, throughout the entire war, and especially from December 1941 until June 1944, this debate continued, and the two theaters received roughly equal allotments of men and material until 1944. The great Japanese victories of early 1942 and the humiliation of the United States at Pearl Harbor in December 1941 and in the Philippines in 1942 gave tremendous impetus to the naval desire to give high priority to the war in the Pacific. Throughout 1942 and 1943 the Pacific theater always seemed more emotional, more threatening, and more accessible to U.S. power than the Atlantic.

While the Soviets and British were able to bear the brunt of the German attack in Europe and the Middle East, the United States was virtually alone in the Pacific. The Soviets were officially at peace with the Japanese, thanks to the 1941 Russo–Japanese Neutrality Pact. The British, absorbed in their own backyard, could make only a limited effort in Southeast Asia. Only the Australians could offer some limited help in the fighting in New Guinea but virtually no significant naval assistance.

The pull of the Pacific exerted the irresistible call of a siren for U.S. policy planners. Despite Operation TORCH, the United States in December 1942 deployed more army troops against Japan (464,000 men) than against Germany and Italy (378,000 men). What is fascinating here is that plans approved earlier that year called for exactly the opposite result, with almost twice as many troops supposed to be deployed in Europe than the Pacific.[29]

And so it went for the next eighteen months. By 1943 the bulk of the United States Navy, now the largest fleet in the world, was deployed in the Pacific Ocean against Japan. Even at the end of 1943, two years in the war, the statistics on U.S. military deployment make fascinating reading. In December 1943 the U.S. military *still* had slightly more manpower deployed against Japan (1.88 million men) than against Germany (1.81 million men). There were seventeen U.S. army divisions deployed against Germany and another seventeen army and marine divisions deployed against Japan. The bulk of the United States Army Air Corps, by a margin of better than 2:1, was located in the European theater rather than the Pacific theater. But this was counterbalanced by the fact that the bulk of the U.S. navy, also by a margin of better than 2:1 (and for naval aviation by a margin of better than 5:1) was located in the Pacific. Thus, even by December 1943, the United States, despite its commitment to the European theater, displayed awesome power in the Pacific—almost 2 million soldiers and sailors, 13 battleships, 188 destroyers, 123 submarines, 3,600 naval planes, 1,440 air force bombers, and 1,900 air force fighter planes.[30]

This passion for the Pacific would last until June 1944. Even during the period of the Normandy invasions and landings a force almost equal to that used in Normandy (20 divisions) set forth under Admiral Nimitz's command to destroy Japanese power in the central Pacific and prepare the way for the final assault on Japan itself. In June 1944 there would be 3.2 million men deployed in Europe and 2.4 million men, backed by the newest planes and ships, in the Pacific. Even in the fall of 1944 U.S. cargo shipping would be split evenly between the two theaters. After the invasion of Normandy, there would finally emerge a strong pull toward Europe. But, as Coakley and Leighton concluded, in 1943 "The flow to the Pacific was still considerably greater than originally anticipated" and until June 1944 "the war against Japan was kept going during that crucial period at almost the same level of intensity as the war against Germany."[31]

The interesting question is why there was such a "pull to the Pacific" when there was a gross asymmetry in the danger posed by the two countries to the United States? That Nazi Germany, as demonstrated by its stunning military victories in Europe, was a significant threat to the United States and its Allies was beyond question. But the same could hardly be said for Japan. Unlike Germany, its economic and industrial base was then very weak. During the war the U.S. economy was six times larger than the Japanese economy and U.S. industrial output was nine times greater. By 1945 the United States would produce 75 million tons of steel while Japan in 1943 produced 7.8 million tons, in 1944 5.9 million tons, and in 1945 2.0 million tons. In war materiel the United States in 1943 would outproduce Japan by a factor of 10:1.[32] The small Japanese islands, heavily reliant on foreign imports of natural resources, were uniquely vulnerable to the application of massive air and naval power, which would easily flow from U.S. industrial superiority.

The early Japanese victories in China before 1941 and in Southeast Asia and the Pacific in 1941 and 1942 had come largely against weak and dispersed forces and at a time of U.S. unpreparedness. Once the United States began even modestly to mobilize its resources, the Japanese offensive would be halted with U.S. victories at Midway and Guadalcanal in 1942. Indeed, in the end the United States would suffer only 78,000 battle deaths against the Japanese compared to 7,000,000 Soviet battle deaths against the Germans.[33] With limited goals and resources, Japan could pose no serious offensive threat to the United States after 1942. By the end of 1942 Admiral Isoruku Yamamoto would write, "How splendid the first stage of our operation was! But how unsuccessfully we have fought since the defeat of Midway."[34] John Costello, in his study of the Pacific War, has observed,

> Forced onto the defensive, they (the Japanese) were discovering that reinforcing the threatened island outposts on their perimeter was draining the reserves of manpower, aircraft and shipping. . . they were fighting a losing campaign to outproduce the huge industrial capability of the United States. . . . The spear of Japan's military superiority had been blunted by the end of 1942.[35]

Top U.S. military leaders did realize the importance of giving priority to Germany over the Pacific. Throughout this period this remained official U.S. policy. In the words of an early staff report, the defeat of Germany "is the key to victory. Once Germany is defeated the collapse of Italy and the defeat of Japan must follow."[36] Why, then, under these circumstances, was there such a massive diversion of resources to the Pacific theater until June 1944?

Several reasons suggest themselves. First, the diversion of resources to fight the immediate Japanese threat fostered a momentum of its own, once victories were won at Coral Sea, Midway, and Guadalcanal in 1942. Second, the U.S. navy, as the main beneficiary of this "pull to the Pacific," did all it could to fight hard for this tendency. In this it was greatly aided by public opinion, which ardently wished to erase the humiliation of Pearl Harbor and the loss of the Philippines. A Gallup Poll in March 1942, for example, found that 65 percent of all Americans wanted to concentrate against Japan compared to only 25 percent who wished to concentrate against Germany.[37] Third, there was the great geographic and strategic importance of the Pacific, especially when the British were unable to provide serious help given their concentration in Europe and in Southeast Asia. This turned the Pacific campaign into a U.S. war and a U.S. ocean by the end of the war.

There were other reasons as well. There was a natural tendency to overrate the Japanese fighting capability. This arose from their early stunning victories over the United States and its European allies, the ferocity of Japanese resistance on the various islands, and the kamikaze phenomena. Additionally, there was uncertainty about whether the United States could devise an effective strategy to fight the Japanese island by island over thousands of miles of Pacific Ocean for a long time without incurring prohibitive rates of attrition. Finally, there was a fierce American emotional desire for retribution against the Japanese, who hitherto had been assumed to be an inferior race by most Americans. As Field Marshal Alan Brooke noted in his diaries about the Americans in May 1943 after a wartime conference, "Their hearts are really in the Pacific."[38]

THE STRANGE ALLIANCE

At this point it might be well to review the relations, often strained, that developed among the three main actors in the alliance to destroy Nazi Germany. (Since there is such a large literature on the subject, we will give only a cursory look at the relationships that developed.[39]) Soviet–U.S. relations were often difficult. Indeed, the title for this section comes from a book by the U.S. military representative in Moscow during the war, General John Deane.[40] The causes of difficulty were manifold, given the fact that this was the only period of real alliance in the seventy years of Soviet–U.S. relations.

The Soviet Union, for its part, was naturally suspicious of its allies, whom it viewed as the leading capitalist powers in the world. More concretely, it intensely resented the Anglo–American failure to open a major second front until 1944, delays in Lend Lease shipments, and the vast disparity between Soviet and Anglo–American losses in this period. It felt that it, and it alone, was carrying the main burden of destroying Nazi Germany. Furthermore, it found hard to understand the British refusal to honor its request for twenty-five to thirty British divisions to fight under British leadership on Soviet soil in the fall of 1941 or President Roosevelt's reneging on his promise to Foreign Minister Vyacheslav Molotov in June 1942 to open a second front in 1942. Even worse was the failure of the Anglo–American allies to open a second front in 1943, at a time when they were fully mobilized, or to seriously respond to Soviet desiderata to alter frontiers in Europe.[41]

In turn, the United States had grave problems in understanding its Soviet ally, given the prior history of serious political differences. During 1941 and 1942 the Roosevelt administration tended to see the Soviet Union in a very positive light, reflecting the dire realties of the battlefield and U.S. incapacity to do much at that time. Initially, in the summer of 1941 the U.S. leadership, like other Western leaderships, was very pessimistic about the Soviet Union's chances to hold out. In June 1941 Secretary of State Frank Knox told President Roosevelt in a memorandum that "The best opinion I can get is that it will take anywhere from six weeks to two months for Hitler to clean up on Russia."[42] That same month, though, Under Secretary of State Sumner Welles was confiding to his diary the hope that "Between them Britain and Russia may frustrate Hitler's aims to rule the world."[43]

In 1942 the Roosevelt administration was openly admiring of the Soviet resistance to Germany and hopeful that it could hold out against the Panzer legions. By December 1942 Roosevelt was telling Henry Wallace of the need, in Wallace's words, "that he, Stalin and Chiang Kai-shek would be playing the game together."[44] Only in 1943 did concern mount with the failure to open a second front and the possibility that extensive Soviet successes might well be the problem, not Soviet failures.

But, at the Teheran conference in November 1943 President Roosevelt often took Stalin's side against Churchill's and he seemed eager to include his somewhat troublesome ally into the new order. By early 1944 the State Department and Averell Harriman, U.S. ambassador to the Soviet Union, would be increasingly concerned about Soviet successes and eager to curtail Soviet truculence through use of Lend Lease. But the imperatives of wartime politics, and especially the need to coordinate the Soviet and Anglo-American campaigns in Europe in 1944 and need to obtain Soviet support against Japan after the war ended in Europe, curtailed the rivalry.

As for the other key relationship, that between the United States and Great Britain, there is no doubt that it was a very special relationship. It was a unique case of wartime collaboration between two sovereign states, one so close that a recent author has spoken of the emergence of a peculiar entity called "Anglo–America."[45] The massive level of Lend Lease aid, the numerous wartime conferences, the almost daily correspondence between Roosevelt and Churchill, the close integration of policies and supplies all testify to something that was historic. In the words of the editors of the secret wartime correspondence between Roosevelt and Churchill,

> One of the most extraordinary aspects of World War II was the high degree of cooperation achieved between Great Britain and the United States. . . . Never before in history had two allies come as near to success in pooling their resources, in meshing their military and diplomatic efforts, and in planning and carrying out a common strategy as did the two great English-speaking nations between 1939 and 1945.[46]

However, it is good not to idealize this relationship. There was a considerable degree of contentiousness in their association, a rivalry that would grow as victory would appear in sight by 1944. Until then the common bonds of history, heritage, and necessity, reinforced by the powerful role played by what would later be the junior partner in this relationship (Great Britain), served to obscure the many differences between the two countries. In this period, though, the conflict would be largely played out in the military arena. The British, as ever, desirous of a peripheral, indirect strategy and preservation of the Mediterranean for their empire, were usually in conflict with the U.S. desire for a more direct approach to warfare, once the means were present. Let us now turn to the Lend Lease program, which served as a powerful bond among the Allies and as an important means of equalizing the burden felt by the three powers.

LEND LEASE

In place of an all-out effort in Europe during this three-year period, the United States did place great emphasis on the Lend Lease program. This program fit well into the U.S. role in the world as the "arsenal of democracy," the provider of a cornucopia of weapons so that other nations could fight the Germans. It played to the U.S. strength—the world's largest economy and the only one to expand enormously during the war. If the Soviet economy in the 1930s was a war economy in peacetime, then in many ways the U.S. economy in the Second World War was curiously a peacetime economy in wartime. No bombs dropped on the U.S. heartland during the war. Suffering was very far away and almost surrealistic in nature, as the bulk of the American people had "a good war."

Lend Lease provided a significant way that the United States could contribute to the British and Soviet struggle without the sending of troops. This allowed the United States to accentuate its greatest strength—its economy—and downplay its greatest problem—accumulation of military strength, and especially infantry fighting power. Through Lend Lease the United States provided over 48.0 billion dollars of war supplies to its Allies, with the overwhelming majority going to Great Britain (31.7 billion dollars) and the Soviet Union (11.0 billion dollars). In total, the United States provided through Lend Lease a stream of war supplies equal to roughly 15 percent of the U.S. war expenses.[47]

The importance of this assistance for Great Britain cannot be denied, especially as it began to feel the impact of the overextension of its resources in late 1943 and 1944. During these two years U.S. Lend Lease provided a phenomenal 19.8 billion dollars in war supplies to Great Britain, a sum equal to roughly 40 percent of domestic British production in these areas. By 1944 fully 13.5 percent of U.S. airplane production and 29.5 percent of U.S. tank production went to the British Empire. At the same time, the continuing importance of Great Britain as a forward base was indicated in one statistic: at the time of the Allied invasion of Normandy in June 1944, an impressive 31 percent of U.S. war materiel came from Great Britain. Overall, then, the United States, while taking a great deal from Great Britain, also did participate fully in providing massive streams of war goods to the British cause in the war.[48]

The impact of the far smaller U.S. assistance to the Soviet Union is harder to gauge. While the Soviet claim that Lend Lease provided only 4 percent of all Soviet weapons and the Americans claim 15 percent, a reasonable estimate is 10 percent, a figure far below that for Great Britain.[49] American aid was not particularly important in most major weapons systems but was of great help in certain crucial aspects of the war effort. The key aid came in such areas as providing over 427,000 trucks, which gave the Red Army badly needed mobility. Specialized products such as aviation fuel, alloy steel, field telephones, and certain petroleum products freed Soviet industry to concentrate on more basic products that could be produced in great quantity. Large supplies of food, explosives, clothes, and rolling equipment were also important. On balance, then, the United States made a significant but not decisive contribution to the Soviet war effort. To put it simply, for the British war effort U.S. Lend Lease became critical, especially in 1943 and 1944, while for the Soviet war effort, it was an important supplement to the impressive Soviet economic performance during the war.[50]

In this chapter we have seen the very diverse roles played by the United States, Soviet Union, and Great Britain in the years leading up to the invasion of Normandy. The fruits of future discord were already well planted by D Day. For the United States the war had been relatively painless. At very low cost until June 1944 it had seen the Allied cause roll back Nazi Germany in the east and south. By June 1944 a large portion of German fighting power was irrevocably destroyed, largely at the hands of the Soviet Union. The great suffering of the Soviet, and to a lesser extent the British, people seemed far away. Fresh and ready for battle, with its war economy at full production, with no bombs having been dropped on its soil, with a wartime prosperity unknown anywhere else, the United States stood ready in 1944 to reap the harvest of the joint Allied effort. Now it could assert what it felt to be its right to lead the world to a new postwar era.

For the Soviet Union the situation was different. Those great accomplishments of destroying the fighting power of the Third Reich had come only at an awesome cost. By June 1944 the Red Army had lost over 11 million soldiers dead or taken prisoner by the Wehrmacht. The western regions of the Soviet Union lay in ruins, millions were homeless, and many millions of civilians had been brutally slaughtered by the Germans. The most developed industrial and agricultural zones of the country, so painstakingly developed in the 1930s, were now utterly decimated in the German retreat. For the Soviet Union there could be no joy or real anticipation in June 1944: only a brutal and determined passion to drive on Berlin and then get onto the massive job of reconstruction that would inevitably follow. But of one thing Stalin and the Soviet people were sure by June 1944—that they, and they largely alone, were responsible for destroying the Third Reich.

And for the third corner of the partnership, the former great power now entering into decay, Great Britain, like the Soviet Union, also felt the bitter sweetness of victory. For the cost had been enormous, enough to set the country on a course of irreversible decline. The sharp decline in British capital and trade (in 1944 exports were one third of 1939), the massive increase in foreign debt, and the total loss of assets equal to one-fourth of the prewar GNP represented a bitter pill to the status and role of the country.[51] War-ravaged Great Britain would face huge problems in the postwar era, and its power and its relations with the United States would deteriorate in the final year of the war.

Military necessity, then, had driven these three countries together to defeat Nazi Germany. But, as the prospect of victory drew nearer and these three countries began to quarrel increasingly about the postwar world, their respective roles and costs in fighting that war would inevitably play a role in their perceptions of each other.

NOTES

1. Speer, *Inside*, p.306.

2. Feis, *Churchill*, p.4

3. See Geyer, "Nationalist Socialist Germany: The Politics of Information," in May, editor, *Knowing*, pp.344–345. For further sources on Hitler's view of the United States, see Compton, *Swastika*.

4. *War Reports*, pp.143–149.

5. *Istoriya kommunisticheskoi*, v. 5, book 1, (1938–1945), p.567 and Dunn, *Second*, pp.212–213.

6. Jung, *Die Ardennen*, p.282.

7. Hancock and Gowing, *British*, p.367.

8. Seaton, *Fall*, p.103 and Urlanis, *Wars*, p.119.

9. Rose, *Long*, p.85.

10. Seaton, *Fall*, p.49.

11. Hastings, *Overlord*, p.60.

12. Butcher, *My*, p.520, Michel, *Second*, p.555; and Dupuy and Martell, *Great*, p.26. In December 1941, 2,040 German planes from a total of 5,178 were on the Eastern front; in March 1943, 3,000 German planes from a total of 10,000 planes were on the Eastern front; and in April 1944, only 1,680 German planes of a total of 5,070 planes were on the Eastern front.

13. Butcher, *My*, p.520.

14. The British were so unprepared even in 1938 that they had but two divisions capable of being deployed in Europe. See *Memoirs of Montgomery*, pp. 46–47; Hancock and Gowing, *British*, pp.67–68; and Kir'yan, *Voenno-tekhnicheskii*, p.52.

15. Hancock and Gowing, *British*, pp.136, 351, 366.

16. Even in June 1940 there were 77,000 British soldiers in the area. See Schoenfeld, *War*, pp. 103, 116.

17. *War Reports*, p.693 and Dunn, *Second*, pp.44–53.

18. Lan, *SShA*, p.55.

19. Hancock and Gowing, *British*, p.373 and Florinsky, *End*, p.264.

20. Weigley, *American*, p.318; Hancock and Gowing, *British* p.368, and Dunn, *Second*, p.x.

21. Thorne, *Allies*, p.131.

22. Goralski, *World*, p.421.

23. Brown, *Applied*, p.85.

24. Vorontsov, *Voennye koalitsii*, p.110.

25. Coakley and Leighton, *Global*, p.798.

26. For the revisionist interpretation, see Dunn, *Second* and Grigg, *1943*.

27. Lewin, *Ultra*, p.216.

28. For the best critiques of the second front in 1943 hypothesis, see the work by Coakley and Leighton, *Global* and Stoler, *Politics*.

29. Huston, *Sinews*, p.430.

30. Millett and Maslowski, *For*, p.433. There was no landing craft shortage for such an invasion. The problem was the continuing diversion of resources to the Pacific. In July 1943 there were 333 landing craft in the Atlantic Ocean and 330 landing craft in the Pacific Ocean. See Dunn, *Second*, p.62.

31. Coakley and Leighton, *Global*, pp.391, 394.

32. Samsonov, *Vtoraya mirovaya*, p.435; Lan, *SShA* and Brown.

33. Costello, *Pacific*, p.675.

34. *Ibid.*, p.383.

35. *Ibid.*, p.384.

36. Thorne, *Allies*, p.134.

37. Costello, *Pacific*, p.222.

38. Thorne, *Allies*, p.288.

39. The classic work of this genre, of course, is that by Feis, *Churchill*.

40. See Deane, *Strange*.

41. See Mastny, *Russia's*.

42. Feis, *Churchill*, p.10

43. Gaddis, *Russia*, p.4.

44. Thorne, *Allies*, p.132.

45. Ryan, *Vision*.

46. Lowenheim, Langley, and Jonas, editors, *Roosevelt* p.3.

47. For the best treatment of the Lend Lease program see Jones, *Roads*.

48. McNeill, *America*, pp.444, 782–792; and Hancock and Gowing, *British*, p.353.

49. Kolko, *Politics*, p.19 and Jones, *Roads*, pp.155, 220–224, 229, 268.

50. Jones, *Roads*, p.235–237; Harrison, *Soviet*, p.257; and Deane, *Strange*, p.94.

51. Hancock and Gowing, *British*, p.500, 516–521, 548, 55l; Marwick, *Britain*, p.257; Balfour, *Adversaries*, pp.46–47; and McNeill, *America*, p.438.

7

Soviet and U.S.
Armies in Battle

In this chapter we turn from a political and military overview of the course of the war to the battles themselves. The names and course of the battles are familiar; what may not be so familiar is a juxtaposition of the action on the fronts that gives a more balanced picture of the actual developments in the war against Nazi Germany. The Soviet accounts of the war naturally magnify the Eastern front to the relative exclusion of all other fronts in this period. Conversely, U.S. accounts of the war tend to glorify U.S. activities in North Africa and Italy, overlooking the great British role in the struggle, and largely downplaying the enormous battles on the Eastern front. Were this just a case of typical nationalist chauvinism it would not be especially harmful. But since the military events of the war played such an important role in shaping the postwar world—and the national perceptions of their roles in the war would be critical in affecting their mutual interactions after the war—the record needs to be set straight. Thus, in this chapter we attempt to provide an overview of the Soviet and U.S. armies in battle, while not ignoring the large and important role of the British Commonwealth.

SOVIET AND U.S. STYLES OF WARFARE

There was a sharp contrast between the Soviet and U.S. styles of warfare. The U.S. style, reflecting the great economic power of the

United States and weaker state of U.S. military power, emphasized money and technology at the expense of land power. In this way the United States could achieve its goals with a minimum of casualties and maximum of influence. By contrast, an economically much weaker and geographically more exposed country like the Soviet Union had to sacrifice human resources to substitute for limited economic resources, no matter how fully mobilized.

During this period, in accordance with their relative economic capabilities, the United States spent over three times more on the war than the Soviet Union. Given the tremendous devastation wreaked by the Germans in this period, and the occupation of territory formerly inhabited by more than eighty million Soviet citizens for much of this period, this expenditure represented an outstanding Soviet effort. At the same time, the Soviets killed perhaps 1,300,000 German soldiers while the Americans killed less than 100,000 German and Japanese soldiers. This meant that it cost the United States roughly $3,000,000 for each enemy soldier killed while it cost the Soviet Union approximately $80,000 for each enemy soldier killed. Thus, it cost the United States almost forty times more than the Soviet Union to kill an enemy soldier.[1]

Of course, several things need to be kept in mind when interpreting these statistics. Most important, is the fact that much of this money went into the huge buildup that did not pay off until the final year of the war. Additionally, part of the Soviet and British successes against the Germans needs to be credited to the United States and its Lend Lease program and strategic bombing campaign. The United States bore extremely heavy transportation expenses in fighting in areas thousands of miles away from North America. If we look at statistics for the entire war, then the figure drops to $800,000 per enemy soldier killed, as the United States was responsible for killing close to 500,000 enemy soldiers in the war. If we factor in Lend Lease, the United States may have been responsible for another 200,000 enemy fatalities, dropping the figure to roughly $600,000. Still, the figure is credible, for if we do a similar accounting for the Vietnam War, the United States spent over 125 billion dollars and killed perhaps 1 million Vietnamese soldiers and civilians, without needing to gain and secure naval superiority in two oceans.[2]

The opposite side, the benefit to the United States and cost to the Soviet Union, was equally extreme in the other direction. The

Soviet losses were huge in this period—almost 6 million soldiers killed and over 5 million soldiers taken prisoner by the Germans. No other army has lost such an enormous number of men—almost 11 million men in all—in any war in history. And certainly no such army has ever gone on to win such a decisive victory as the Red Army in World War II. This is not to mention the 10 million civilians killed or massacred by the Nazis and the awesome destruction wreaked by them in the East.

The comparison with the official battle losses for the U.S. army and its air force in the same period is striking: 500 killed in 1941, 3,600 killed in 1942, 15,700 killed in 1943, and 100,400 killed in 1944 (mainly after the Normandy invasion). If we factor in naval losses and divide 1944 properly, we come to the conclusion that the United States lost perhaps 100,000 men and the Soviet Union 11,000,000 men from June 1941–June 1944. Thus, the United States gave liberally of money and minimized its casualties while the Soviet Union gave liberally of men and of such money as it had.[3]

SOVIET AND U.S. MILITARY OPERATIONS

A comparison of the U.S. and Soviet campaigns against Nazi Germany from June 1941 until June 1944 begins to sound like Soviet propaganda. And it is true that the Soviet Union did not seriously contribute to the naval and air struggles with Germany, nor did it have to face a second front in the Pacific (having maintained its neutrality with Japan). However, taking all this into consideration, as well as the shorter Soviet lines of communication and transportation and advantages of fighting on one's own soil, one fact remains inescapable: the Red Army bore the brunt of the land fighting against the Third Reich for the entire three-year period before the Normandy invasion in June 1944.

While the United States and Great Britain confronted something between six and twenty-six German divisions in North Africa and Italy, the Soviet Union faced up to two hundred German divisions and several dozen allied divisions on its own soil. Roughly 90 percent of all German war losses at this time came on the Eastern front.

Although these facts have receded into the mists of time and have been largely ignored due to the Cold War, they were generally appreciated and acknowledged by Western leaders at the time. In May 1942, President Franklin Roosevelt wrote to General Douglas MacArthur that "the Russian armies are killing more Axis personnel and destroying more Axis material than all other 25 United Nations put together."[4] In July 1943 President Roosevelt, in his weekly radio broadcast, after the collapse of the Mussolini regime in Italy, commented forthrightly that Great Britain and the United States were fortunate to contribute "somewhat" to the Soviet war effort for "the heaviest and most decisive fighting today is going on in Russia."[5] In 1944 Winston Churchill made his famous and apt appreciation of the Soviet effort when he commented that the Red Army "tore the guts out of the German Army."[6] As the head of the U.S. military mission to the Soviet Union after November 1943, General John Deane, later observed,

> There can be no doubt that the Soviet Union alone absorbed the fury of the German attack in the period of nearly a year and a half that elapsed between the fall of France and our invasion of Africa. I say this in full recognition of the suffering endured and courage displayed by the British in the Battle of Britain and of the gallant battles fought by the British Empire in the Middle East. Western Russia was Russia and it was completely destroyed. By her valor and suffering Russia blunted the edge of the German sword and when she finally turned the tide at Stalingrad the outcome of the war was no longer in doubt.[7]

JUNE 1941–JUNE 1943:
OPERATION BARBAROSSA AND NORTH AFRICA

There was a great distance between the struggles of the Soviet Union in the East and the United States in North Africa during this period. For the Soviet Union it was a time of life-and-death struggle of tremendous magnitude. For the United States, protected by its oceans and supported by its Allies, the invasion of North Africa was merely a voluntary policy option adopted by the Roosevelt administration.

The Russo–German war in the East assumed titanic proportions during these three years. The initial German conception of Operation BARBAROSSA was for an extremely ambitious ten-week summer campaign that would destroy the Red Army, occupy Moscow, and reach a line 1,000 miles inside Soviet territory running from Arkhangel'sk in the north to the Caspian Sea in the south. For this mammoth undertaking the Germans deployed roughly 170 divisions (including some allied divisions), 3,300 tanks, and 2,000 airplanes. With 3.2 million men under arms and a series of rapid blitzkrieg victories under its belt, the ever-victorious Wehrmacht looked hopefully, and even somewhat confidently, to the East.[8]

In the early weeks of the invasion launched in June 1941 the German army fully met its initial expectations. The massive air raids on the first day of the war destroyed over 1,000 Red Army planes. The German army smashed through weak and disorganized Soviet units. Within ten days the Germans had seized much of the Baltics, western Belorussia, and western Ukraine. By October a great German surge had covered the almost 700 miles to Moscow in the center and the 500 miles to Leningrad in the north. In the south the battle of the Kiev salient, a few weeks earlier, had netted the astounding total of 550,000 prisoners. By October 1941 the Red Army, now down to only 2.4 million men, was fighting for its very survival in front of Moscow and Leningrad. It had also lost the bulk of the Ukraine and nearly all of western Soviet Union. The great losses included territory that had produced 62 percent of its coal production and 47 percent of its grain production before the war. The situation was desperate and the Germans seemed on the verge of another great military triumph.

At this point, though, the Red Army rallied, with an able assist from German military errors and the weather. The German army faced lengthening supply lines and inadequate preparation for winter. Red Army resistance stiffened as the war moved to the Soviet heartland. The advance knowledge provided by the Soviet spy Richard Sorge that the Japanese would attack the United States rather than the Soviet Union enabled the transfer of ten Siberian rifle divisions to the Moscow front. Stalin rallied the Soviet people and used the Soviet population reserves to create a numerically superior Red Army force to defend Moscow. The strategy worked, and not only did the Red Army defend Moscow successfully but it even threw the German army back an average of 100 miles in savage winter fighting. This marked the first major defeat then suffered by German land forces in World War II.

Despite this setback, the German army was far from exhausted and still retained a distinctive advantage over the Red Army. In the spring and summer of 1942 the Soviet leaders prepared for an attack in the central sector, a renewal of the thrust on Moscow. Instead, the Germans launched their thrust only to the south, rather than the three axes to which they deployed in 1941. Here the Germans again achieved notable successes. In open battle the Germans took over 200,000 Soviet prisoners in the fighting around Kharkov in May, and in June they seized Sevastopol. Once again the Wehrmacht seemed invincible as their armies swept south towards Stalingrad, a key industrial city on the Volga. Once across the Volga the Germans could reach the Soviet oil fields at Baku and also hope to cut the Soviet Union in two.

Stalingrad thus emerged as a critical battle which would mark the high-water point of the German advance in the Soviet Union. The Russians prepared extremely carefully for the battle. They replicated those tactics that had worked well in the defense of Leningrad and Moscow, notably the use of a huge quantity of civilian labor to build three enormous defense lines ringing the city. They learned from the mistake in Leningrad when they had failed to evacuate much of the civilian population. By September 1942 the German army was lured into a war of attrition in the streets of Stalingrad. Even as the 300,000 German troops under General von Paulus surged forward, Stalin resisted the temptation to commit his reserves carefully accumulated and trained east of the Volga.

Some of the worst fighting of the war occurred in the streets of Stalingrad where the two armies fought savagely for control of districts, streets, homes, and even floors of buildings. Finally, in November 1942 the German offensive ground to a halt in Stalingrad, after capturing most of the city. At this point the Red Army, using its reserves, launched a vast counteroffensive, initially aimed at exposed Romanian positions on the flanks of the German forces. The Romanians were soon routed and within a week the German army at Stalingrad was encircled. Here Hitler made a key mistake by refusing to allow a breakout until it was too late, and a breakin attempt just barely failed. Over the next two months the Soviet troops kept shrinking the circle under German control until von Paulus, now a field marshal, surrendered his frozen and disintegrating hordes at the beginning of February 1943.[9]

The great Soviet victory at Stalingrad was one turning point in the war. The image of German invincibility had now been permanently shattered and the Soviet Union had survived its darkest moments. With minimal Allied aid in the first eighteen months of the war, the Soviets had survived a German onslaught that had seized territory on which 40 percent of the population (80 million people) had lived before the war. The Soviets had produced no less than 78 percent of their pig iron, 63 percent of their coal, 58 percent of their steel, and 42 percent of their electricity in these areas before the war. The massive relocation of 17 million people and over 1,360 major plants in the east was a tremendous accomplishment under these conditions.[10] And the great Soviet victory at Stalingrad, with its destruction of twenty German divisions, contrasted sharply with the much smaller Allied liquidation of six German divisions in the North African campaign.

Nevertheless, the great Soviet triumph in the battle of Stalingrad, no matter how glorious, did not mean that the war was over. Far from it. Early in February 1943 the German army still retained at least 185 divisions in the Soviet Union and disposed of over 2,000 planes. Yet more ominous, the lack of an effective second front in 1943 allowed the Germans to transfer over 30 divisions from the West to reinforce their troops in the East.[11]

The U.S. situation was vastly different. After the Japanese attack on Pearl Harbor and the German declaration of war in December 1941, the United States, ill prepared for war, desperately sought some way to get into the action. But the United States in 1942 was hardly ready to fight any major actions, given its weak military mobilization and lack of military experience. Furthermore, first priority had to be given to winning the battle of the Atlantic, as German U-boats sank six million tons of shipping that year. In addition, the Japanese advance in the Pacific and the strong German gains in the Soviet Union and North Africa in 1942 meant that powerful Axis forces still retained the strategic initiative. Under these circumstances the cancellation of Operation SLEDGEHAMMER (invasion of France) in 1942 and postponement of planning for an invasion of France (Operation ROUNDUP) until 1943 were objective necessities.

In the summer of 1942 the great Allied victories at El Alamein and Stalingrad and the U.S. offensive at Guadalcanal still lay several months in the future. The U.S. desire to do *something* merged with the British desire to pursue their peripheral strategy and provide indirect aid to their embattled forces fighting Rommel's Afrika Corps. French North Africa, controlled by Vichy

France, seemed like an ideal target. Given traditional French hostility to Germany, the Allied invasion of neutral territory could expect low resistance from the 300,000 Vichy French troops in North Africa. The Allies could hope to clear the Germans from North Africa and then the Middle East, secure a forward base to attack southern Europe, enhance their control of the Mediterranean Sea, and keep Spain and Vichy France neutral.

In November 1942 the Allies, under the command of General Dwight Eisenhower, successfully launched their invasion of North Africa. An initial Allied force of 90,000 men (later built up to 290,000 men), sailing from British and U.S. ports, descended on Rabat, Oran, and Algiers. Here politics came to the aid of the Allies. The head of Vichy France, Marshal Henri Philippe Pétain, gave a free hand to Admiral Jean François Darlan, the commander of the Vichy forces in North Africa. Darlan ordered an end to all French resistance and ensured French cooperation with the Allies. As a consequence Darlan became the high commissioner for North Africa and Morocco and Algeria moved into the Allied camp. On the military front French resistance ended after only one day in Algiers, three days in Oran and Casablanca. By December 1942 the Allies controlled all of North Africa from the Atlantic to the Nile, except for Tunisia, as Montgomery's victory at El Alamein combined nicely with the Allied victory in North Africa.[12]

Unfortunately for the Allies, Tunisia proved to be an extremely stubborn nut to crack. The Germans poured in reinforcements from France, and the battle for Tunisia turned into a stalemate. At the Kasserine Pass in February 1943 the Germans even inflicted a sharp, if brief, defeat on the inexperienced U.S. army. The weather and terrain made fighting conditions difficult and favored the Germans. Only six months later in May 1943 was the German surrender finally realized in Tunisia. No less than 240,000 German and Italian troops surrendered, a sizable victory for the Allies.[13]

The victory, though, highlighted many of the shortcomings of the Allied (and especially the U.S.) war effort. Despite a better than 2:1 manpower superiority and 9:1 tank superiority, it had taken the Allies seven months to drive the Germans out of North Africa. Furthermore, almost half of the Axis manpower came from low-quality Italian forces. By the end of the campaign there were 33 Allied divisions in the Mediterranean versus 7 undersized German divisions and 5 Italian divisions. In this light, given overwhelming Allied air, tank, and numerical superiority, the capture of 125,000 German troops after a 7-month campaign was less than overwhelming. And the costs were high: 70,300 Allied casualties and the delay of the invasion of Normandy for another year.[14]

One other aspect of Operation TORCH was to be especially troubling. Despite the overall command of the operation by General Eisenhower, the U.S. role in nearly every facet of the campaign was overshadowed by the British role. Indeed, when General Eisenhower was confirmed as the Supreme Commander of Allied Forces in the western Mediterranean at the Casablanca conference in January 1943, the British General Harold Alexander was confirmed as his deputy, to run the daily land battles. This was not an accident. By the end of the campaign the 8 U.S. divisions under General George Patton (and then General Omar Bradley) paled beside the 22 British infantry and armored divisions and 3 French divisions in the area. In the major battles of the campaign British soldiers accounted for roughly 75 percent of the Allied manpower. Similarly, the British took over 50 percent of the casualties while the Americans suffered only 26 percent of all Allied casualties, a figure in line with their overall contribution. In short, then, the weakness of the U.S. war effort was demonstrated by the fact that even more than a year after Pearl Harbor the United States could mount only a modest attack against weak German forces on the periphery of the Third Reich. And, at that, it could only do so with British help that overwhelmed U.S. help by a figure of 3:1.[15]

OPERATIONS HUSKY AND CITADEL: SUMMER 1943–SUMMER 1944

By the summer of 1943 the tide had turned in the favor of the Allies, against both Nazi Germany and Imperial Japan. On the Eastern front the Soviets had stopped the Germans at Stalingrad and now hoped to gain their first victory in summer as well. For the Anglo–American allies, their victories in the Atlantic and over the skies of Nazi-occupied Europe led to new questions of the proper path to victory. They chose the conservative but surer path of continuing the peripheral strategy that had worked well the previous year.

The Germans, in retreat, decided to try one last great offensive in the East—this time, Operation CITADEL, aimed at the Kursk-Orel salient. Here, in July 1943, while the Allies faced 2 German divisions in Operation HUSKY in Sicily, the Red Army confronted the massed might of 50 German divisions, backed by 2,700 tanks and self-propelled artillery pieces, 10,000 guns and mortars, and over 2,000 planes. Altogether the Germans deployed 900,000 troops in this last great endeavor, compared to 50,000 troops in Sicily.

The Red Army, for its part, prepared a powerful and elaborate defense zone to blunt the German offensive. The Red Army committed a huge force of 76 divisions, 1,337,000 men, 19,300 guns and mortars, 3,300 tanks and self-propelled artillery pieces, and 2,650 planes. For two weeks in the beginning of July the German forces strove to smash the Soviet defenses, but to little avail. The largest tank battle in military history occurred over one small village—1,200 tanks took part. Finally, with the German offensive power spent (and very little to show for it), the Red Army went over to the offensive and gained a resounding triumph at Kursk-Orel.[16]

The great Soviet victory at Kursk-Orel unleashed the most powerful Soviet offensive of the war. That summer and fall of 1943 the Red Army, using over 200 divisions and more than 2.6 million men, completed the liberation of two-thirds of all Soviet territory originally occupied by the Germans. In major offensives the Red Army advanced 300 miles in the center and 800 miles in the south. The Red Army especially focused on retaking most of the Ukraine, seizing such key cities as Kharkov and Kiev in the process. This broad-scale offensive on a 1,500 mile front was so successful that by January 1944 the Red Army was even prepared in one sector to leave Soviet territory and move into Poland.[17]

By the beginning of 1944 the Germans were in retreat everywhere, but nowhere more than in the East. By January of that year the Red Army, despite massive losses, deployed a huge army of 6.4 million men replete with 95,600 cannon, 5,250 tanks, and 10,200 planes against the German army. These numbers would only change slightly by June 1944. In January Red Army troops went over to the offensive and finally lifted the siege of Leningrad, which had caused more than 600,000 civilian deaths—alone twice more than all U.S. battle deaths in World War II. A spring offensive took the Red Army into the Crimea and thrust the Germans out of the Ukraine.[18]

By June 1944 a large and powerful Red Army stood poised to clear the last remaining German troops from its territory in Belorussia and the Baltics. This force had held down and mauled the bulk of German land power in Europe for almost three years. In short order it would be able to manifest strong offensive capabilities to drive the German army out of Eastern Europe as well and even enter into Germany itself. Yet the losses had been awesome—perhaps 16 million civilian and military deaths at this point. When Elliot Roosevelt visited General Eisenhower in England in May 1944 on the verge of the invasion of Normandy, he observed,

> But the eastern front was a war of unbelievable brutality and suffering. Members of the Russian high command were complaining to him that the Red Army "suffered more casualties before breakfast every morning than the Allies suffered in a month."[19]

For the United States the situation was again markedly different. After the Allied victory in North Africa in May 1943, logic almost dictated an Allied assault on Sicily and Italy later that year. It was now too late to mount an assault that summer in France, and the Allies were not disposed to letting their growing resources stand idle. The most promising and easiest target would be Mussolini's Italy, which, they hoped, could be knocked out of the war and even turned into an ally like Vichy France. The Italian people were known to be tired of war and relatively friendly to the West. The Italian army was rated as extremely weak and likely to collapse under Allied pressure. The Allies would have complete air and sea mastery and face only a small force of 2 German divisions backed up by 9 weak Italian divisions. In sum, the Allies would face 50,000 German troops and 315,000 Italian troops on the island. How could the Allies resist the siren call of Sicily less than 100 miles across a calm sea from North Africa?[20]

Under such circumstances success seemed ensured for Operation HUSKY. Taking no chances, the Allies landed 9 divisions in the initial assault, eventually augmenting that number to an impressive 13 divisions (ultimately 478,000 men). A powerful naval task force included no less than 6 battleships, 6 cruisers and 24 destroyers. Allied air power included over 1,000 planes. Even in the initial assault the Allies brought in 1,800 artillery pieces and 600 tanks. So overwhelming was the invasion that the initial landing involved more troops (181,000 men) and ships (2,500 vessels) than were used in the initial assault at Normandy.[21]

At the outset, Italy seemed a replay of North Africa. The morale of the Italian Sixth Army was low. When the initial assault went well and Mussolini was overthrown and replaced that month by Marshal Pietro Badoglio, a glorious future seemed to await the forces of Patton and Montgomery as they raced to crush the enemy and move on to the Italian mainland.

Fate, however, had another destiny in mind for the Allies. The mountainous terrain, strong German resistance, and an unimaginative battle plan slowed the Patton and Montgomery advance to a crawl. What should have been a quick victory wound up taking thirty-eight days to accomplish. Even worse, the Allies failed to trap the German divisions: 40,000 German soldiers crossed safely into Italy, and only 5,500 were taken captive in the campaign; no less than 60,000 Italian soldiers escaped the slow-moving Allies as well. The Axis forces even managed to escape with 50 tanks, 94 cannons, 10,000 vehicles, and 17,000 tons of supplies. The Allies did finally triumph, killing and taking prisoner 250,000 troops, mainly Italian, of the Axis. But after such a massive effort and with such advantages, Operation HUSKY was disappointing.[22]

One other feature of the campaign also replicated the North African adventure—the British continued to be the dominant force. While the initial landing brought in far more British Empire soldiers (115,000 men) than U.S. soldiers (66,000 men), this was eventually evened up with the deployment of 7 U.S. divisions and 6 British divisions. But the British role remained predominant. Montgomery took pride of place over Patton in the campaign. While General Eisenhower did retain overall control, all three of his key deputies were British. The Allied ground forces commander was General Sir Harold Alexander, the air chief was Marshal Sir Arthur Tedder, and the admiral of the fleet was Admiral Sir Andrew Cunningham.[23]

The record of the Allied military thrusts—and especially the U.S. contribution to those thrusts—left little to boast of by September 1943 when Sicily was finally liberated. The United States had been at war with Nazi Germany, which it rightfully considered the main threat to its national security, for almost two years. In that time its forces had managed to confront only 8 German divisions—6 in North Africa and 2 in Sicily. The U.S. army had helped to destroy the 6 divisions in North Africa, which constituted less than 2 percent of the more than 300 German divisions then in existence. And at a time when the Red Army was facing and pushing back close to 200 German divisions, it could not even confront this tiny handful of German divisions in the far outposts of the Third Reich without a predominant role reserved for its British ally.

Of course, there were some mitigating circumstances. The United States was playing a predominant role in the war against Japan and had played a major role in winning the battle of the Atlantic against German submarine warfare in 1943. It was building up its strength for an all-out assault on the European heartland in 1944. And its growing air power would inflict serious damage on the Third Reich in 1943 and 1944. Still, all things considered, the record of the U.S. army left a great deal to be desired and hardly reflected the role of the United States as a superpower less than two years hence.

The final Allied campaign before the Normandy invasion— the invasion of Italy—was even more logical than the Sicilian campaign and even less fortuitous for the Allies. Obviously, the conquest of Sicily would lead directly to the invasion of Italy. Again, as in North Africa and Sicily, the political situation seemed promising. Already, as we have seen, in July 1943 Marshal Pietro Badoglio had taken power, dissolving the Italian Fascist Party and ousting Mussolini. In August the new government began peace negotiations with the Allies, reaching an armistice in September 1943.

On the surface, then, all seemed propitious for the Allied landing on the mainland that same month. One of the three members of the Axis, Italy, appeared ready to desert Nazi Germany and stand with the Allies. There was only one problem: the Germans refused to accept this and rapidly occupied the bulk of the country. The 18 German divisions in or near Italy in September 1943 soon escalated to 24 German divisions in the country by December. An Allied assault at Salerno managed to seize Naples by the end of September, but after that the Allied advance slowed to a crawl. In the next three months the U.S. Fifth Army advanced only 70 miles at a cost of 40,000 casualties and 50,000 sick men, while Montgomery's Eighth Army did even less well on the east coast. A January 1944 Allied assault at Anzio failed to break the stalemate. Only in June 1944, nine months after the landing on the mainland, would Allied forces take Rome. At that, as we will see, the Italian campaign would be far from over.[24]

The Allies had chosen one of the worst places in Europe to concentrate their forces, for the Germans had built a powerful defense belt, known as the Gustav line, in the Apennine mountains 100 miles south of Rome. This rugged and mountainous terrain, the limited resources available to the Allies, the inability to make use of Allied advantages in tanks and trucks in such an environment, and the ease with which the Germans could reinforce their troops all hampered the effort. Beyond this, even once the Allies reached Rome, the Germans would be able to make equally good use of the rugged terrain in the north of Italy. As a result, Italy drained the Allies of great resources with little to show for it. By June 1944 the Allies had committed 28 divisions to the campaign, greater than the number of U.S. divisions then in Great Britain waiting to assault France. For their massive effort they were holding down only 26 German divisions, could carry out strategic bombing of Germany, and had secured the Mediterranean.[25]

The record of joint U.S.–British military operations for the entire period from June 1941 until June 1944 was poor. The Allies had wasted their considerable resources on the periphery of Europe with few results. Even by June 1944 they found themselves in Rome, still facing a long and arduous campaign that would only take them to the foothills of the Alps. During these several years they had failed to do more than annoy the Third Reich and certainly had not come close to threatening its existence. Two and one-half years after Germany had declared war on the United States, Washington had failed to mount a credible challenge to German power. In May 1944 its forces were part of an Allied operation that had forced Germany to commit only 26 divisions, or perhaps 10 percent of its might, to control its offensive. And, once again, even this small U.S. effort had been impossible without large-scale British help, and was conducted under the overall command of the well-known British General Harold Alexander. Even if we take all the mitigating circumstances into account—war in the Pacific, development of naval and air power, lengthy lines of transportation and communication—the U.S. record is still weak, especially when one considers that one year later the United States would emerge as the world's leading superpower.

The Soviet and U.S. armed forces, then, reached June 1944 in very different states. The Soviet military was ravaged by 1,000 days of unrelenting devastation on the Eastern front. No other army in world history has faced the loss of 11 million soldiers and several million others seriously injured—and survived and even triumphed to fight another day. If the losses were astounding, so too was the progress. The Red Army had rebounded from the most devastating blow ever inflicted by one army against another in 1941 and 1942. By June 1944, largely on its own efforts, it had not only survived but had recaptured nearly all of the vast territory it had lost in those first sixteen dark months of the war. In short order it would be able to complete the recapture of all of its prewar territory and move onward into Eastern Europe.

The Red Army dramatically disproved the contention of Hitler and most other Western skeptics that it would easily collapse under sustained German pressure. Not only did it not disintegrate as in World War I, but it more than held its ground against a German army three times greater than in World War I. In three years of continuous warfare it had repeatedly mauled the famed German army and permanently removed no less than 2 million soldiers from its ranks. By 1944 the Wehrmacht was but a shadow of its former grandeur. Now, despite the huge losses, the Red Army stood on the threshold of doing something that Russia had long dreamed of but had never been able to accomplish in the last century: an invasion of Eastern Europe and triumphal march into Germany itself.

The contrast with the U.S. military was compelling. The United States by June 1944 had established its naval dominance in the Atlantic and its air dominance over German-occupied Europe. Its land adventures, though, had been puny and small scale compared to Soviet campaigns. In North Africa, Sicily, and southern Italy the United States had engaged a grand total of less than 35 German divisions over a two-year period—this at a time when the Red Army was daily engaging upwards of 200 German divisions on the Eastern front.

Even worse, as we have seen at length, this small U.S. role was only possible because of a powerful British contribution to the joint U.S.-British ventures. In the Atlantic Ocean, in the skies over Europe, in the battlefields of North Africa, the Middle East, and Italy, the British Commonwealth forces were everywhere. Until the middle of 1943 their role was predominant and in the last year before the invasion of Normandy their role was at least equal to the U.S. war effort in battle. This magnificent British effort, which had lasted almost five years since the start of World War II, so overtaxed British resources that the British role would diminish sharply in the last year of the war. But while it lasted, the British role was a powerful reason for the containment and ultimate defeat of the Nazi menace to Europe and the world.

Until June 1944, then, the Soviet Union and Great Britain had played a predominant role and the United States only a supporting role in the struggle against Germany. In the process, though, these two great powers had seriously strained their human and material resources to carry on the fight. By contrast, in May 1944 the United States was still a fresh and apparently great untested power, with seemingly endless human and material resources at its disposal. Its initial small-scale encounters with the German army in North Africa and Italy had shown little and not contributed a great deal to the destruction of the Wehrmacht. Now, at long last, as D Day approached, the United States would finally test itself seriously against Germany.

NOTES

1. Perrett, *Days*, p.400.
2. *Ibid.*
3. Grigg, *1943*, p.81.
4. Feis, *Churchill*, p.42.
5. Gaddis, *United* p.5.
6. See Feis, *Churchill*.
7. Werth, *Russia*, p.xiv.
8. See the most valuable books on the Eastern front in World War II by Erickson and Seaton. See Erickson, *Road to Stalingrad* and its companion volume, *Road to Berlin*. See also the fine work by Seaton, *The Russo-German War 1941–45*.
9. *Ibid.*
10. Dupuy and Martell, *Great*, p.3.
11. Feis, *Churchill*, pp.115–119.
12. Eisenhower, *Allies*, pp.121–125; Stoler, *Politics*, pp.52–64; McNeill, *America* p.218; Leahy, *I*, pp.111–136; and Grigg, *1943*, pp. 37, 55.
13. Grigg, *1943*, p.81.
14. Dunn, *Second*, pp.33, 248.
15. *Ibid.*, p.33 and Bradley, *General's*, p.158.
16. Dupuy and Martell, *Great*, pp.76, 85 and Sivachev and Yakovlev, *Russia*, pp.186–187.
17. Dupuy and Martell, *Great*, p.106; Sivachev and Yakovlev, *Russia*; p.187 and Kolko, *Politics*, p.19.
18. Samsonov, *Vtoraya mirovaya*, pp.359–360.

19. Eisenhower, *Eisenhower*, p.235.

20. Lan, *SShA*, p.57.

21. Lamb, *Montgomery*, p.24 and Morison, *Two*, p.247.

22. Grigg, *1943*, p.95.

23. Morison, *Two*, p.246 and Lamb, *Montgomery*, p.24.

24. McNeill, *America*, p.286; Feis, *Churchill*, pp.162, 187; *War Reports*, p.167; and Grigg, *1943*, p.114.

25. Millett and Maslowski, *For*, p.425; Weigley, *American*, p.327; and Matloff, editor, *American*, p.482.

Section 4
The Soviet and U.S. Destruction of the Third Reich June 1944–May 1945

8

Soviet and U.S.
Armies in Battle

The passage of over four decades since the last year of World War II in Europe has dimmed our memories of those fateful events. What stands out are the highlights of that historic victory over Nazi Germany—the Normandy landings, the liberation of Paris, the courageous defense of Bastogne, the drive across the Rhine at Remagen, the linkup with Soviet troops on the Elbe, the Nazi surrender on V-E Day. All these events seemed to confirm the awesome power of the United States over a crumbling evil empire of the Third Reich. The emergence of the United States as the predominant superpower in the postwar era seemed to flow inexorably from this vast display of U.S. military might.

The problem with this popular image is that it is only partially true. The United States did play a strong role in the ultimate defeat of Nazi Germany. What is omitted from this story, though, is as important as what is told—the formidable power of the Third Reich in the last year of the war and the great role played by the Red Army in the achievement of final victory. The simple, if unpalatable, truth is that U.S. military power, and especially land power, was less effective than usually believed. Without the formidable power of the Red Army, victory in Europe in 1945, or even 1946, would have been impossible for the Allies to achieve.

OVERVIEW OF THE LAST YEAR OF THE WAR IN EUROPE

Overall, four reasons can help explain this apparent paradox. First, the Red Army, and not the U.S. and British armies, had largely been responsible for mauling the Wehrmacht before June 1944. To the extent, then, that the U.S. and British forces faced an exhausted and depleted German army in the West in the last year of the war, the credit largely lay with the Red Army. Table 8.1, drawing on German statistics for casualties to its field forces, makes this point dramatically.

The contrast between the two sides is massive. The Red Army inflicted almost 4.2 million casualties on the Wehrmacht, the U.S. and British armies barely 300,000 casualties. The minor losses suffered by the German army in North Africa, Sicily, and Italy could be easily repaired by the large population reserves of the Third Reich. The industrial damage inflicted by Allied strategic bombing was similarly reparable by the large German labor force, supplemented by six million foreign laborers. By contrast, the Red Army, by inflicting over 2 million permanent losses on the Wehrmacht, had made serious inroads into its fighting strength.

Of course, the Anglo-American contribution was not as miniscule as portrayed above. The Western allies had liberated North Africa and much of Italy, kept Vichy France and Spain neutral, protected the Middle East oil fields, sent large Lend Lease supplies to the Soviet Union, held down significant German forces in the West, gained air and sea superiority over the Third Reich, and borne the brunt of the war against Japan. All this is true. But, it cannot gainsay the brutal fact illustrated in the Table 8.1: it was the Red Army that had destroyed most of the Wehrmacht fighting power. Without this Soviet devastation of German fighting power, no Anglo-American landings at Normandy would have been possible. Had Nazi Germany remained at the level of military brilliance displayed so convincingly in the 1939–1942 period, culminating in the easy destruction of France and occupation of huge Soviet territories, the Allies would have faced an extremely difficult, if not impossible, task in 1944. Worse, without massive British help, which exhausted the British Commonwealth, even this lesser Western effort by the United States would have been impossible.[1]

Second, the image of a weak and prostrate Germany, which looms so large in our minds, is a picture drawn only from the

Table 8.1 Wehrmacht War Casualties, June 22, 1941–June 4, 1944

Casualties	Eastern Front	Other Fronts
Dead	766,300	35,400
Wounded	2,882,700	119,500
Missing	545,800	147,900
Total	4,194,800	302,800

Source: 1. Hermann Jung, *Die Ardennen-Offensive 1944/45* (Frankfurt: Musterschmidt Gottingen, 1971), pp.282, 289.

final months of the war. In June 1944, and even in November 1944, Nazi Germany remained a formidable, if shaken, foe. In June 1944 the forces of Nazi Germany stood everywhere outside of the borders of Germany. The Third Reich encompassed nearly all of Western, Central, and Eastern Europe and a small part of the Soviet Union (Belorussia and the Baltics). Equally important, the 80 million Germans in the Third Reich still adored and revered their Fuehrer.

The German military was far from finished in June 1944, despite the loss of air and naval supremacy in the West and serious land defeats in the East. During 1944 the Third Reich could field armed forces of over 9.4 million men, declining only slowly to 7.8 million men in early 1945. Its tanks (especially the Panthers and Tigers), artillery and antitank weapons were equal to or better than anything possessed by the Allies, especially in the West. The new weapons that were being brought into production—jet planes, U-boats, flying bombs, supersonic missiles—promised to seriously outclass anything likely to be produced by the Allies. Despite years of retreat, the German army, with excellent officers and soldiers, remained qualitatively superior to any of the enemy armies. Colonel Trevor Dupuy has found that in 1944 the German ground soldier inflicted 50 percent more casualties on the U.S. soldiers than their numbers warranted. This has led Max Hastings, noting the "immense and extraordinary fighting power of the German army," to comment that "throughout the Second World War, whenever British or American troops met Germans in anything like equal strength, the Germans prevailed."[2]

Nor was the German economy, and especially the war economy, anywhere near exhaustion. The Germans had massively exploited Europe for their own benefit and imported 6 million foreign laborers to bolster their economy. With German GNP in 1944 still 17 percent greater than in 1938, Berlin could spend almost 40 billion dollars on the war effort, a sum nearly half of the U.S. war effort that year. The production figures for 1944— including 2.9 million rifles, 18,300 tanks and self-propelled artillery pieces, 34,100 planes—were very respectable under the circumstances.[3] As the war moved closer to the homeland, the Germans could use excellent interior lines of transportation and communication to fight the invaders more efficiently.

Third, the Soviets and the Americans faced very different obstacles in the final year of the war. For the last six months of 1944 German soldiers continued to fight well on both fronts. But during the final five months of the war the morale of German soldiers and civilians disintegrated on the Western front while remaining strong on the Eastern front. Although there was occasionally tough resistance in the West, this was the exception rather than the rule after the final mop-up in the Ardennes in January 1945. In March 1945, after Montgomery crossed the Rhine against no resistance (he took thirty-one casualties), an exuberant Winston Churchill exclaimed, "My dear General. The German is whipped. We've got him. He is all through."[4] At the end of April 1945 General George Patton, in letters to his family, observed that "the war is sort of petering out. We go anywhere we want and with very limited opposition. . . . This part of the war is rather dull, sort of a 'last roundup.'"[5]

The diary entries of Propaganda Minister Joseph Goebbels in March 1945 best reflected the view from Berlin,

> I cannot understand the fact that hardly any resistance was offered in Köln (March 7). . . . Particularly in the West a fairly severe dent has now been made in our fighting morale, which is slowly beginning to sink (March 9). . . . Gauleiter Stohr gives me over the telephone an extraordinarily tragic account of the present situation in the Saar territory. . . the people's morale and that of the Wehrmacht has sunk to an extraordinarily low level (March 20). . . . At the present moment the enemy is having an easy time in the West. Neither the troops nor the civil population are putting up an organized courageous resistance against him so that the Americans in particular can drive about the countryside at will (March 26) . . . large-scale demoralization has set in in the West . . . a vast army of stragglers is on the move eastwards (March 29).[6]

The contrast with the Eastern front was startling. There, rather than petering out, the war reached a new level of frenzy in the final months of World War II, culminating in the titanic battle for Berlin in May 1945. The Germans, having committed mass genocide in the East, were afraid of the rightful revenge which the Soviets would administer for having slaughtered 20 million people, most in cold blood. The Nazi propaganda campaign for more than a decade had sought to convince the German people that Bolshevism would bring the Dark Ages back to Germany and that millions of Germans would be liquidated, raped, robbed, or sent to Siberia as slave laborers. Driven by hatred, fear, and patriotism, the Germans fought ever more desperately as the Red Army invaded German territory. In the words of William McNeill,

A second factor which slowed the Red Army's rate of advance was German fear of the Russians—a fear which impelled the German soldiers to fight far more determinedly on the eastern than the western front. Thus, while Eisenhower's armies plunged into the vitals of Germany and met only scattered resistance, the Red Army found the going much more difficult. This German behavior did not fail to sow seeds of distrust between Russia and the West.[7]

Two statistics illustrate this point dramatically. In the final battles of the war, from the Rhine to the Elbe, the U.S. army lost over 9,000 men while just in the battle of Berlin alone the Red Army suffered 305,000 casualties.[8] And in the eleven months from D Day to April 1945, *before* the battle of Berlin, the Red Army inflicted 1,405,200 casualties (dead and wounded) on the German field armies in the Eastern and the Southeast theaters; the U.S. and British armies inflicted 443,500 such casualties in the Western and Southwestern theaters.[9]

The Germans not only fought much more fiercely in the East, especially in the last five months of the war, but they also kept the bulk of their divisions there throughout the final year of the war. The Americans and British troops usually faced no more than one third of the German forces, and often not the better third at that. The Red Army drained off most of the Wehrmacht fighting power, even in 1944 and 1945 (as it had done throughout the war), opening the way for the West to score easier victories in Western Europe. Table 8.2 makes clear the extent to which the Anglo-American forces depended on the Red Army to engage the bulk of the Wehrmacht.

The Anglo-American forces, except during the Battle of the Bulge, usually faced only one-third of all German divisions. This was true in terms of number of men as well as in the somewhat trickier number of divisions. Throughout the entire last year of the war the Germans maintained over two million combat troops in the East and over one million combat troops in the West.[10] This high priority of the East was maintained at all costs. When the January 1945 Red Army offensive obliterated the German lines and threatened Berlin itself, over half of the western Panzer divisions, one-third of the infantry forces, and almost all of the new armored production were rushed eastward.[11] At the end of March 1945, when General Dwight Eisenhower was asked at a press conference which would be the first army to enter Berlin, he candidly replied, "I wouldn't want to make any prediction. They have a shorter race to run although they are faced by the bulk of German forces."[12]

But even against this limited force the Anglo-American armies were unable to mount an overwhelmingly numerically superior force, relying instead on air power and tank forces to compensate for their deficiencies. This is remarkable if we consider that the population of the United States and Great Britain alone was more than double that of Germany, and this gap was only partially accounted for by transport problems or the war in the Pacific.

A comparison of the Soviet and U.S. war efforts makes this more comprehensible. While both sides mobilized roughly similar 12 million man armies, the distribution of these forces was markedly different. As we will see in the coming chapter, the United States poured fully 50 percent of its manpower into the navy and air force, the Soviet Union a mere 7 percent. By contrast, the remaining 50 percent of U.S. manpower went to fill only 90 field divisions while the remaining 93 percent of Soviet manpower created 488 divisions by January 1945. In short, this meant that the Red Army had roughly 6.0 million men in active field divisions, the U.S. Army 1.5 million men. And when the lower U.S. slice of actual fighting men in divisions and the U.S. second front against Japan are taken into account, it means that in 1945 the Red Army had perhaps 3.6 million combat troops in Europe in the East while the United States had .6 million combat troops in the West.[13] Although the United States did compensate for this deficiency through the use of British Commonwealth and French troops, massive air power, and tank superiority, it still faced a

Table 8.2 German Troop Dispersal Among Fronts, June 1944–April 1945 (number of divisions)

Date	Eastern Front	Western Front
June 1944	189	96
September 1944	172	82
January 1945	153	117
April 1945	133	77

Sources: 1. Albert Seaton, *The Russo-German War 1941–45* (New York: Praeger, 1970), pp.439, 621.
2. David Eisenhower, *Eisenhower: At War 1943–1945* (New York: Random House, 1986), p.610.
3. Charles MacDonald, *The Last Offensive* (Washington, D.C.: Government Printing Office, 1973), p.5.
4. Charles MacDonald, *The Siegfried Line Campaign* (Washington, D.C.: Government Printing Office, 1963), p.15.
5. John Strawson, *Hitler As Military Commander* (London: B. T. Batsford Ltd., 1971), p.216.
6. Samuel Mitcham, Jr., *Rommel's Last Battle: The Desert Fox and the Normandy Campaign* (New York: Stein and Day, 1983), p.28.
7. Herbert Feis, *Churchill, Roosevelt, Stalin* (Princeton: Princeton University Press, 1967), p.447.
8. A. Russell Buchanan, *The United States and World War II*, (New York: Harper and Row, 1964), Vol.2, pp.417–418.
[a]The Eastern front includes all German forces in the Soviet Union, Finland, Eastern Europe, and the Balkans. The Western front includes all German forces in Scandinavia, France, Italy, and West Germany.

serious problem of not being able to gain significant numerical superiority until near the end of the war. By contrast, the Red Army was able to maintain a strong numerical superiority of 2-3:1 against the far larger German army in the East throughout the last year of the war.

Table 8.3 highlights the difficulties that the United States, even with strong British help and with the majority of German divisions drained off to the East, had in establishing clearcut numerical supremacy over the Wehrmacht.

The table shows the difficulties the Western allies had in mounting a successful campaign against Germany. Of course, the numbers are not as bad as they seem given the German penchant not to disband shattered divisions and the U.S. passion for keeping divisions at full strength. Thus by March 1945 U.S. divisions were generally at least twice the size of German divisions.

Table 8.3 Comparison of Anglo-American and German Divisions Deployed on the Western and Southwestern Fronts, June 1944–May 1945 (number of divisions)

Date	Anglo-American	German
October 1944	82	85
December 1944	87	97
January 1945	107	100
February 1945	105	106
March 1945	119	79

Sources: 1. F. E. Ellis and A. E. Warhurst, *The Defeat of Germany* (London: Her Majesty's Stationery Office, 1968), pp.143, 173, 295.
  2. Albert Seaton, *The Fall of Fortress Europe 1943–1945* (New York: Holmes and Meier, 1981), p.182.
  3. Forrest Pogue, *George C. Marshall: Organizer of Victory 1943–1945* (New York: Viking Press, 1973), p.657
  4. Albert Kesselring, *A Soldier's Record*, translated by Lynton Hudson (New York: William Morrow, 1954), p.286.
  5. Herbert Feis, *Churchill, Roosevelt, Stalin* (Princeton: Princeton University Press, 1967), pp.478–479.
  6. David Eisenhower, *Eisenhower At War 1943–1945* (New York: Random House, 1986), p.478.

Table 8.3, however, conceals one less positive fact about the U.S. contribution. This was that roughly 40 percent of the total manpower in the West was being supplied by the British Commonwealth and France, not the United States.[14] This meant that the U.S. troops in Europe, except near the end of the war, were always outnumbered even by the relatively thin layer of German troops in the West.

The arithmetic is inescapable. If two-thirds of the German forces were on the Eastern front and the Americans were providing 60 percent of the manpower on the Western front, then the U.S. army was confronting 20 percent of the Wehrmacht while the Red Army was confronting 66 percent of the Wehrmacht. If we then add in that the Germans, especially in the last five months of the war, were fighting much harder in the East than in the West, only then do the casualty figures for the final year of the war begin to make sense. In the last year of the war, the Americans suffered 135,000 battle deaths in Europe, the Soviets over 1.2 million battle deaths.[15]

THE SUMMER OF 1944: BELORUSSIA AND NORMANDY

The Anglo-American decision to open a second front in northern France in June 1944, which had been confirmed at the Teheran conference in November–December 1943, brought the war to a new intensity. Now, finally, all three great powers would be fighting simultaneously, and on a large scale, to crush the Third Reich from opposite ends of the continent. The Allied decision to invade France was an acknowledgment that the Italian campaign, while making progress (Rome was seized the day before the invasion occurred), was doomed to be a slow and limited effort leading the Allies into a cul-de-sac. France promised to be a much more desirable arena for the destruction of German power and opening the road into Germany itself.

It is customary in the West to lay the greatest possible emphasis on the Normandy landings. There is no question that they were important and, as Hitler had declared the previous winter, would be decisive for the fate of Nazi Germany. But we should first turn to Operation BAGRATION, the Red Army campaign that summer which would do even more to unhinge the remaining power of the Third Reich. General von Mellenthin has cited figures that show that from 1 June 1944 to 31 August 1944, the German armed forces lost 293,800 men in the West, but 916,800 men in the East.[16]

The massive Red Army summer campaign represented a new stage in the development of Soviet capabilities. The Red Army developed a powerful offensive on a wide front, followed by mass armor thrusts and mobile units pouring through the gaps to destroy enemy reserves and rear lines of communication. The Red Army had truly arrived as a modern and efficient army.

On 22 June 1944, the Red Army, aided by the large-scale actions of 140,000 partisans in the forests and swamps of Belorussia, began a giant offensive aimed at the destruction of Army Group Center, the hinge of the whole German front in the East. Before 22 June , despite all the Red Army gains of the last eighteen months, the German army still held positions in Belorussia on the approaches to Moscow 290 miles away. The Red Army, by contrast, was yet at best 550 miles from Berlin.

After months of careful preparation, the Red Army unleashed a mammoth offensive with 124 divisions, under Rokossovsky, Bagramyan, and Chernyakhovsky, against the 40 German divisions of Army Group Center. Operating with 3:1 manpower superiority,

4:1 artillery superiority, and almost 6:1 tank superiority, the Red Army devastated the Wehrmacht, despite the natural defensive protection of bogs and thick woods. In less than two weeks 28 German divisions had vanished with the loss of 350,000 German soldiers dead, wounded, or captured. So rapid was the advance that no less than 31 of the top 47 German generals were killed or captured. In July, 57,000 German prisoners would be paraded in the streets of Moscow.

Within three weeks the Red Army, having torn a 250-mile gap in German lines, advanced over 200 miles. By the time the advance halted at the Vistula in the middle of August the Red Army had advanced almost 200 miles in the north and 300–435 miles in the center. The Red Army had liberated Belorussia and much of the Baltics and threatened East Prussia and Czechoslovakia. The Soviets had now moved into Poland and were on the outskirts of Warsaw as their drive died. There, in a highly controversial move, they were both unwilling and unable to come to the aid of the Polish resistance forces, which staged a futile and gruesome uprising against the German occupation forces in August 1944. Large German units were now cut off in the Baltics. Overall, 30 German divisions had been liquidated and another 30 German divisions had been badly mauled.[17]

In the south this massive thrust was supplemented by a second offensive launched by Konev's 80 divisions against the 45 divisions of Army Group North Ukraine. This secondary campaign was also crowned with success. By August Konev's troops had advanced 400 miles to the Vistula where they threatened the whole German position in Romania and Hungary. The door was now open to destroy the entire German domination of Eastern Europe.[18]

Let us now turn from the killing zones in the East to their counterparts in the West. The role of the Soviet Union and British Commonwealth was decisive in the U.S. victory in France. With only 58 German divisions in France (and many of them of poor quality) and 189 German divisions (including most elite divisions) on the Eastern front, any significant transfer of 20–40 good German divisions and 5–10 more Panzer divisions to the West would probably have spelled disaster for the Americans.

This was especially true given the thinness of U.S. manpower reserves with only a 90-division army. The 37 Anglo–American divisions assigned to the invasion task force were already outnumbered by General Gerd von Rundstedt's 58 German divisions in France. Furthermore, the slowness of Anglo–American progress in Normandy in the first seven weeks of the campaign and the near disaster on Omaha Beach on the very first day illustrate that the margin of victory in Normandy was thin. The massive Red Army Operation BAGRATION in June 1944 decisively shattered not only Army Group Center and Army Group North Ukraine but also any chance that the Germans might be able to move troops to their embattled positions in France and destroy the invaders.[19]

The power of the Red Army had affected the German army in other ways that benefited the U.S. army. The urgent demands of the Eastern front had stripped the Western front of most of its better divisions. On D Day only 24 of the 58 German divisions in France were rated as fit for service on the Eastern front. Thirty-four of the 58 divisions were essentially low grade static or reserve divisions, filled with underage or overage men, non-German soldiers (no less than 30,000 frontline soldiers in Normandy were not Germans), and minimal equipment. For several years the relatively inactive Western front had been a vast rest and rehabilitation ground for units chewed up on the Eastern front. As a result, experienced soldiers were scarce and many units were mere skeletons of real fighting units. The cumulative impact of the three years of horrendous struggle on the Eastern front were seen in one statistic: in 1944 the fighting capability of a standard German armored division was rated by the Wehrmacht at 33 percent of the level of 1939.[20]

The great aid rendered indirectly by the Soviets on the Eastern front was matched by the direct aid provided by the British Commonwealth on the field of battle. For the last time the British were able to make a very important contribution to the Allied cause. Over the next eleven months their influence and role would steadily fade. But in the climactic invasion of Europe, appropriately enough launched from the British isles, the armies of Winston Churchill were to play an indispensable role.

This role started even before the invasion began. In January 1944 at Strategic Headquarters of the American Expeditionary Force headquarters in London 50 percent of the 489 officers and 67 percent of the 614 men there were British. In 1944 British Generals Maitland Wilson and Harold Alexander remained the commanders for the Mediterranean and Italian theaters. For Operation OVERLORD, of course, two Americans, General Dwight Eisenhower and General Bedell Smith, were nominally in charge as commander and chief-of-staff of the invasion. However, all of the key assistants actually running the operation were British. Air Marshal Sir Arthur Tedder was deputy supreme commander, General Bernard Montgomery was commander of the land forces, Admiral Sir Bertram Ramsay was commander of the naval forces, and Air Chief Marshal Sir Trafford Leigh-Mallory was commander of the air forces.[21]

On D Day a similar pattern prevailed. At least 60 percent of the landing craft and 79 percent of the warships used that day were British, not U.S. The U.S. formed only 43 percent of the soldiers to hit the beach on D Day, although they did account for over 90 percent of the men in the airborne assault that day. Appropriately, there were 2 U.S. beaches (Utah and Omaha) and 3 British and Canadian beaches (Gold, Juno, and Sword) on the first day. Almost 50 percent of the air power on D Day was provided by the RAF, not the USAAF. The 19 U.S. divisions waiting to disembark in France were matched by 17 British Commonwealth divisions and 2 French and Polish divisions.[22]

Even though the role of the British Commonwealth ebbed throughout the final year of the war, it still played an important subsidiary role to the main U.S. effort. During the three-month campaign in France, the British Commonwealth provided almost 40 percent (or 830,000 men) of the total forces and suffered 40 percent (84,000) of the casualties. Without this massive effort, as well as the generalship of officers like Montgomery, it is not only doubtful but highly unlikely that the U.S. army could ever have broken out of Normandy, much less crossed the Seine.[23]

The Allies pursued a very successful strategy in the preparation of the invasion. They gained absolute air and sea superiority before the invasion. So overwhelming was this supremacy that on D Day 11,000 Allied planes swept the paltry 500 German planes from the skies. The vast Allied naval flotilla with 6,900 vessels could not be challenged by a weak German naval presence. The Allied deception plan, centered around General George Patton and a mythical army, was so successful that the 19 divisions of the German Fifteenth Army (plus 5 Panzer divisions) were held around Pas de Calais for nearly two months awaiting an invasion that never came. As a result, only the German Seventh Army, with 6 divisions in the Normandy area and 13 divisions overall (plus 3 Panzer divisions), was immediately available to counter the landings.[24]

The essential German problem was that with fifty-eight

divisions in France and the Low Countries they had to protect a 3,000-mile coastline. This gave them a linear density of one division per 50 miles, five times less than what is generally considered to be necessary for effective defense. This problem was reinforced by the fact that Rommel's intense program to greatly strengthen the Atlantic Wall was interrupted when it was only partially completed.[25]

Given the low quality, and weak training and equipment of most of the German troops, any serious invasion was likely to meet with some success. This was especially true if the Allies could gain total air and naval superiority and launch a good deception program, as they did. The only way for the Germans to compensate was to pour in their Panzer units, which they ultimately did, with 1,300 tanks. But these could not compensate for the other deficiencies.[26]

The Allied assault on D Day was wildly successful (except for a near disaster on Omaha beach). At a cost of only 9,000 casualties on the first day, the Allies put 132,700 ground troops ashore along a 60-mile-wide sector of the coast. Another 16,400 airborne troops floated into Normandy. The massive air and naval display played a key role in this accomplishment. So too did the liberal use of firepower and good Allied equipment compared to the severe limitations on German equipment and ammunition in the West.[27]

The Allies also proved adept at rapidly widening their beachhead and pouring men and material into it at a rapid rate. By 1 July 1944 the Allies had landed over 1 million men in Normandy, replete with one-half million tons of supplies and 177,000 vehicles. One month after D Day the Allies had already landed a formidable force of 35 divisions, which would only gradually grow to 39 divisions by the end of the campaign.[28]

Despite all these advantages, the Allies made only slow progress in Normandy for the first seven weeks. By 15 June the Allies were ashore but barely seeming to get anywhere. Caen, supposed to be taken on the first day of the invasion, was uncaptured on the twenty-first day. On 1 July the Allied beachhead, now seventy miles wide, was as little as five miles deep and, except near Cherbourg, nowhere even twenty miles deep. The stalemate in Normandy was provoked by a number of factors, including the excellent defensive terrain of hedgerows and earthen dikes, the first-rate German defense under difficult conditions, the relatively mediocre Allied command strategy, and the lack of clear-cut Allied numerical superiority such as that attained on the Eastern front. As Max Hastings concluded in his study of the Normandy campaign, despite the poor quality of German troops, after D Day,

> In the weeks that followed, despite the Allies' absolute command of the sea and air, their attacks were repeatedly arrested with heavy loss by outnumbered and massively outgunned German units. None of this, of course, masks the essential historical truth that the Allies eventually prevailed. But it makes the campaign seem a far less straightforward affair than chauvinistic post-war platitudes suggested.[29]

The Allies responded to this frustrating deadlock, in which they could advance little despite all their advantages, by resorting to the use of massive firepower. In late June, when the British launched a large-scale attack in Operation EPSOM with 675 guns, they suffered heavy casualties and made small gains. Then in the middle of July another massive British attack, this time with 750 tanks and 7,000 tons of bombs, made all of 7 miles. Although a tactical failure, Operation GOODWOOD did begin to exhaust the Germans and draw their armor totally to the British sector.

A week later, when Operation COBRA was launched, the world saw the first modern carpet bombing, in which 2,500 Allied planes dropped over 4,000 tons of bombs on a 15-square-mile area; over 600 U.S. troops (including General Lesley McNair) were killed or wounded. But the German resistance finally broke, and the Allies could now move into open country, where they could utilize the talents of officers like General Patton. After a failed German armored assault near Avranches, the Allies encircled a large German force at Falaise. Although 35,000 German soldiers, including 16 of 29 corps and division commanders, did escape through the Falaise gap, still 10,000 Germans were killed and 50,000 Germans were taken prisoner.[30]

While the Allies were racing across northern France in August, a second amphibious assault was mounted in the south in the middle of the month. General Johannes Blaskowitz commanded a weak force of 7 understrength and generally low quality German divisions, with only 200 planes and 450 heavy guns along the entire coastline. On August 15th a predominantly French invasion force (ultimately 7 French divisions, 3 American divisions) went ashore, backed by strong support from 25,000 armed French resistance fighters. Operation ANVIL went smoothly with light opposition on all but one beach. Within two weeks, and having suffered only light casualties (4,000 French, 2,700 American casualties), the Allies had taken the prize of Marseilles and over 57,000 German troops.[31]

This blended in with the even greater success in the north. At the same time the Allies were seizing Paris in late August, Antwerp and Brussels in the beginning of September, and hurtling towards the German border. By the middle of September the Allies were well beyond the Seine, and German resistance seemed to be cracking fast. The liberation of France was a great Allied victory that cost the Germans over 200,000 dead and wounded, 210,000 prisoners, 1,300 tanks, and 2,000 assault and artillery guns captured and destroyed. For the Allies the cost of victory had also not been light, including 204,000 dead and wounded and 20,000 missing. There is no doubt, though, that this was a most important victory, dooming the Third Reich.[32]

BALKAN TRIUMPH AND WESTERN STALEMATE

In early September it looked as if victory in Europe could be attained in 1944, with the scenario of November 1918 being repeated. But, this was not to be, as the German army rallied its strength after the crushing defeats in Normandy and Belorussia. The Allies bogged down in front of the Siegfried line and suffered a series of setbacks. Not until early in the New Year, after absorbing a strong German counterblow in the Ardennes, would they regain the initiative. Meanwhile the Red Army pushed on, now focusing its attention on the strategically valuable countries of Eastern Europe, especially in the Balkans.

The Red Army, however, also scored significant successes in the north. In Finland, where the Red Army had launched a serious attack back in June, the campaign achieved success. With the Finnish defense line in ruins in the far north, the Finnish government asked for an armistice at the end of August. In the middle of September the armistice was initialed, with the Soviet Union regaining Finnish territory lost in 1940 and Finland agreeing to pay reparations, in return for Soviet respect for Finnish independence.[33]

The Finnish victory was accompanied by a more significant

advance by the Red Army into the Baltics. There a massive Red Army attack using 125 divisions on a 300-mile front caved in the elaborate German defense line and seized Riga by October. Equally important was the isolation of 30 divisions of Army Group North in Kurland, where they remained trapped until the end of the war. This deprived the Third Reich of extremely powerful forces that it badly needed in the remainder of the war.[34]

The most important Soviet thrust, though, came in the Balkans where the Red Army crushed German resistance in three major countries: Romania, Bulgaria, and Yugoslavia. Here, for the first time, politics emerged as predominant on the battlefield. The Soviet thrust into the south, far away from Berlin, was politically motivated—Moscow was eager to secure its hegemony in an important and troublesome region of Europe. At the same time the deep hatred of the Germans, who had alienated the local populations and elites by their actions, and popularity of the Soviet Union in Yugoslavia and Bulgaria, eased the way for the Red Army. This was particularly significant given the German reliance on local national forces in the region.

The key to the Balkans turned out to be Romania. Situated in the region was the most powerful German force—General Friessner's Army Group South Ukraine. This army consisted of 45 divisions (24 German, 21 Romanian) with 600,000 men, 400 tanks, and 800 planes. For the campaign Generals Malinovsky and Tolbukhin possessed 92 divisions, 19,000 guns, 2,100 tanks, and 1,900 planes. Even more important, they could count on Romanian antipathy to the Germans. When the Red Army attacked on 20 August, the Romanian army refused to fight and began to disintegrate. Only three days later Romanian King Michael staged a coup, arrested the Antonescu brothers, and announced that Romania would no longer fight. This led to catastrophe for the German forces, already reeling under the impact of a massive Soviet offensive, who now had to face two Romanian armies now fighting against them rather than for them. By 27 August the Red Army announced an end to the war with Romania, which now proclaimed its desire to fight on the side of the Soviet Union.

The results were a great victory for the Red Army. Only eleven days after the campaign began, the Red Army was in Bucharest, where it now had new allies. Bessarabia and northern Bukovina went back to the Soviet Union. Romania agreed to fight Germany and pay reparations in exchange for regaining Transylvania from

Hungary and the Soviet (temporary as it turned out) agreement to allow the Romanian army and government to remain intact. Militarily, this was a powerful victory as in one week the Red Army destroyed eighteen German divisions, took 98,000 German POWS, killed 100,000 Germans, and turned the Romanian army from foe to ally.[35]

Now the Red Army could easily kick the props out from the entire German position in the Balkans. And it proceeded to do exactly that with alacrity. The very next week the Red Army declared war on neighboring Bulgaria. Here pro-Soviet sentiment was traditionally strong, and the pro-Soviet Fatherland Front (a coalition of anti-German parties) very popular. Bulgaria had never actually declared war on the Soviet Union, only the United States and Great Britain. Here there was not to be any fighting at all. When Tolbukhin's twenty-eight divisions entered Bulgaria, he met with no resistance from the 450,000-man Bulgarian army. Rather, the next day the Fatherland Front seized power and Bulgaria broke relations with Germany. The following month an armistice was reached in which, similar to the Romanian accord, the Red Army could run the national armed forces, move freely in the country and establish an Allied Control Commission for direction of political activities. Once again, the Third Reich was shrinking fast.[36]

Next in line came Yugoslavia, which had been the scene of many of the worst depredations of the war (1.7 million Yugoslavs were killed in the war). The Red Army could rely on significant aid from the most successful European partisan movement, 400,000-man strong under Marshal Tito. The German army was not terribly strong there, with only 14 divisions reinforced by 5 Hungarian divisions. The October 1944 Red Army drive into Yugoslavia was successful despite strong German opposition. That month the Red Army liberated Belgrade, after killing 15,000 Germans and taking 9,000 German POWs.[37]

Finally, in October the Red Army, under Generals Malinovsky and Tolbukhin, turned their sights on Hungary, as a backdoor into Germany. Events here would not go so smoothly. Had matters been left only to the Hungarians there would have been little problem. The Hungarians were tired of war and wanted an armistice as much as their neighbors did. In August 1944 Admiral Horthy had taken power and in October announced his desire to surrender Hungary to the Red Army. But here the Germans intervened, seizing and deporting Horthy back to Germany.

German units poured into Hungary as Hitler decided to try to make Budapest unassailable. The late September 1944 Red Army offensive stalled in the middle of November in front of Budapest, which would be taken only after extremely heavy fighting in February 1945.[38]

Meanwhile, the Western Allies found the going much rougher in the fall than in the summer. On paper this seemed absurd. After all, the German army was reeling, having lost France, its remaining territory in the Soviet Union, and several Eastern European countries. The losses in the West had been serious and morale was extremely low. General Gerd von Rundstedt estimated that his 63 German divisions on paper were equal to only 25 full-strength divisions. The 5 German divisions in the Channel Islands and coastal fortresses were as good as lost. A September 1944 SHAEF Intelligence summary declared that the German army was "no longer a cohesive force but a number of fugitive battle groups, disorganized and even demoralized, short of equipment and arms."[39]

By comparison, the Allies looked unbeatable. They enjoyed in early September a 2:1 manpower advantage, 2.5:1 superiority in guns, 20:1 superiority in tanks, and 23:1 superiority in planes. Their casualties in the French campaign had not been onerous (224,600 men), especially compared to the 2.2 million Allied troops now in Western Europe. General Eisenhower, now in operational command of the forces, had 39 full-strength Allied divisions (22 U.S., 17 British and Canadian) in good material and morale shape. The biggest Allied problem seemed to be whether to adopt Eisenhower's broad-front strategy or Montgomery's single thrust approach.[40]

What happened? There are at least four explanations for the Allied failure to continue on in the fall of 1944 into Germany. The most important reason, and one often downgraded, had nothing to do with the Allies. As we observed earlier, Germany remained a powerful country even at this time. As the war came to the German heartland Hitler was able to rally the German people for defense of the fatherland. German logistic problems became minimal as its supply lines shrunk. The Nazis were able to mobilize from August to October 700,000 new men into the Wehrmacht, which still had close to 300 divisions. No less than 50 new Volkssturm divisions appeared in the second half of 1944. The 600,000 men who returned from France helped form 18 new divisions. German war production reached its wartime peak in the summer and fall months, despite massive Allied strategic bombing. Overall, then, even after having lost territory on both fronts equal to three times the size of Germany, the German army, still formidable even in retreat, could still regroup behind Germany's natural frontiers.[41]

Second, the Allies faced almost impossible logistical problems, similar to those that forced frequent lengthy halts for the Red Army in the East. The speed of the Allied advance had far outstripped the Allied capacity to support any great extension of the armies. The Allies were supposed to reach the German border in 330 days: it took only 100 days. This was especially serious given the need to import most of the supplies through overcrowded and now distant ports. The inability to use the port of Antwerp until December was especially harmful to the effort.[42]

Third, there were natural reasons. The terrain on much of the German border, reinforced by the Siegfried line, was extremely difficult. It effectively neutralized much of the massive Allied tank, artillery, and airplane superiority so critical to success. At the same time, these problems were reinforced by the weather, with rain, sleet, and later snow, supplemented by mud, providing excellent support to the German defenders.

Finally, who could gainsay the great skill of the German officers, as once again demonstrated in Normandy? Under such fine leadership, an inferior force on the defensive, with great space to maneuver, could be very dangerous to the Allies. This was especially true for the Germans, given their superior experience and skills in land warfare. Knowing that they were going to win unless they made serious blunders, the less experienced Anglo–American commanders tended to be more conservative and rarely took any risks (except for Operation MARKET-GARDEN). The Allied commanders made some serious mistakes, such as failing to pursue the fleeing Germans at all costs and failing to clear the Scheldt estuary approaches to the crucial port of Antwerp.[43]

The dreary events of the fall are well known and merit only a brief review. The most spectacular failure, of course, was Operation MARKET-GARDEN, an uncharacteristically bold gesture by General Montgomery to end the war. The plan was to drop 34,000 troops by parachute and glider to secure the Rhine crossing at Arnhem in September 1944. They would then hold their ground while army units were supposed to link up with them by moving sixty-five miles in two days over five rivers and canals.

Unfortunately, it truly was "a bridge too far." The army could not move fast enough over all the obstacles, the paratroopers were scattered over a fifty-mile area, the weather turned bad, and the Germans managed by accident to seize a copy of the Allied orders from a paratrooper. Even worse was the accidental presence of elements of two SS Panzer divisions in the area, as well as Field Marshal Model lunching in Oosterbeek only two miles from the drop sight. It was a risky plan, poorly but bravely executed, and the tragic result was failure and over 13,000 Allied casualties.[44]

The general Allied drive against the Siegfried line also was intensely disappointing, especially after the spectacular victory in France. Failure was not total in these four months: the Canadians did finally open the port of Antwerp in November, the British took part of the Netherlands, the Americans took Lorraine and the west bank of the Upper Rhine. But the main thrust against the Siegfried line went very slowly and at great cost. On 1 September 1944 the U.S. patrols first crossed the border. More than three months later, after incurring 200,000 casualties, the American forces had penetrated no more than twenty-two miles into Germany.[45]

The great surprise, though, was the daring German offensive in the Ardennes forest in December 1944. Suddenly, the supposedly defeated Germans were mounting a large-scale operation threatening to drive the Allies back to Antwerp. In the middle of December General von Rundstedt hurled 24 German divisions, including two Panzer armies with 1,800 tanks and self-propelled artillery pieces, at 4 U.S. divisions guarding a 75-mile front in the Ardennes forest. The Americans were initially taken by surprise given the excellent natural defense positions in the forest, the bad weather, and the weakened state of the German army. At the beginning the Germans made rapid progress, eventually overrunning 700 square miles of Belgium and Luxemburg and taking almost 30,000 prisoners.

The rest of the story is so famous that it needs only a brief retelling. After being momentarily thrown off balance, the U.S. army rose to the challenge. General Patton brilliantly redirected his troops in a forced march against the German southern defenses that relieved Bastogne, after a heroic stand by outnumbered defenders, on 26 December. Once the weather cleared, the U.S. air force, flying 63,700 sorties at a loss of 647 planes, massively disrupted the German offensive. With

Montgomery in charge in the north and Patton in the south, the Americans managed to contain the German drive well short even of its minimal objectives. In early January 1945 two U.S. armies had lopped off the salient and a month later the Germans were back at their starting positions.

The cost was high on both sides: 76,900 U.S. casualties and 30,000 Americans taken prisoner, 81,800 German casualties and 50,000 Germans taken prisoner. But the U.S. victory in its largest campaign of the war had drained the Germans of all their reserves and deprived them of any further offensive capability in the remaining months of the war.[46]

THE FINAL ASSAULT ON GERMANY: EAST AND WEST

The Allies, as would be seen in the Yalta conference in early February 1945, entered the new year justifiably confident of final victory. The U.S. repulse of the German offensive in the Ardennes forest, the long Soviet buildup in the central sector since August, and the Soviet advances in the Balkans all foreshadowed the imminent destruction of the Third Reich. By early 1945 the question was no longer whether Nazi Germany could be destroyed, but simply when.

By January 1945 the Allies were once again prepared to regain the offensive. The Red Army had now regrouped its forces for another massive campaign against the German homeland. Stalin had 372 rifle divisions at or near the front and another 67 rifle divisions in reserve, with a grand total of 439 rifle divisions. This mammoth force of 6.7 million men in the active army supported by 107,300 cannons, 12,000 tanks, and 14,700 planes now prepared to invade Germany. With the Yalta conference scheduled for February and with the Anglo–American armies still bogged down in the Ardennes, Stalin decided to strike a major blow that would assert the primacy of the Soviet Union in the destruction of the Third Reich. With his Red Army offensive stalled in front of Budapest by major German offensives, he reoriented his strategy to direct a massive thrust towards Berlin on the most direct axis through East Prussia and Poland.[47]

This campaign was focused on the Central front, which had come to a rest five months earlier outside of Warsaw. There Generals Georgii Zhukov and Ivan Konev had accumulated a force of 163 infantry divisions, including 2.2 million men, 32,100 cannons and mortars, 6,500 tanks and self-propelled artillery pieces, and 4,800 planes. This huge force—only one of four Soviet armies to go into action—now enjoyed, in part because of the diversion of German forces to the West, a commanding advantage of 5.5:1 in manpower advantage, 5.7:1 in tanks, 7.8:1 in cannons, and 17.6:1 in airplanes. This force was supplemented by the large armies of Chernyakhovsky and Rokossovsky in the north and Malinovsky and Tolbukhin in the south, where they also prepared to go over to the attack.[48]

The Red Army offensive in January, utilizing almost 300 divisions, was a tremendous success, bulldozing everything in its path. Within four days the gigantic Soviet offensive had torn a nearly 350-mile hole in the German defense lines from East Prussia to the Carpathians. Moving as fast as 10–20 miles a day, the Red Army advanced 200 miles in the south and 300 miles in the center in only three weeks. By the time the offensive came to a halt for lack of fuel and ammunition in the third week of February, the Red Army lined up on the Oder and held a bridgehead only 40 miles from Berlin. Warsaw, and the rest of Poland, and most of East Prussia (except for Koenigsberg) were safely in Soviet hands. The Red Army not only conquered much valuable territory but, equally important, destroyed 45 German divisions, took 350,000 German prisoners and inflicted perhaps 800,000 German casualties. John Erickson has nicely summarized the "speed, frenzy and savagery (that) characterized this advance,"

> After one week's fighting, the German defensive system had been staved in, overrun or bypassed. Fourth Panzer and Ninth Armies, reduced to a drifting mass of men and mangled machines, were left far to the rear and oozing in a glutinous military mass in the direction of the Oder and hopefully home.[49]

The central sector now became quiet for two months. The six week offensive exhausted Red Army supply capabilities and caused serious casualties. Many Red Army divisions in East Prussia, after the fierce fighting, were down to 3,000-4,000 men. Tank losses in February alone exceeded 4,600, a huge number. At the same time the Germans busily transferred over 20 divisions to the East to shore up their defense lines. With the Red Army firmly entrenched on German soil and threatening Berlin, Hitler was able to rouse the Germans one last time to protect the fatherland from Bolshevism. New units were formed from stragglers, deserters, overage men to supplement the remaining regular troops. The drastic shortening of the German front to only 200 miles long greatly aided the German defense efforts.[50]

The main action now switched in February and March to the constituent parts of the old Austro–Hungarian Empire. There in the middle of February, after a protracted four-month battle, the Red Army finally conquered Budapest. This battle alone saw 50,000 German and Hungarian troops killed and 110,000 Axis troops taken prisoner. However, Hitler would not easily acquiesce in the loss of Hungary, his vital southern flank, and he prepared one last surprise for the Allies. He carefully husbanded his last reserves and gathered a strike force of 31 German and Hungarian divisions, replete with 5,600 guns and mortars and almost 850 planes for an offensive in the Lake Balaton region in western Hungary. This last German offensive took General Tolbukhin's force of 37 depleted Red Army divisions and 6 Bulgarian divisions by surprise. Only 10 days later was the German offensive halted in central Hungary with the loss of over 40,000 Germans and Hungarians and 500 tanks and self-propelled artillery pieces.[51]

The Red Army next turned its attention to cleaning up German strongholds elsewhere. In March and April it concentrated its actions on attacking the remaining fortresses in East Prussia, such as Koenigsberg. In the middle of the month, it opened a campaign to seize Vienna, a bitter campaign that lasted a month before success was achieved. Always, though, all eyes were on Berlin. By the middle of April the Red Army was now ready to renew its offensive in the central sector, an area that had remained dormant for over two months.[52]

There is no way to talk about the battle of Berlin except in superlatives. Here, in one small space, was the greatest concentration of forces ever seen for a single battle—2.5 million Red Army troops (1.6 million of them combat troops), 42,000 cannons, 6,250 tanks and self-propelled artillery pieces, and 7,500 planes. Generals Zhukov, Konev, and Rokossovsky, with 190 Red Army divisions, enjoyed a massive advantage over General Gerhard Heinrici's 47 German divisions in Army Group Vistula and assorted other forces totalling 38 divisions. Even by Russian statistics, the Red Army had a 2.5:1 manpower advantage and 4:1 advantage in guns and tanks. On the other side, Berlin, the capital of the Third Reich, was now strewn with the wreckage of over one-third of its houses from Allied bombing raids that had dropped the equivalent of 65 kilotons of explosives on the city.

Yet the battle was to prove extremely difficult. The Germans fought with a level of fanaticism and courage that had not been seen in the West for years. The terrain, with numerous streams, soft grounds, and hills such as the Seelow Heights (500 feet high), strongly favored the defense. So, too, did the well-built city of Berlin, with its numerous natural strongpoints sprawled over 320 square miles. And the German defenders had strengthened their position by building five defense lines and three defense belts covering Berlin. The U Bahn, underground tunnels, and bridges also offered great maneuverability for the defenders.

The level of ferocity in this two-week battle that began on 16 April was extraordinarily high. The Red Army relied on overwhelming numbers and tremendous firepower, greater than anything seen on the Western front. The attack began, appropriately enough, with a 20-minute blast of 500,000 shells, mortars, and rockets on German positions. During the next two weeks the Soviet air force flew over 91,400 sorties while the army fired over 4.1 million artillery and mortar shells with an explosive value of 25 kilotons at the Germans. Behind this hurricane of explosives came wave after wave of heavily armed Soviet assault squads and thousands of tanks. In fierce hand-to-hand fighting of a savagery not seen since Stalingrad, the battle went on day and night without letup.

Within nine days the Red Army completed the encirclement of Berlin, with the Third Reich's fiefdom reduced in this area to only 35 square miles. On 26 April the Red Army launched its final assault, spearheaded by 464,000 troops and backed up by 12,700 guns, 1,500 tanks and self-propelled artillery pieces, and 4,000 Katyusha launchers. The area controlled by the Hitler bunker continually shrunk until Hitler and his cronies committed suicide at the end of April. Despite furious resistance on an unparalleled scale, the Red Army, at horrendous cost, surged forward to final victory with the raising of the red flag over the Reichstag on 2 May.

The cost was appalling: over 680,000 casualties on the two sides in less than two weeks. For the Red Army the figure was astronomical: 305,000 casualties. This was *greater* than all the Allied casualties (260,000 men) suffered from January until May 1945. And the physical destruction was also mindboggling. An emaciated German army, facing certain defeat, still destroyed

2,156 tanks and self-propelled artillery pieces, downed 527 planes, and eliminated 1,220 guns and mortars.

On the other side 60,000 German troops were dead, perhaps 200,000 were casualties, and 120,000 were taken prisoner. In addition, 100,000 German civilians became casualties of the fighting. Hitler was finally dead, the world was saved from the scourge of fascism that had killed 11 million people in its concentration camps—but at what a cost to the Red Army and the Soviet people![53]

The contrast with the final Anglo–American campaign in the West in the final months of the year was striking. The Allies did amass a large force, ultimately numbering 4.5 million men, 970,000 vehicles, and 18 million tons of supplies in Western Europe alone. The 91 divisions in Western Europe were supplemented by another 18–31 divisions in Italy, making the 5.5 million Allied soldiers in the West not grossly inferior to the 6.5 million Red Army troops in the East. But the distribution of men and equipment was different. A similar numerical force made up roughly 110 divisions in the West but 450 divisions in the East. On the other hand, the Western Allies, with 28,000 combat planes in 6 tactical air forces and 2 strategic air forces, possessed vastly greater air power than the Soviet Union. And, with over 10,000 tanks in combat, they had a significantly greater tank force as well.[54]

Another familiar pattern, but less prominent than before D Day, was the continuing role of U.S. allies in the achievement of final victory. Even on V-E Day, despite the fading role of the British Commonwealth and limited role of France, U.S. allies contributed almost 40 percent of the Allied divisions in the West and Italy (41 of 109 divisions) and took almost 40 percent of the casualties. The British also contributed almost 50 percent of that vast armada of planes that swept the Luftwaffe from the air and rained bombs incessantly over the Third Reich. Without this great help from the British Commonwealth and even greater aid from the Red Army draining off the bulk of German land forces in the East, the United States could hardly have contested the still considerable power of Nazi Germany on the European continent in the last year of the war.[55]

Having contained and then defeated the German drive in the Ardennes, the Allies, bolstered by the great Red Army drive in the East that forced a large-scale transfer of troops from the Western front, now could resume their offensive. With a force of 72 divisions (49 of them U.S.), 50,000 cannons, 16,100 tanks, and 16,700 planes in the West, the Allies advanced against a depleted Wehrmacht with 73 understrength divisions equal to perhaps 39 Allied divisions. This 2:1 numerical superiority was reinforced by the freshness of the U.S. forces, which in the past six months had suffered (despite the Ardennes) relatively light losses of 55,000 dead and 280,000 wounded.[56]

After heated controversy, General Eisenhower decided to reject the British proposal for a single main thrust north of the Ruhr in favor of a double offensive. The main thrust, under General Montgomery, was to come in the north, supplemented by a secondary thrust in the south under General Patton. General Montgomery's Twenty-First Army Group, with 27 divisions (15 of them U.S.), confronted only 10 German divisions west of the Rhine. In February 1945 General Montgomery kicked off his campaign with an artillery barrage of 5 1/2 hours from over 1,000 guns aimed at the relatively weak German defenders, who made the mistake of not retreating behind the Rhine. Operation VERITABLE was soon coupled with Operation GRENADE in February to overcome the weak German defense lines and place the Allies finally on the Rhine.

By the middle of March 1945 these two operations had shattered 19 understrength German divisions, inflicted 49,000 German casualties, and taken 51,000 German POWs. All this was achieved at a light cost of 22,300 Allied casualties (70 percent of them British and Canadians). This is not surprising given the weakness of the German forces. In Operation GRENADE, for example, the Allies enjoyed a 5:1 numerical advantage and even greater firepower superiority as they attacked a German force along the Roer that had only 30,000 men and 85 assault guns. In the words of Charles MacDonald's official study of the final Allied offensive of the war, the advance over the Roer was done "with relative ease," "against this enemy whose numbers were small, whose arms were weak, whose spirit faltered."[57] Compare the ease of the Allied advance with light casualties against weak opposition to the difficulties of the Soviets confronting fierce opposition at that same time in East Prussia and Hungary.

In the south, General Patton, despite very limited forces, was having an even easier time. From 29 January to 22 March his Third Army advanced rapidly in the south in a drive on the Saar. In that period, at a cost of only 5,200 casualties, he captured 140,000 German soldiers and inflicted 99,000 casualties on the

Germans. Seizing 6,500 square miles, his Third Army advanced so readily against minimal opposition that Patton would say at a news conference on 30 March, "Our losses in this operation have been extremely small. We have been trading about 12 to 1."[58] One other statistic makes clear the disintegration of German opposition in the West. In February and March the Germans lost 500,000 men west of the Rhine, 350,000 of whom were POWs, many of whom surrendered readily. In the latter part of March the Germans were losing 10,000 men a day as POWs.[59]

While Patton took the Rhine on the run in the south in March 1945 and the Allies exploited the famous German lapse at Remagen to pour troops across the Rhine, General Montgomery prepared his set piece assault in the north. In Operation VARSITY the Allies poured 21,700 men across the Rhine in parachutes and gliders while in Operation PLUNDER General Montgomery pushed 27 divisions, or almost one million men, across the river with nominal losses (31 killed the first day). Montgomery's advance beyond the Rhine also met little opposition as the German defense folded. The Rhine campaign, then, was a great success with the level of resistance indicated in the statistics: 60,000 German casualties and 250,000 German POWs in March 1945.[60]

The final full month of the war in April 1945 in the West was as easy for the Anglo–American forces as the battle of Berlin in the East was hard for the Soviets. General Eisenhower's 90 divisions (61 of them U.S.) confronted a weak and disintegrating German force equivalent to perhaps 26 full divisions. Even these German divisions were "ill-equipped, lacking ammunition, drastically short of fuel and transport, artillery and tanks."[61] Their morale was low and they lacked any coherence, as they were formed from a hodgepodge of Luftwaffe men, SS troops, antiaircraft troops, Volkssturm units of old men and boys, teenage officer cadets, and remnants of shattered units.

The Allies moved almost at will in April 1945. Field Marshal Model's forces, entrapped in the Ruhr, surrendered in the middle of April, with 317,000 Germans taken prisoner. The cost to the Allies: 341 killed, 121 missing, and 2,000 wounded. In many towns the Americans were able to pick up the telephone and arrange a leisurely and peaceful capitulation with the Buergermeister of the next town. Many commanders became more concerned about road accidents and injury from friendly fire than enemy fire. In the first eleven days of April the U.S. forces moved eastward over

300 miles. In the north Montgomery drove steadily towards Hamburg without difficulty as German General Gunther Blumentritt "had made a gentlemanly arrangement with the British, even going so far as to despatch a liaison officer to warn the enemy of an area containing a cache of gas bombs."[62]

While the war reached new heights of frenzy in the battle of Berlin, it simply petered out in the West. The biggest Allied problem seemed to be not German resistance (which was slight) but whether or not to drive on Berlin. With over 2 million Soviet soldiers preparing to storm the city from a distance of less than forty miles, this really was a more academic question than is usually presented. Given the fact that the Soviets were still U.S. allies and that the United States wished to avoid any serious casualties, the storming of Berlin by the Red Army at this point in time was inevitable. Had the Allies seriously wished to take Berlin, they would have launched a second front in 1943 rather than 1944.[63]

The Allied linkup on the Elbe with the Red Army symbolized the end of the war. In the last weeks of the war the German resistance simply melted away, turning the war from hot combat into gentlemanly pursuit. The last word, appropriately, belongs to General Bernard Montgomery. As he observed in his memoirs written in 1948, by late April "the German Army was now fast approaching disintegration," while by 1 May,

> The countryside north of the Elbe was now packed with a mass of German soldiery and refugees, fleeing from the Allied advance and from the Russians. It could now be said that the enemy had decided to abandon the fight and, apart from small groups of fanatics, nothing more than token resistance was to be expected from German armed forces south of the Kiel Canal.[64]

The last year of the war set European boundary lines that have lasted, with only minor changes, for over four decades. The decision of the United States and Great Britain to invade France in force in June 1944 sealed the fate of the Third Reich. Except for the German counteroffensive in the Ardennes in December 1944, the Germans viewed the Soviets as the more dire threat. Accordingly, they kept roughly two-thirds of their troops there throughout the final year, and the level of resistance to the Allies was far greater in the East than the West. The powerful Anglo–American strategic bombing campaign did even the score somewhat for the Western side, but it cannot solely account for the massive discrepancy between German casualties East and West and between Soviet and U.S. casualties in the last year of the war. Air power, while important, cannot win wars by itself: the lowly ground troops must go in and ultimately win the war.

There is a natural tendency, both in the East and in the West, to Stalinize the past, to see everything as inevitable, to praise solely the military exploits of one's own country, and to downplay or ignore the contributions of one's allies. For the United States, which, after a brief period of time, downgraded the enormous contribution of both the Soviet Union and the British Commonwealth to what it interpreted as "its" victory, this has been especially true. Only in Korea and Vietnam, where the United States lacked powerful allies to ease the path to victory, would it suddenly find the serious limits on its own conventional military power. In the next two chapters we turn to a comparative analysis of the strengths and weaknesses of the Soviet and U.S. war efforts, at home and on the battlefield, to help us to understand not only 1945 but also the postwar era in general.

NOTES

1. General George Marshall, in his official War Report to the Secretary of War, has confirmed the very minimal losses suffered by the Axis at the hands of the Western Allies before 1944. He estimated that in Tunisia and Sicily the Axis lost 24,600 dead, 21,000 permanently disabled, and 137,100 captured. And this included both German and Italian losses. These losses paled before the estimated 263,000 Axis deaths and the 4,200,000 German losses before V-E Day on the Eastern front after D Day. See *War Reports* p.276.

2. Hastings, *Overlord*, pp.24, 184–316; Van Creveld, *Fighting*, p.66; and Dupuy, *Genius*, p.253–254.

3. *Istoriya vtoroi*, v. 12, p.200; Brown, *Applied*, pp.61–64; Pollard, *Peaceful*, p.311; and Speer, *Inside*, pp.551, 560, 581.

4. Ryan, *Last*, p.140 and MacDonald, *Mighty*, p.449.

5. Huston, *Sinews*, p.694. So weak was even the attempted resistance in many areas that the German civilians spoke of the local army units putting up "sixty-one minute roadblocks." These were roadblocks at which the U.S. soldiers would laugh for sixty minutes and then tear down in one minute. See MacDonald's excellent study, *Last*, p.410.

6. Trevor-Roper, editor, *Final*, pp.38, 87, 89, 180, 233, 265.

7. Shulman, *Defeat*, p.279; Toland, *Last*, p.5; and McNeill, *America*, p.569. McNeill's volume, almost thirty-five years later, remains of enduring

value and interest. Perhaps the flavor of this obdurate German resistance to the Soviets was given in an interview with the thirty-four-year-old former Hitler Youth division commander, Major General Kurt Meyer, in a POW camp after the war: "Germany fought this war for the preservation of Western culture and civilization. The menace of the East was always appreciated by the Fuehrer and his one object was to save Europe from the menace of Bolshevism. We had no quarrel with the English or the French. . . . The peoples of the East want to sweep away all of Western culture as we know it, and set up in its place their own half-developed, animal-like existence. This Germany tried unsuccessfully to prevent." See Shulman, *Defeat,* p.314.

8. Sivachev and Yakovlev, *Russia,* p.205.

9. Jung, *Die Ardennen,* pp.282–289.

10. Matloff, editor, *American,* p.495; Seaton, *Russo-German,* p.547, Feis, *Churchill,* p.296; and Ziemke, *Stalingrad,* p.456.

11. Westphal, *German,* p.190 and Wilmot, *Struggle,* p.663.

12. Butcher, *My,* p.788.

13. Seaton, *Russo-German* p.9 and Willmott, *June 1944,* p.15.

14. Michel, *Second,* p.684.

15. For U.S. casualties, see Matloff, editor, *American,* p.497; for Soviet casualties see *Istoriya vtoroi,* v. 12.

16. Sivachev and Yakovlev, *Russia,* p.191.

17. *Istoriya vtoroi,* v.12, p.224; Erickson, *Road to Berlin,* pp.199–200, 214, 326, 224–230; Carell, *Scorched,* p.482; and MacDonald, *Siegfried,* p.508.

18. Eisenhower, *Eisenhower,* p. 402 and Erickson, *Road to Berlin,* pp.231–232.

19. The importance of this point was stressed by Averell Harriman, among others. He observed that Allied plans "were based on the premise that we could not land successfully in Normandy if there were more than about 30 mobile German divisions in the west of Europe. . . the transfer of a relatively small number of divisions from the Eastern front could have been disastrous." Considering that there were 23 mobile German divisions in the West and roughly 200 German divisions in the East at that time, the transfer of even 5 percent of those divisions from the East could have been fatal, according to Allied planners. See Harriman, *America,* p.31. See also Flower and Reeves, editors, *Taste,* p.861 and Mitcham, *Rommel's,* p.55.

20. Willmott, *June 1944,* pp.60–61 and Shulman, *Defeat,* p.92.

21. Morison, *Two,* p.386 and Belchem, *Victory,* p.13.

22. Lamb, *Montgomery,* pp.71, 101; Ready, *Forgotten,* p.277; Majdalany, *Fall,* p.357; and Hastings, *Overlord,* p.346.

23. Lucas and Barker, *Battle,* p.164 and Belchem, *Victory,* pp.181- 182.

24. Jacobsen and Rohwer, editors, *Decisive,* pp.324–325; MacDonald, *Mighty,* p.261; and Lamb, *Montgomery,* p.89.

25. Downing, *Devil's,* p.185. Fortunately for the Allies Rommel did not have time to complete his work. He did plant 5 million mines but wanted

200 million mines. Only two of his four lines of water gadgets were completed, and they were visible to the Allies. His antiglider stakes with shells were never installed (pp.184–188).

26. Chandler, editor, *Papers of Eisenhower*, III–IV, p.2103.

27. Majdalany, *Fall*, p.363; MacDonald, *Mighty*, p.279; and Ellis, *Victory*, v.1, p.80.

28. MacDonald, *Mighty*, p.291 and Mitcham, *Rommel's*, pp.99–100.

29. Hastings, *Overlord*, p.177. The problem posed by the lack of powerful numerical superiority was considerable. At the time of Operation COBRA in July 1944 Field Marshal Alan Brooke said to General Eisenhower, "I told him that in view of the fact that German density in Normandy was two and a half times that on the Russian front while our superiority and strength and strength was only in the nature of some twenty-five percent, as compared to three hundred percent Russian superiority on the eastern front, I did not consider that we were in a position to launch an all-out offensive on the eastern front." See Eisenhower, *Eisenhower*, p.383.

30. Lamb, *Montgomery*, pp.115, 177; MacDonald, *Mighty*, pp.302, 319; and Irving, *War*, pp.211, 226.

31. Ready, *Forgotten*, p.317; Buchanan, *United*, v.II, p.405; and Craven and Cate, editors, *Army*, v.3, pp.426-427.

32. Chandler, editor, *Papers of Eisenhower*, III–IV. p.2103 and Samsonov, *Vtoraya mirovaya*, p.413.

33. Feis, *Churchill*, pp.411–412.

34. Erickson, *Road to Berlin*, pp.412–421.

35. *Ibid.*, pp.346–347, 364; McNeill, *America*, p.467; and Ziemke, *Stalingrad*, p.350.

36. Erickson, *Road to Berlin*, pp.376–377 and McNeill, *America*, pp.470–472.

37. Erickson, *Road to Berlin*, pp.381–387 and Shtemenko, *Last*, pp.201–202.

38. McNeill, *America*, p.474 and Feis, *Churchill*, pp.419–421.

39. Whiting, *Siegfried*, p.8; MacDonald, *Siegfried*, p.5; and Essame, *Battle*, p.6. Eisenhower in a secret cable to top commanders on 4 September 1944 reported that "enemy resistance on the entire front shows signs of collapsing." The eleven weak infantry and Panzer divisions north of the Ardennes, he told his commanders, were "disorganized, in full retreat and unlikely to offer any appreciable resistance if given no respite." See Chandler, editor, *Papers of Eisenhower*, v.IV, pp.2115–2116.

40. Weigley, *Eisenhower's*, p.356 and MacDonald, *Siegfried*, p.5.

41. Eisenhower, *Eisenhower*, pp.437, 522 and MacDonald, *Siegfried*, p.393.

42. Ambrose, *Eisenhower*, p.494 and Weigley, *American*, pp.349–350.

43. This famous September 1944 discussion was also based on a degree of unrealism, bred by the euphoria of the great victory in France. Germany, as we discuss in the coming pages, was reeling but far from

finished. The Western Allies were at the end of their tether and, as subsequent events showed in the coming four months, had far less offensive capability than was generally believed at this time. It was natural for the Allies, in the wake of the great victories in both theaters, to hope the war would be over. But it was not a somber military judgment, even more so given Hitler's determination to fight to the end and the willingness, even eagerness, of the bulk of the German people to follow him blindly.

44. Lamb, *Montgomery*, pp.217, 251 and Eisenhower, *Bitter*, p.79.

45. MacDonald, *Siegfried*, pp.251, 432, 616.

46. Eisenhower, *Eisenhower*, pp.533–535; Polenberg, *War*, p.181; Westphal *German*, p.186; Ellis and Warhurst, *Victory*, p.181; and Lamb, *Montgomery*, pp.303–325.

47. *Velikaya otechestvennaya* (1984), p.388; Ziemke, *Stalingrad* p.416; and *Istoriya velikoi*, v. 5, p.27.

48. *Ibid.*, p.57.

49. Erickson, *Road to Berlin*, p.460, 480; Bialer, editor, *Stalin*, pp.462, 472; and Blond, *Death*, pp. 122, 140.

50. Erickson, *Road to Berlin*, p.517 and Irving, *Hitler's*, p.787.

51. *Ibid.*, p.419 and Erickson, *Road to Berlin*, pp.440, 446, 510, 514.

52. *Ibid.*, pp.542, 550.

53. *Istoriya vtoroi*, v.12, p.218; Chuikov, *End*, p.140; Dupuy and Martell, *Great*, pp.219, 234; Michel, *Second*, p.697; Erickson, *Road to Berlin*, pp.535, 621; and Werth, *Russia*, pp.990, 996.

54. Leebaert, editor, *Soviet*, p.497; MacDonald, *Last*, p.477; and Ellis and Warhurst, *Defeat*, p.407.

55. Leebaert, editor, *Soviet*, p.497.

56. *Velikaya otechestvennaya* (1984), p.388; *Istoriya velikoi*, v.5, p.31; and MacDonald, *Last*, p.5.

57. Breuer, *Storming*, p.22; Weigley, *Eisenhower's* p.606; Lewin, *Montgomery*, p.247; and Lamb, *Montgomery*, p.352.

58. Blumenson, *Patton*, pp.660–678.

59. Shulman, *Defeat*, p.276.

60. Breuer, *Storming*, pp.199–120 and MacDonald, *Last*, pp.209, 319.

61. Ryan, *Last*, p.131 and MacDonald, *Last*, p.322.

62. Toland, *Last*, pp.383, 396; Weigley, *Eisenhower's*, p.680; and Ryan, *Last*, pp.133–134.

63. For a good discussion of this subject, see Ambrose, *Eisenhower*.

64. Montgomery, *Normandy*, pp.343–345.

9

Soviet and U.S.
War Efforts

Why was the United States unable or unwilling to translate vast economic and political superiority into great military power in World War II? Why was the Soviet Union, in such an inferior economic and military position, nevertheless able to mount such an impressive war effort?

To answer these questions we will first look at aspects of the comparison between the two countries. Then we will briefly review the political relationship in the final year of the war. Finally, we will compare three vital military aspects of the war efforts of the future superpowers: infantry fighting power, nature of officers and men, and war production.

ASPECTS OF THE COMPARISON

There was a great asymmetry in the global political and military position of the United States and Soviet Union throughout the war. This would inevitably have a strong influence on the way the war was fought. There were seven principal differences between the two great powers: the war in the Pacific, the nature and extent of logistical difficulties, air power versus land power, Lend Lease, the extent of wartime devastation, the nature and power of allies, and the strength of their economies. The latter four differences, all political/economic in scope, are discussed in the next chapter.

The first three factors constitute the standard U.S. explanation for weak U.S. land performance in the war. First, it is argued, no true comparison is possible because the United States was fighting on two fronts and the Soviet Union only on one front. Second, the United States, because of its geographic remoteness from the battlefield, suffered a great disability in fighting the war, which the Soviet Union did not face. Third, finally, the emphasis herein presented on the course of World War II omits the most important aspect, the air war.

These three problems unique to the United States do not begin to compare with the enormous difficulties unique to the Soviet Union. These, of course, were the extensive devastation wrought by the Germans on Soviet soil, the loss of 11 million Soviet soldiers killed or taken prisoner by June 1944 and the almost complete absence of reliable allies to provide troops and equipment on the Eastern front (save Lend Lease).

War Against Japan

The U.S. second front in the Pacific did by choice divert significant resources from the European theater. But, as we have shown, by 1944 the final defeat of Japan was inevitable and the continuing diversion of massive resources to the east was a political judgment, as much as a military one. This reflected the economic superiority of the United States over Imperial Japan by a factor of roughly 10:1. During the 1939–1945 period the United States produced 11.9 times more steel, 10.3 times more coal, and 6.9 times more electricity than Japan.[1] Table 9.1 dramatically shows a similar enormous gap in the crucial area of war production, with the United States producing almost 38 times more tanks and self-propelled artillery pieces, 5–7 times more machine guns and rifles, and almost 4 times more planes, cannons, and large fighting ships than Japan during the war. And, of course, there was significant help from Great Britain and Australia, not to mention the lesser help of China, in fighting Imperial Japan.

As an island empire heavily dependent on overseas trade for many vital resources and as a small geographical entity, Japan was uniquely vulnerable (as the Soviet Union or Germany were not) to naval strangulation. By late 1943 the United States had come to realize that it probably would not be necessary to destroy Japanese land power in Asia to reach Japan itself. By the summer

Table 9.1 U.S. and Japanese War Production, January 1942–August 1945

Weapon	United States	Japan	Ratio
tanks and self-propelled artillery	98,600	2,600	37.9:1
machine guns	2,594,100	380,000	6.8:1
rifles and carbines	12,292,100	2,328,000	5.3:1
military planes	190,000	49,000	3.7:1
cannons	543,500	148,700	3.7:1
large fighting ships	733	205	3.6:1

Source: 1. *Istoriya vtoroi mirovoi voina 1939–1945* (Moscow: Voenizdat, 1982), Vol. 12, pp.181, 202.

of 1944 U.S. air and naval predominance was so overwhelming that the fate of Japan had already been sealed. As Robert Coakley and Richard Leighton have observed, by late 1944 the "supposedly preliminary campaigns had already reduced Nipponese power to a shell."[2] As Ronald Spector recently echoed this sentiment in his study of the war against Japan,

> Following the Battle of Midway, United States forces did not confront a major Japanese fleet until mid-1944. They did not engage even a medium-size Japanese army until the end of 1944. Yet by that time Japan had been effectively defeated. Her supply lines had been severed by American submarines, her air power had been dissipated in costly air battles over the Solomons and New Guinea, Rabaul and Truk; and her cruiser and destroyer forces had been worn down in countless night clashes in the Solomons. That war of attrition—and the even more deadly attrition by submarines and heavy bombing in 1944–45—finally spelled Japan's defeat.[3]

In the Pacific, with a 3:1 naval advantage by July 1944, the U.S. navy could smash through the Japanese outer island defense system and push on towards Japan. The numerous Japanese small island outposts could easily be cut off by superior Allied naval capabilities and overrun at leisure by masses of U.S. soldiers, backed by overpowering air, sea, and artillery firepower. Unlike in the European theater, where the German army, even in decline, could inflict greater casualties on the Allied armies than it suffered, the same was hardly true in the Pacific.

Imperial Japan gained little advantage from possessing a large army, which even in July 1945 numbered 5 million men. The results of land campaigns were overwhelmingly one sided. In the 1945 campaign in Luzon and the Philippines, 10,400 Americans and 256,000 Japanese died; in Okinawa 12,500 Americans and 110,000 Japanese soldiers died. In the brutal battle on Iwo Jima more than three times as many Japanese soldiers as American soldiers perished. Under these circumstances, it is important to realize that the United States, despite the brutality of the fighting for small islands like Tarawa and Iwo Jima, suffered roughly 78,000 battle deaths against Japan while it took almost three times that many against Germany—and the Soviet Union took 90 times that many against Germany.[4]

Similarly, with many wooden structures concentrated into a few cities, Japan was highly vulnerable to devastating air raids. One fire raid alone in March 1945 on Tokyo destroyed almost 16 square miles, caused 124,000 casualties and devastated 267,000 buildings.[5] This meant that air power could be decisive against Japan in a way it could not be against Germany.

In short, the war in the Pacific was a difficult and protracted exercise for the United States, and primarily its navy. But, especially in the last year of the war, in no way could there be a serious comparison between the difficulties of a land assault against a still powerful Third Reich, dominating all of Europe, and a rapidly weakening Imperial Japanese island empire. The U.S. style of war, with its emphasis on high technology and massive air and naval power, could be far more effective against an accessible Imperial Japan than a remote Nazi Germany. Under these circumstances, the still major diversion of men and resources to the Pacific (roughly one-third of the war effort) in the last year of the war represented a policy option, rather than dire necessity, against a dying and fading empire.

The Soviets, too, had to maintain a second front against Japan, albeit a passive one until the summer of 1945. The Japanese threat to the Soviet Union was taken very seriously until the winter of 1941, when the Japanese moved south rather than westward. The large Japanese Kwangtung Army represented an ongoing threat to the Soviet Far East. In response, the Red Army force there rose from 30 divisions in November 1944 to 47 divisions in May 1945.

With 1.2 million men, 20,700 guns and mortars, 2,300 tanks and self-propelled artillery pieces, and 4,300 planes, the Red Army presence in the Far East by V-E Day was roughly comparable to the British war effort in Europe (1.3 million men) at that time. And, in August 1945, after victory in Europe, the Red Army would crush the Japanese Kwangtung Army in a lightning campaign.[6]

Logistics

The second aspect of comparison is U.S. geographic remoteness. The logistics issue is not as simple as it is usually presented. Of course, the geographic remoteness of the United States from the European and Asian theaters of battle hindered the U.S. capacity to project its power against Germany. But at the same time, this liability was also a great asset. While German predominance in Europe from 1939–1944 wrought extreme devastation to the Soviet Union and Great Britain, the United States, ill prepared for war, was shielded from German power by the enormous reaches of the Atlantic Ocean. This allowed the United States the luxury of arming and mobilizing for war out of reach of the Wehrmacht and Luftwaffe. For as General of the Army George Marshall reported to the Secretary of War in September 1945,

> The security of the United States of America was saved by sea distances, by the Allies and by the errors of a prepared enemy. For probably the last time in the history of warfare those ocean distances were a vital factor in our defense.[7]

When the United States did need to conquer the Atlantic Ocean to get back into the war, it did not need to do so alone. As we have shown earlier, the Royal Navy played a powerful role in this effort right through 1944. And the enemy, the German navy, was always hindered by Germany's continental orientation and its traditional weakness vis-à-vis the British and U.S. navies. In addition, Great Britain provided a powerful and secure advance base for operations on the European continent only 20 miles away. While the battle was difficult in 1942, by the summer and fall of 1943 the battle of the Atlantic was won against the Germans. Losses after that time to U-boats were relatively minimal.

While the U.S. logistical effort was ultimately adequate, it was handicapped by many innate difficulties. The U.S. war effort staggered under the burden of carrying quantities of vehicles, food, and supplies far in excess of those used by other forces. The U.S. soldier used roughly twice as many supplies on a daily basis as the German soldier, with no appreciable benefit. As James Huston wrote in his study of U.S. logistics,

> People who have studied the records, or who have actually participated in industrial mobilization and procurement activities of World War I and World War II, for instance, never cease to be amazed at how the lessons of the first were ignored in the second and how frequently the same mistakes were repeated.[8]

The Red Army also faced serious logistical problems of its own. Unlike the U.S. army, it lacked any secure and powerful advanced base from which to sally forth against the Germans. The massive German scorched earth policy during the great Russian advance from 1943–1945 meant that the Red Army had to advance through zones of enormous destruction and barrenness. What a contrast to the Anglo–American advance through France and the Low Countries, which had been far less devastated by the Germans in their retreat.

Air Power Versus Land Power

The third major aspect of comparison is the very different strategies used by the two powers—a predominantly air and sea strategy of the United States and land strategy of the Soviet Union. The crucial point is clear: simply because the two sides did not use the same strategy does not vitiate the comparison. The key question is not how they used military power but what they achieved. In the end how much each contributed to the destruction of the Third Reich is the bottom line.

A second aspect of this question is the key assumption that U.S. air power, and especially strategic bombing, was so effective that it cleared the way for the Soviet ground advance. Certainly it helped, but how much and at what cost is the question. Our basic contention is that while tactical air power was highly cost effective, strategic bombing had only a limited impact on the German war effort and at such a high cost as to seriously weaken the other aspects of U.S. military power.

The scope of the U.S. commitment to air power was impressive. Roughly 40 percent of the entire budget was devoted to the air force. During the entire war as much money was spent on building airplanes (34 billion dollars) as was spent on all of the ordnance requirements of the army (34 billion dollars).[9] By May 1945 the United States Army Air Corps, with 2.3 million men and 243 operational groups in Europe, had over 2,000 bombers available for missions. During the final year of the war the U.S. Army Air Force dropped 1.1 million tons of bombs in Europe and .3 million tons in the Pacific. The air war killed 305,000 Germans, seriously injured 780,000 more, and destroyed or damaged 6 million German homes.[10]

The U.S. air campaign did achieve important results. Without the defeat of the Luftwaffe by the spring of 1944, the invasion of Normandy and subsequent successes would have been very difficult, if not impossible. The German army was forced to operate without air cover in the final year of the war, a situation both mentally depressing and militarily dangerous. Millions of Germans—4.5 million by the fall of 1944—were diverted from the army and war production to defend the homeland against air attacks, to clear the debris and reconstruct factories, and to produce fighter planes to counter the campaign. The strategic campaign did bear fruit over time in the destruction of significant German industrial assets and morale. By January 1945 arms production was 18 percent below 1944 levels, and in March 1945 52 percent below 1944. By April 1945 the German economy was in shambles. The attacks on oil and transportation were particularly devastating. The strategic bombing campaign, especially in tandem with the tactical air campaign, had an impressive impact on the German war effort.[11]

Yet was it worth the mammoth effort devoted to it? The strategic air campaign had a significant impact only at a time when the ground campaign had already achieved decisive success and broken the back of the Third Reich. Only when the Red Army seized the Ploesti oil fields in Romania or the Allied armies occupied the V-2 launching sites in the Low Countries were the vital objects of the German war effort finally destroyed. While the Red Army scored major victories over the Germans without any strategic air power (tactical air power was useful), the U.S. armed forces placed too many resources into strategic air power. In addition, 40 percent of all operational Allied bombers in the last year of the war were flown by the Royal Air Force. While Alan Milward has characterized the strategic air campaign as "a study of failure," Maurice Matloff concluded that strategic air power "failed to prove the decisive instrument many had expected . . . the application of power of the ground armies finally broke the German ability and will to resist."[12] Recently John Kenneth Galbraith, who conducted the postwar bombing survey with Paul Nitze and George Ball, has reminisced,

> The overall conclusion was that wars were won by the slogging progress of troops across France and into Germany, with a good deal of help from tactical air power: support for actual movement of troops on the ground. It was an extended form of artillery. Strategic bombing was designed to destroy the industrial base of the enemy and morale of its people. It did neither. Need I say that this conclusion was less than popular at the time?[13]

The overall impact of strategic bombing was limited. During 1943 it reduced German war production by 9 percent, in 1944 by 12 percent, and in the first five months of 1945 by 7 percent. Despite massive strategic bombing, German weapons production rose from a base of 100 in January 1942 to 234 in 1943, 384 in July 1944, and still 284 in January 1945. The Germans produced over 3,000 fighter planes in September 1944 and 1,600 tanks and assault guns in November 1944. During 1944, at the height of the bombing campaign, only 6.5 percent of German machine tool stock was damaged. War production peaked in the summer of 1944 and only decisively fell off in early 1945 as the Third Reich disintegrated on both fronts.[14]

The problems with strategic bombing were numerous. The biggest difficulty was its lack of technological precision. With an emphasis on area bombing, the fact that bombers in the final year of the war had an average CEP (circular error probability) of two miles meant disaster. The postwar bombing survey, not surprisingly, found that only 3 percent of all bombs actually hit a damageable target. Over 12 percent of all U.S. bombs were duds. The U.S. Army Air Force had only a vague understanding of German industry, whose power it underestimated. The Germans effectively dispersed their industries, mounted an impressive repair and reconstruction effort, created huge stockpiles of raw materials, and used smoke and air defense in a skillful manner. Poor weather and darkness also aided the German efforts. The German defense was conducted so capably that the Anglo–American attackers lost 87,000 airmen and 14,900 heavy bombers (18,400 planes in all) in their attacks on the Third Reich.[15]

At such a cost the United States, with British help, did inflict damage on perhaps 10 percent of the German economy and divert another 10 percent of the manpower resources annually in the last two and one-half years of the war. But the massive effort could not make any strong impact on the German war effort until 1945 when the war was already virtually over. In the words of one standard work on the economic history of Europe in this century,

> The German economy does not appear to have suffered from shortages of machine tools, general machinery or plant facilities—except temporarily in a few isolated cases. On the contrary, machine tool and machinery capacity were generally in excess in needs.[16]

As a consequence (and here would be a pattern that would later be repeated in Korea and Vietnam) the U.S. army would be starved of manpower and resources to support an air effort whose impact would not be commensurate with its costs. A small U.S. army, with only ninety divisions (sixty of them deployed in Europe), could not by itself achieve the massive superiority necessary to achieve victory over a stubborn and skillful opponent. In the end the lowly infantry soldier had to go in and occupy enemy ground—and the U.S. army, unlike the Soviet army, often found itself short in this vital category.

The Strange Alliance Revisited

The story of the strains in the wartime alliance of the three great powers is so well documented that there is little need to review it here. What needs to be pointed out, though, are several overall themes. One is that the fixation of the literature on analyzing Soviet–U.S. conflicts that laid the basis for the Cold War largely ignores extensive tensions between the United States and Great Britain.[17] While there definitely was a special bond between the two countries, the differences between them grew in scope as victory became certain. By 1944 the British war effort was in decline while the U.S. war effort was in full bloom. The unifying factors were still there. The two powers shared a common heritage and language, Anglo Saxon elites, a history of decent relations since the 1890s, and a strong anti-Axis bond.

However, as the power relationships changed and the prospect of peace came into sight, all of the old problems surfaced. They ranged from simple differences in such key issues as trade, national identity, histories, and power, to disputes over the entire nature of the postwar era. The British desire to hold its fabled empire, to maintain a restricted "sterling bloc," and to support a continuation of the "balance-of-power" system all ran directly counter to the U.S. vision of the postwar world. As Christopher Thorne has written in his study of the Anglo–American wartime alliance, the common ties

> . . . did not outweigh either the latent strength of Anglophobia in the United States or the widespread distrust of that country which existed in Whitehall. Disagreements over debts, tariff barriers, disarmament and the wide issues involved in the search for international peace and security all helped to create a relationship that was far removed from that "hands-across-the-seas" version that was later to be projected outward from the temporary alliance in arms of 1941 to 1945.[18]

The simple truth is that the three allies had very dissimilar backgrounds and interests and were only drawn together by the necessity of defeating a powerful foe out to dominate the world. This common need could draw the Allies together, as at the Teheran conference, when Stalin successfully pushed for a definite commitment for a second front in Europe in 1944. But when the common bond would wither as the defeat of the Third Reich seemed more certain by the summer of 1944, the natural differences in power, interests, and perceptions would inevitably assert themselves, and the very different war experiences of each of the three powers would serve to push them apart, rather than draw them together, as the war came to a close.

There is a significant body of literature that asserts that the British and Soviets were skillful politicians pushing for military means to support political ends.[19] The British desire for actions in the Mediterranean to secure their lifeline to the British Empire or the Soviet moves into the Balkans in the fall of 1944 are frequently cited in this regard.

But the other side of this coin, the idea that the Americans were naive and only utilizing military means for military ends, leaves much to be desired. After all, President Franklin Roosevelt and his advisors were skillful politicians (Roosevelt was elected for an unprecedented four terms). They were hardly unaware of the kind of world which they hoped to create after the destruction of Germany, and then Japan. The whole second front debate, as Mark

Stoler has well argued, reflected differing national interests in which the United States demonstrated a keen awareness of the political ramifications of the issues.[20] Indeed, the United States, as seen in the creation of the Bretton Woods accords, United Nations, International Monetary Fund, and World Bank, was strongly interested in using its power to shape a new postwar era. The increasing tension between the United States and its two allies reflected this increasing U.S. desire to use its power to create a more desirable postwar world.

INFANTRY FIGHTING POWER

The Soviet capacity to develop infantry fighting power was greater than that of the United States, and rested on several factors: number of divisions, teeth-to-tail ratio, and nature of divisions. The most basic U.S. problem was its inability to create an adequate number of divisions, despite a population considerably larger than that of Nazi Germany and not greatly inferior to a depleted Soviet Union. Table 9.2 makes this point sharply.

Table 9.2 shows that the Soviet Union created roughly 6 times more divisions (albeit smaller ones) than the United States, which possessed less than 6 percent of all divisions in existence during the war. Even worse, the United States, fighting a two-front war, had roughly only 60 divisions available for the European theater. Although the United States actually had a larger armed forces (12.0 million men) than the Soviet Union (11.3 million men) by 1945, it put 50 percent of all its manpower into the air force and navy. Of the remaining half, it placed only 23 percent into combat units. By contrast, the Red Army put 93 percent of its manpower into the army and 80 percent of its army manpower into combat units. During the final campaign in Europe in 1945 the roughly 450 active Red Army divisions dwarfed the 60 U.S. divisions in action against the Germans. In raw numbers the 4.5 million Soviets in active Red Army divisions towered over the 1.1. million Americans in active U.S. Army divisions in Europe.[21]

The second problem was the far smaller teeth-to-tail ratio in the U.S. army than the Red Army. While fully 80 percent of all Soviet division personnel actually were combat soldiers, the corresponding figure in the U.S. division was a mere 53 percent. John Erickson has observed that the Soviets maintained such a

Table 9.2 Number of Divisions of Major Powers in World War II

Country	Number of Divisions
Soviet Union	550
Germany	313
China	300
Japan	120
United States	90
Italy	70
Great Britain	50
Others	70
Total	1,563

Source: 1. *The War Reports of General of the Army George C. Marshall, General of the Army H. H. Arnold and Admiral of the Fleet Ernest King* (Philadelphia and New York: J.B. Lippincott, 1947), p.266.

high ratio of combat strength by centralizing logistics, conducting training in operational frameworks, and holding down the size of formations and units. The Red Army traveled in a much more primitive fashion than the U.S. army would ever consider. The result was that 3.6 million Soviet combat troops confronted the Germans on the Eastern front while only .6 million U.S. combat troops faced the Germans on the Western front.[22]

Third, the two armies had very different organizational philosophies. The U.S. army, reflecting U.S. tradition and technological orientation, emphasized the concept that all 90 of its divisions should be equally good, interchangeable parts capable of performing the same tasks. The Soviet army, emulating the German example, created a large number of divisions, easy to maintain, with limited mobility and less qualified men for defense. This allowed the concentration of limited resources on specialized high-quality units (guards units) for difficult, high-risk tasks such as breaking through German defense lines. This approach proved highly beneficial to the Soviets and was utilized by the U.S. navy with its Marine divisions.[23]

Many U.S. generals were upset, in Russell Weigley's words, over the U.S. "inability to mobilize for the European war the margins of manpower superiority on which U.S.Grant had relied against the Confederacy."[24] In February 1944 General Lesley McNair wrote to Major General L. E. Jones about "the invisible horde of people going here and there but seemingly never arriving."[25] In May 1945 the colorful General Joseph Stilwell complained to General Marshall about the "disappearing ground combat army," which "could be pregnant with disaster if we have a tough ground fight with Japan."[26]

Why did the United States undertake, to use Maurice Matloff's phrase, "the 90 divisions gamble?" From December 1942 until the end of March 1945 the U.S. Army grew by 2.0 million men, yet only 6 percent of this increase went into the ground combat units. The rest went into service units (.8 million men) the army air force (.6 million men), and overhead (.4 million men). The original 1942 plan for 334 divisions shrivelled to 90 divisions by 1944 and 1945. The passion for air and naval power, the proven reliability of Soviet and British fighting power, the pull of the Pacific (primarily a naval war), and the reverses of the German and Japanese forces made U.S. infantry power a low priority. So too did the Allied insistence on a peripheral strategy in 1942 and 1943 and the traditional weak role of ground forces in U.S. military history.[27]

OFFICERS AND SOLDIERS

Any detailed comparison of the officers and men of the two armies inevitably begins to discuss fundamental differences in the nature and style of the two societies and countries. The differences between the opulence of the U.S. war effort and poverty, even primitiveness, of the Soviet war effort at times were startling. Nowhere was this clearer than in the life styles of the general officers of the two armies.

Even before the invasion of Normandy, the U.S. officers had already taken over many of London's most opulent hotels for use as officers' billets. Although General Eisenhower set an example of personal modesty, the same could hardly be said of the bulk of the general officers. In September 1944 Eisenhower's headquarters, with a huge staff of almost 5,000 people, was set up in the Trianon Hotel in Versailles. General Everett Hughes, chief-of-staff for the European Theater of Operations, lived in a suite in the sumptuous

Hotel George V amid the not totally faded splendor of Paris, where over 600 hotels were taken over for Allied officers. By November 1944, at a time that Allied casualties only 200 miles east of Paris were totalling as high as 2,000 men a day,

> Life in Paris for Eisenhower's generals was still a round of cocktail parties, Red Cross nurses, newspapermen, suspenseful trials of alleged collaborationists and the Folies Bergères. As GIs flooded in, a frenetic black market was building up.[28]

Nor did matters improve in 1945, even after Eisenhower moved in February to Rheims where his residence was a large chateau. While General Omar Bradley lived in an eighteenth-century Belgian chateau outside of Namur, General Courtney Hodges resided in the splendor of the Hotel Britannique in the renowned watering hole of Spa. And General George Patton lived first in a palatial home in Nancy and then, later, in a castle in Regensburg.[29]

The contrast between the grand life-styles of the top U.S. officers, with their huge staffs (by May 1945 the SHAEF staff numbered 30,000 people), and the simplicity and small staffs of the Soviet top officers was overwhelming. When General John Deane visited the Vilna front in July 1944 he found a scene that bore almost no resemblance to what he was used to seeing in the U.S. army. There was no post exchange, no USO, no doughnut wagon, no morale agencies, and especially no large staff. Instead, he found an army staff of fifteen-twenty officers working and living in a few small trailers scattered in the woods. Their conference room and mess was a huge hospital tent. Most of the officers did not even have a stenographer. Similarly, when Western visitors met with Marshal Fyodor Tolbukhin, a front commander, in March 1945, they were astounded to see only 100 small cottages, few sentries, and no telephone lines. The Red Army did pay a price in the neglect of advance planning, weak recordkeeping, and poor coordination of subordinate units. But the message that was sent to the soldiers was simple and extremely powerful: the general officers were near the front and at one with them in their life-styles.[30]

A similar contrast was evident in the officers of the two armies. The U.S. officers, recruited largely on the basis of intelligence, came primarily from the middle and upper classes. Fifty-two percent had gone to college and 87 percent had graduated from high school. By contrast, the majority of the Red Army commanders came from the lower classes, with a mere 3 percent having gone to college and 22 percent to high school.[31]

The mechanics of the officer corps also differed sharply between the two armies. The U.S. army, with 891,000 officers by 1945, had a very weak nucleus of 14,000 regular army officers and 21,000 National Guard officers from 1940. Furthermore, many of them were poor, reflecting the low pay and status of officers in peacetime. With seniority and not merit as the path to advancement, the results were predictable. A large number of the newly created officers during the war also left much to be desired. This naturally reflected the U.S. emphasis on intelligence rather than leadership and character, which the army saw as merely a function of human engineering. It also reflected the weak battle experience of the U.S. army before Normandy.[32]

Most military analysts concur in their appraisal of the U.S. officer corps in the war. The top commanders—men such as Omar Bradley, George Patton, Courtney Hodges, and Dwight Eisenhower—are generally seen as good but not great commanders. The real problems came in the rest of the officer corps, filled with inexperienced men. Men such as Bradley and Patton repeatedly complained of the lack of initiative, toughness, and imagination of U.S. officers. Much like its ideal organizational model, the officer corps functioned in a predictable and cautious mode in strategy and tactics. The officers, viewing war as an organizational game, were seldom seen near the front lines. While many top Soviet commanders (such as Generals Ivan Chernyakhovsky, Lev Dovator, Mikhail Kirponos, and Alexander Bodin) were killed at the front, only one top U.S. commander was killed by enemy fire (General Lesley McNair was killed by friendly fire) in the European theater during the whole war. That officer, General Maurice Rose, as the son of a rabbi, was scarcely a typical representative of U.S. general officers.[33]

The Soviet officer corps functioned in a radically different environment. Much like the Israeli officer corps, Soviet officers were promoted primarily on merit and leadership capability demonstrated on the field of battle. As in other revolutionary armies, only combat was seen as the true test of merit for officers. Especially after the summer of 1942, the role of military commissars was downgraded and competence became the sole judge for advancement. While the lower level of officers was often weak, reflecting the war devastation, the Great Purges, and the low level of Soviet society, the top commanders were seen as very good, and often excellent. Many analysts have praised the great capabilities of Stalin's talented, and often very young generals and marshals. Men such as Marshals Zhukov, Rokossovsky, Shaposhnikov, Vasilievsky, and Voronov, are often highly praised. As Seweryn Bialer has concluded, the quality of field command improved "radically" during the war, and "according to both German and Western sources, it was excellent for the most part during the second half of the war."[34]

Similar differences pervaded the soldiers in the two armies. The Red Army enjoyed two natural advantages that overcame the obvious superiority of the U.S. army in terms of quality of manpower. First, the massive devastation and depredations committed by the Germans in the Soviet Union created a passionate hatred of Germans and desire for revenge that propelled the Red Army, despite huge losses, from Stalingrad to Berlin. The Red Army had an efficient propaganda machine of 138,000 political workers by January 1945 and the help of gifted writers as Ilya Ehrenburg, who called for "two eyes for an eye" and "a pool of blood for a drop of blood." This violent anti-German mood fed a virulent nationalism that sought to erase the deep humiliation of the Soviet Union by the devastating German victories in the early phases of the war. It promoted a tremendous sense of pride in each new victory over the detested German foe, a pride deepened by the quest for medals and distinctions. And it permitted the average Soviet soldier to accept a very low standard of living for the sake of that great shared goal of destruction of the Third Reich.[35]

The other great advantage enjoyed by the Red Army was the existence of an elite and self-sacrificing force in the Communist party. By 1945 no less than 25 percent of the soldiers were Communists and another 20 percent were Komsomolites. During the war 6.8 million soldiers were taken into the party as members or candidates. They functioned as the Soviet samurai, as the critical glue that held the army together in the face of enormous adversity. Party membership for soldiers was important as a promise of advancement after the war. No less than 3 million Communists died in the war on all fronts. Although no more than 25 percent of the army, Communists accounted for over 40 percent of all casualties and nearly 74 percent of all Heroes of the Soviet Union.[36]

These two advantages lacking in the U.S. army offset the massive qualitative superiority of the U.S. soldier over the Soviet soldier. After all, the U.S. officers did not have to face a soldiery, as did the Soviet officers, whose average level of education was four years of schooling.[37] The will to fight, though, among the U.S. soldiers was naturally far weaker than among the Soviet soldiers. The war was seen not as a crusade but as a painful necessity against a remote and often only dimly understood adversary. The war seemed to be a dangerous, but inescapable, interruption in the normal flow of U.S. life—something to be endured and survived.

The U.S. infantry soldier often left much to be desired. As in Vietnam, the infantry was a very low priority, taking what was left over after the air force, navy, and specialized services got the cream of the crop. The infantry became "a wastebin for men considered unsuitable for any other occupation."[38] The uneducated, unskilled, and unmotivated disproportionately wound up in the infantry. The lack of battle experience before June 1944 only compounded the problem. Worst of all, the foot soldiers felt neglected and ignored by the system. This is evident in their telling phrase, "The Navy gets the equipment, the Marines get the glory, the soldier gets very little."

The basic problem was that the army did little to promote social cohesion of units. The small number of divisions meant that units were seldom rotated. The constant replacement of casualties and the failure to return wounded and ill soldiers to their units undermined small-unit cohesion and prevented the consolidation of primary groups. A callous replacement system sent men without preparation right into the front where they often perished. There was no social homogeneity as divisions were called up without a geographic base. The weak quality of officers, often derided (and accurately) as "90 day wonders," reduced unit capabilities. The soldiers, feeling a lack of confidence in their own abilities and largely ignored and shunted around in a vast impersonal system, did not develop the military capabilities so necessary for effective fighting power.

A few statistics illustrate the malaise that often pervaded the ranks. In the period from June until November 1944, 26 percent of all U.S. soldiers in combat divisions were treated for combat fatigue, a rate almost 10 times higher than in the Wehrmacht. In typical battles of the period only 15 percent-30 percent of the riflemen actually fired their weapons. The number of desertions mounted as it became evident that the supreme weapon—court martial and shooting for desertion—would never be implemented on a wide scale. In short, as Russell Weigley has reported, "The enemy did not rate American infantry highly: American officers had to concede a lack of aggressive zeal."[39]

Only the application of overwhelming artillery firepower and close air support would remedy the situation, even against a German foe already suffering from three years of combat against the Red Army.

WEAPONRY

The greatest accomplishment of the Soviet Union, and one given very little attention, was its remarkable production of weapons during World War II. Earlier in this book we have seen the vast economic gap between the Soviet Union and United States, a gap that widened to a chasm by 1945 when the U.S. GNP was four times greater than Soviet GNP. The enormous devastation of Soviet territory and occupation of 40 percent of the Soviet Union by Germany for over two years also opened up an huge gap between the Soviet Union and Nazi Germany. Consider Table 9.3, comparing Soviet and German economic production. In short, during World War II Nazi Germany enjoyed a better than 2:1 advantage over the Soviet Union in key economic indicators.

Given the great economic preponderance enjoyed by the United States and lesser preponderance possessed by Nazi Germany over the Soviet Union in the war years, how then did the Soviet Union manage to fight the war on a relatively equal footing? For the unalterable fact is that the Soviet Union produced war equipment in quantities often equal to and even surpassing both its enemy and its ally. Table 9.4 makes this point dramatically.

Table 9.4 shows that the Soviet Union actually outproduced Nazi Germany, often by a wide margin, and was competitive with the United States in certain key areas, especially in infantry and tank weaponry. In the next chapter we will look at how this feat was accomplished.

The Soviet accomplishment also reflected radically different priorities and circumstances than those faced by the United States.

Table 9.3 Soviet and German Economic Production,[a] 1941–1945 (millions of tons)

Product	Germany[b]	Soviet Union[c]	Ratio
coal	2,151.0	441.5	4.9:1
cast iron	98.1	31.5	3.1:1
steel	133.7	45.5	2.9:1
electricity	334.0	147.3	2.3:1
oil	62.0	91.3	1:1.4

Source: 1. *50 let vooruzhennykh sil SSSR* (Moscow: Voenizdat, 1968), p.457.
[a]All figures are expressed in millions of tons except for electricity, which is expressed in billions of kilowatts.
[b]The figures for Germany are for the 1941–1945 period.
[c]The figures for the Soviet Union are for the period July 1941–July 1945.

Table 9.4 Weapons Production[a] of the Soviet Union, United States and Nazi Germany in World War II

Weapons	Soviet Union	United States	Nazi Germany
rifles	12,139,300	12,330,000	8,525,200
machine guns	1,515,900	2,614,300	1,096,400
cannons	482,200	548,900	311,500
tanks and self-propelled artillery pieces	102,800	99,500	43,400
military planes	112,100	192,000	80,600

Source: 1. *Istoriya vtoroi mirovoi voina* (Moscow: Voenizdat, 1982), Vol.12, p.168.
[a]For the Soviet Union these figures are for the period from June 1941 until August 1945. For the United States these figures are for the period from December 1941 until August 1945. For Nazi Germany these figures are for the period from January 1941 until April 1945.

As with its manpower, the Soviet Union placed primary, indeed overwhelming, emphasis on army needs, with lower priority for the air force and minimal concern for the navy. Furthermore, Lend Lease aid, while not critically important in itself, did allow the Soviet Union to focus in certain areas by providing key specialty goods and a large volume of motor vehicles for mobility. By contrast, the U.S. armaments program, as we will see in greater depth in the next chapter, focused primarily on ships and planes to the exclusion of precisely those items on which the Soviet war industry concentrated. In 1944 and the first eight months of 1945, the United States spent 43.7 billion dollars on producing planes and ships but only 18.1 billion dollars on producing combat and motor vehicles and their ammunition.[40]

The Soviet accomplishment was not degraded by low standards of Soviet military production. In a war in which artillery remained the "king of battle," Soviet artillery retained its traditional pride of place, both in quantity and quality. Soviet Katyusha rockets were considered an outstanding military weapon. Most importantly, Soviet medium (T-34) and heavy (KV-1) tanks were as good or better than anything possessed by the Germans. Overall, Soviet tanks, artillery, and rockets were also as good as comparable U.S. weapons. Only in areas of traditional U.S. high-technology specialization, such as ships, planes, electronics, and the atomic bomb, did the United States possess a clearcut lead. This lead was undercut by the weakness of U.S. weapons, especially in the vital tank arena with the old durable Shermans no match for either their more powerful and heavier Soviet or German counterparts.[41]

Against enormous odds and at staggering cost, the Soviet army managed to develop a credible infantry fighting power that the U.S. army often seemed to lack. The gap between awesome U.S. economic and political power and brute force on the battlefield remained a problem throughout the war and would later recur in different circumstances in Korea and Vietnam. The United States, with great help from its allies, was able to mount a credible, but no more than that, show on the battlefield in Europe in the last year of the war.

Here, then, was a great contrast: with so many assets the United States barely managed to eke through in Europe, while with seemingly so little the Soviet Union managed to accomplish so much. For the Soviet Union the great victories in the war not only marked survival and triumph over a great foe but also a major improvement over Tsarist Russia's abominable performance in World War I. For the United States, the war would mark confirmation of its great power in all power indexes.

NOTES

1. *Istoriya vtoroi,* v.2, pp.176, 193.
2. Coakley and Leighton, *Global,* p.394.
3. Spector, *Eagle,* p.xiv.
4. Lan, *SShA,* p.71; *War Reports,* pp.654, 684; Bradley, *Soldier's,* pp.1012, 1090–1091; Divine, editor, *Causes,* p.316; Vorontsov, *Voennye koalitsii,* p.129; and Costello, *Pacific,* p.675.
5. Spector, *Eagle.* pp.504–505.
6. Kesselring, *Soldier's* p.240; Erickson, *The Road to Berlin,* p. 266; Deane, *Strange,* p.247; and Ellis and Warhurst, *Defeat,* p.406.
7. *War Reports,* p.290.
8. Huston, *Sinews,* pp.ix, 530–531 and Dunn, *Second,* pp.171–173.
9. Coakley and Leighton, *Global,* p.830.
10. Matloff, editor, *American,* p.463; Webster and Frankland, *Strategic,* v.3, part 5, p.3; *War Reports,* p.458, Craven and Cate, editors, *Army,* v.3, p.801; Sivachev and Yakovlev, *Russia,* p.174; and Trevor-Roper, editor, *Final,* p.24.
11. Speer, *Inside,* p.560; Craven and Cate, editors, *Army,* v.3, pp.786, 804; and Clough, Moodie, and Moodie, editors, *Economic,* p.323.
12. Milward, *War,* p.298; Matloff, editor, *American,* p.497; and Webster and Frankland, *Strategic,* p.3.
13. Terkel, *Good,* p.209.
14. Marwick, *War,* p.134; Clough, and Moodie, Moodie, editors, *Economic,* pp.321-323; Dunn, *Second,* pp.33, 254, 156–158; MacDonald, *Last,* p.7; Craven and Cate, editors, *Army,* v.3, pp.288, 644; and Milward, *War* pp.333–334.
15. Verrier, *Bomber,* p.253; Craven and Cate, editors, *Army,* v.3, pp.670, 790–795; Webster and Frankland, *Strategic,* pp.221–223, 242; Michel, *Second,* p.547; *War Reports,* p.435 and Millett and Maslowski, *For,* p.439.
16. Clough, Moodie, and Moodie, editors, *Economic,* p.316 and Jung, *Die Ardennen.*
17. Vorontsov, *Voennye koalitsii,* p.133; Willmott, *June 1944,* p.108; Greenfield, Palmer, and Wiley, *Organization,* pp.194, 163; *War in the East,* p.116; and Eisenhower, *Eisenhower,* p.485.
18. Thorne, *Allies,* p.20.
19. See, for example, Feis, *Churchill.*
20. Stoler, *Politics,* pp.165–167.
21. See the sources in note 17.
22. Erickson and Feuchtwanger, editors, *Soviet,* p.32; *War Reports,* p.135; and Erickson, *The Road to Berlin,* p.81.
23. Dunn, *Second,* p.114.
24. Weigley, *Eisenhower's,* p.12. This is an excellent work of the first order.
25. Greenfield, Palmer, and Wiley, *Organization,* p.236.

26. *Ibid.*, p.255.

27. *Ibid.*, pp.175; and Hastings, *Overlord*, p.30.

28. Irving, *War*, pp.8, 9, 88, 274,324.

29. Summersby, *Eisenhower*, p.222; Irving, *War*, pp.332, 337, 406; Whiting, *Siegfried*, p.48; and Matloff, editor, *American*, p.464.

30. Michel, *Second*, p.615; Deane, *Strange*, pp.210–211; and Toland, *Last*, p.179.

31. Jones, *Red*, pp.8, 92; van Creveld, *Fighting*, p.136.

32. *Ibid.*, pp.127, 150; *War Reports*, p.124; and *Statistical History*, p.736.

33. Whiting, *Siegfried*, pp.154, 156, 27–28; and Blumenson, *Patton*, p.517.

34. Bialer, editor, *Stalin*, p.406; Werth, *Russia*, p.226; and Essame, *Battle*, p.487.

35. Harriman and Abel, *Special*, pp.3, 6, 319; Toland, *Last*, p.56; and Werth, *Russia*, pp.763, 764.

36. *Istoriya velikoi*, v.6, p.365.

37. *War in the East*, p.106.

38. Hastings, *Overlord*, p.16.

39. Bradley, *Soldier's*, p.446 and Hastings, *Overlord*, pp.246, 248.

40. Milward, *War*, p.74.

41. *War Reports*, pp.255, 258; and McNeill, *America*, p.123.

10

Soviet and U.S. War Economies

The preceding chapter left open one big question: given the enormous deficiencies suffered by the Soviet Union in the war, how did it ever manage to even come close to matching U.S. war production in many key areas? Of course, part of the answer is that the Soviets only matched the Americans in infantry and armored weapons, eschewing the more expensive and high-technology weapons systems of ships, planes, electronics, and atomic bombs. Another part of the answer is that the Soviet Union had the advantage of being an advanced forward base area, in which the Soviets were able to move their new weapons forward rapidly and at minimal cost. And a final part of the standard answer is that U.S. Lend Lease supplies to the Soviets were a powerful force in ultimate Red Army triumph.

Since we have discussed these points earlier, we will only briefly summarize them here. The fact that the Americans chose a capital-intensive, high-technology warfighting style emphasizing the air force and navy while the Soviets chose a labor-intensive, lower-technology style stressing the army does not *ipso facto* make one or the other innately better. In war, as nowhere else, the proof of the pudding is in the eating. The massive disadvantage of having the German army occupying almost 40 percent of the Soviet Union's territory and industrial and agricultural capacities far outweighed any advantages accruing to being an advanced forward base. Lend Lease, while useful in certain specialized areas and especially in providing much needed mobility to the army, was only a peripheral factor in Red Army victories in 1944 and 1945 and of minimal value in 1941 and 1942. The 11 billion dollars of U.S. Lend Lease supplies represented less than 4 percent of U.S direct war costs (288 billion dollars) and roughly 10 percent of Soviet government spending.[1]

These standard explanations for U.S. and Soviet war performance ignore the enormous economic gap between the two countries and the overwhelming devastation inflicted on the Soviet Union while the United States escaped the ravages of war. These points are reflected dramatically in Table 10.1.

Table 10.1 shows that even beyond the 4:1 overall economic advantage enjoyed by the United States over the Soviet Union, the gap grew to an average of roughly 6:1 in such vital industrial indicators as steel, electricity, and pig iron. And this does not even reflect the powerful economic and military aid rendered to the United States by it allies while the Soviet Union stood almost alone.

Table 10.1 reflects several phenomena. The United States experienced a wartime boom at the same time that the Soviet Union, already in an inferior position, underwent the great trauma of war with Germany. No other nation in modern military history has had to fight with over 40 percent of its industrial, agricultural, and human resources—and its most valuable ones at that—in the hands of its enemy for several years. Even worse, as the Red Army moved westward in the last two years of the war, it liberated vast areas of Soviet territory torched and scarred by brutal fighting and German destruction and removal of all valuable property.

SOVIET WAR ECONOMY

The situation was grim. By the fall of 1942 the Soviet Union had lost territory on which fully 40 percent of the prewar population, or 80 million people, had lived. Even worse was the fact that 42 percent of the electricity, 58 percent of the steel, and 71 percent of the pig iron produced in 1940 had come from these areas. Almost half of all fixed capital (46 percent, to be exact) was lost in 1941 and 1942, which called into question the very basis of Soviet existence. This forced a massive evacuation of men and material to the East. There a whole new war effort had to be launched on a

Table 10.1 Soviet and U.S. Economic Production, 1945 (millions of tons)

Product	United States	Soviet Union	Ratio
oil	235.8	19.4	12.1:1
electricity[a]	271.3	43.3	6.3:1
steel	72.3	12.3	5.9:1
pig iron	48.8	8.8	5.5:1

Sources: 1. Roger Munting, *The Economic Development of the USSR* (New York: St.Martin's Press, 1982), p.126.
  2. G. Warren Nutter, *Growth of Industrial Production in the Soviet Union* (Princeton: Princeton University Press, 1962), pp.582–593.

[a]Electricity is measured in billions of kilowatts.

previously small base, something unprecedented for a nation in wartime.[2]

The situation even deteriorated further in the course of that gruesome and protracted struggle in the East. By 1945 roughly 25 percent of the prewar capital stock had been permanently destroyed, a level twice that for its archrival Germany (13 percent) which had also suffered greatly during the war. Devastation was everywhere. Twenty million people were dead, 25 million people homeless, 5 million people crippled, 17 million cattle and 7 million horses lost. Over 1,700 towns and 70,000 villages lay in ruins, while 26,000 miles of railroad track had been ripped up. Leningrad alone had suffered 10 times more deaths than Hiroshima would suffer from the atomic bomb. In Stalingrad one building was intact in the whole city. Rubble was everywhere. The cost of the war, which was equal to 6–7 years of 1945 national annual income, was greater or at least equal to the total wealth created during the advance of the 1930s.[3]

The Soviet economy lay in shambles in 1945. Despite great sacrifice, Soviet national income and GNP in 1945 was 20 percent lower than in 1940. Steel production was down 33 percent, pig iron production down 41 percent, tractor production down 76 percent. Soviet agriculture was so hard hit that it would not fully recover until 1952, and even then per capita production was less than in 1928. By 1945 a disastrous harvest brought in a mere 49 percent of the 1940 crop. Wheat production had declined even further, by 58 percent, and meat by 56 percent. Famine menaced the land.[4]

Under these horrendous circumstances, how did a country only so recently removed from dire poverty survive and even outproduce the far more powerful German economy and come close to the enormously rich U.S. economy in the production of many vital war goods? The most basic reason is also the simplest. The Soviet people, under Stalinist leadership, sacrificed themselves and nearly everything they had to win the war while the U.S. people enjoyed a relatively luxurious "good war." The data are incontrovertible on this point.

Only by reducing civilian consumption to a bare minimum— and sometimes not even that—could a truncated Soviet economy manage to find adequate resources for the war economy. Under the slogan, "Everything for the front," the first and absolute allocation priority for reduced output of food, clothes, and consumer goods was the large Soviet army. The low standard of living of 1940 soon appeared as a distant mirage of unattainable luxury to the Soviet people. On top of all this were long and difficult Soviet winters that became almost unendurable for the civilian population.

The statistics are horrifying. By 1945 the real wages of the workers and employees in the national economy had declined a shattering 60 percent from the already low level of 1940. Housing was extremely weak, with a tiny 3.9 square meters per capita of housing space available in urban areas in 1944. In liberated areas ravaged by the war, many people lived in holes in the ground, in cellars under ruins, or in lean-tos and shacks hastily thrown together. Food was so scarce and tightly rationed that many Soviets were hungry or even died from starvation, cold, and overwork, especially in the dark days of 1942 and 1943. Agricultural production in 1943 was a pathetic 41 percent of the 1940 level and even by 1945 had only climbed to 51 percent of 1940. On a per capita basis Soviets ate only 45 percent as much food in 1944 as in 1940, and only 24 percent as much sugar. Even by the end of the war, "hunger stalked the Soviet land in 1945 . . . grain production that year was little more than half that of 1940."[5]

The tragic living conditions of the Soviet people extended beyond their meager diet and housing, their selection of consumer goods was pitiful. The output of consumer goods in general declined a massive 58 percent and consumer durables by 88 percent in 1945 over the 1940 level. Clothes became very hard to come by as cotton fabric production slid 55 percent. Boots and shoes were virtually irreplaceable as production collapsed 70 percent and many of the few remaining were reserved for the army. Simple consumer goods, such as radios, sewing machines, phonographs, bicycles, and cameras, virtually vanished from the stores. All the gains made since the October Revolution were abolished by the German invasion and the Soviets slid back into a dire poverty not seen even in the Soviet Union or Tsarist Russia for several generations.[6]

Various Western observers have commented on the conditions the Soviets endured on the road to victory. Alexander Werth, on the scene, observed scurvy in Moscow and desperate hunger in Leningrad.[7] Alec Nove has pointed out that the rural and urban hardships of World War II were far greater than those that led to the collapse of Tsarist Russia.[8] And William McNeill, in a classic work on the origins of the Cold War, wrote over thirty years ago,

> The expansion of munitions production was achieved only at the cost of enormous civilian sacrifice....What is amazing is not the failure of Russians to restore or maintain their pre-war levels of production, but rather the fact that they were able to keep going at all. Consumption was cut to bare survival level; heartbreaking and back-breaking burdens were put upon the working population; yet, despite grim conditions, the Russian government was able to demand and to get sufficient war production to keep the Red Army strong.[9]

UNITED STATES WAR EFFORT

The contrast with the U.S. war effort was overwhelming. The United States had a "good war," with a rise in the standard of living, great increase in U.S. economic and political power, minimal casualties, and geographic protection from the European and Asian battlefields. Full employment and wartime prosperity left most Americans markedly better off than during the tragic decade of the Great Depression. Despite wartime restrictions, in 1943 nearly 70 percent of all Americans, during the greatest armed struggle in world history, reported that the war had not required any real sacrifice. As Richard Polenberg found in his fine study of the U.S. homefront in World War II,

> For most Americans World War II spelled neither hardship nor suffering but a better way of life. In part this was because the war

followed a decade of distress: high earnings and full employment contrasted sharply with conditions during most of the 1930s and millions of people gained a chance to get back on their feet, clear up old debts and make a new start.[10]

Of course, some Americans did make great sacrifices and all suffered from the wartime restrictions. There was wartime rationing of gas, tires, sugar, coffee, and fuel oil. Consumers were forced to do without large consumer durables as the production lines for cars and electric household devices were closed down. There were lines for buses, restaurants, and theaters. With an end to car production and mass movement to the cities for war jobs, public transportation—buses and trains—became overcrowded. This same migration, combined with a decline in housing starts, led to a critical housing shortage. Television was not developed in favor of war-mandated demand for radar. Vacations were few and work hours were increased. Millions of American families suffered an intense loneliness for their sons and husbands stationed far away, often in remote countries of the world of which they had previously been only dimly aware.[11]

However, the overall level of U.S. sacrifice was minimal compared to the intense suffering in the Soviet Union. By the end of the war 50 million Soviets were dead, homeless, or crippled: in the United States the comparable figure was 500,000. More Americans were killed in civilian industrial accidents at home than were killed in the war. While the average Soviet citizen eked out a desperate existence with a 60 percent decline in real consumption, the standard of living of Americans rose sharply during the war. By 1944 per capita real disposal income had risen 43 percent over the 1940 prewar level. While consumption of durable goods rose only 6 percent, that of nondurable goods rose 97 percent, and that of services 50 percent from 1940 to 1944, before inflation is taken into account. While luxuries were limited (women's leather shoe production dropped 22 percent), consumption of food alone more than doubled, and recreation spending soared by 74 percent. With a GNP that more than doubled between 1940 and 1944, the Roosevelt administration was able to pursue a policy of "both guns and butter," ensuring a popular war for the American people.[12]

What is remarkable is how the wartime boom distributed prosperity among so many sectors of U.S. society. Many Americans became rich as liquid individual assets skyrocketed from 50 billion dollars in December 1941 to 140 billion dollars in

December 1944. The old pyramidal U.S. social structure now gained a large bulge in the center as many millions of Americans entered the middle class for the first time. U.S. trade unions saw their membership rise from 10.5 million members in 1941 to 14.8 million members in 1945. With the average labor weekly pay check swollen by 70 percent over the prewar level (fattened by heavy overtime) and with a prominent labor role in the government (personified by "Clear It With Sidney" Hillman), labor's future seemed rosy indeed. But this did not come at the expense of big business, which also flourished. After the debacle of the Great Depression, big business regained visible power and public esteem by its strong role in the war effort. Net business profits before taxes almost tripled between 1940 (9.5 billion dollars) and 1944 (26.5 billion dollars) and nearly doubled even after onerous taxes. Corporate assets almost doubled between 1939 and 1945 while business received nearly 25 billion dollars in new plants and equipment.[13]

The U.S. war effort, then, promoted a major expansion of civilian consumption as well as military production while the Soviet war effort sacrificed civilian consumption, along with investment and nonmilitary government expenditures, totally for military production. This difference was highly important since war potential is historically defined as gross production less the amount of civilian consumption and investment which may be foregone without disrupting the political and social system.[14] In the Soviet Union, an authoritarian socialist system, combined with popular mass resistance to the German invaders, was able to cut civilian consumption and investment to the bone, or even below in 1942 and 1943. In the United States, a democratic capitalist system, not facing direct invasion, chose to forgo much military production by actually allowing civilian consumption to rise sharply in wartime.

The United States, for historical reasons as well as current military and political realities, devoted much of its resources to creating planes, ships, and electronics equipment. Long-range bombers, aircraft carriers, cruisers, and cargo vessels devoured huge amounts of industrial manpower and resources. By contrast, the Soviet Union allocated the great bulk of its industrial manpower and resources to developing a powerful army that could destroy the greatest military force in history that was occupying much of its territory.

MANPOWER MOBILIZATION

The Soviet Union carried out a more thorough mobilization of manpower than the United States. Fortunately for Stalin the Soviet Union, even after the massive loss of territory in 1941 and 1942, still had (after evacuation of 17 million people eastward) 130 million people left by the end of 1942. By 1945 this figure would rise to 170 million people. This meant that, in 1942, the Soviet Union still had a population equal to that of the United States and far greater than Nazi Germany, even if its educational level was significantly lower. And this advantage would increase as the Red Army moved westward in the last two and one-half years of the war.[15]

Stalin carried out a ruthless and thorough mobilization of all available manpower. The massive drain of young males to the army, on top of serious army losses of manpower, made this an urgent task. By the end of 1942 all possible manpower had been put at the service of the state. Moscow could now direct at will all of the unemployed, women, youth, elderly, and invalid not formerly in the workplace. This mobilization, in addition to the redirection of 3 million employees into industry, construction, and transportation during the war, necessitated a massive training program of 14.2 million workers on the job and 2.8 million vocational school graduates. Through these efforts the Soviet leaders were able to maintain an industrial work force that reached 7.2 million people by 1945, only 1.1 million short of the 1940 figure. This was a remarkable achievement under the circumstances.[16]

The centerpiece of the mobilization was the use of female labor on a scale not seen either in the United States or Nazi Germany. The utilization of female labor was not new in the Soviet Union, where, in 1940, already 52 percent of the collective farm workers and 38 percent of nonagricultural workers were women. Indeed, much of the great success of the 1930s was due to the massive employment of female labor. What was unique, though, was reliance on women as the main labor force, something without precedent in modern history. By 1944 women formed 80 percent of all collective farm workers, 50 percent of the industrial work force, and even 36 percent of the building and construction workers. While the number of men declined 8.0 million (37 percent) among wage and salary earners from 1940 to 1945, the number of women increased (despite war losses) by 2.7 million.

The Soviet army, even, would use 800,000 women, at times as snipers and machine gunners and partisans. The war was won by the use of female labor in every possible area.[17]

The United States did not need total mobilization of manpower, especially of women, to win the war, and it did not do so. It could easily expand its industrial work force by 70 percent to 17.0 million people by 1944. The United States could voluntarily draw in over 8.5 million unemployed workers and millions of other youth, women, and older people eager to work at higher salaries than ever known before. While the Soviet civilian labor force declined by 11 million people between 1940 and 1945, the U.S. civilian labor force in the same period expanded by almost 10 million people. This reflected the great labor reserves unused by the United States due to the Great Depression. There would be no compulsory mobilization of labor or military discipline in the workplace in the U.S. system as in the Soviet system.[18]

Under these circumstances the United States never made full use of untapped labor reserves, especially those of women. Only 4.5 million women were drawn into the labor market during the war. At their peak in 1945 women formed only 36 percent of the U.S. civilian labor force compared to over 60 percent in the Soviet labor force. Furthermore, while the great majority of all Soviet women were mobilized into the work place during the war, only 32 percent of all American women over the age of 14 years old were employed in 1944.[19]

CENTRALIZATION

This leads to our final point, the greater and more effective centralized direction and control of the Soviet war economy than the U.S. war economy. Without such a system, it is highly unlikely that the Soviet regime would have survived, much less triumphed, in World War II. The enormous military losses of 1941 and 1942, of territory with a population greater than that of the Third Reich and well endowed with natural and industrial resources, would have destroyed most of the economies in the world.[20]

The State Committee of Defense, under Stalin, Voroshilov, Beria, Malenkov, and Molotov, developed impressive control over the war economy from an early date. In this they were greatly aided by the experience of the 1930s, which had witnessed the rapid development of a war economy in peacetime. Building on this experience, the Stalinist elite could effectively and swiftly mobilize the entire economy around war needs. By 1942 already 55 percent of national income was going for defense. Fully 70 percent–80 percent of all industrial production went for the war that terrible year. Despite a 29 percent drop in national income from 1941 and the mass evacuation of vital industries from west to east, the Soviet Union still managed to increase its arms output 33 percent in 1942 over the 1941 level. This type of performance continued throughout the war. In 1944 national income was still 12 percent below the 1940 level, but arms output was 251 percent greater than that last peaceful year.[21]

Nothing showed the mettle of the Stalinist regime as much as its survival in 1941 and 1942. The twin tasks of conversion to a full war economy and mass evacuation of industries and people from threatened areas to the East under conditions of military disaster preoccupied a regime fighting for its very existence. The real emergency lasted from June 1941 until December 1942, a period marked by hasty and ruthless improvisation and rule by emergency mobilization. The prewar industrial and plant contingency plans, the authoritarian nature of the regime and its lengthy experience with other emergencies (such as the civil war and collectivization) greatly eased the transition to a war footing. The evacuation of 13 percent of Soviet industrial assets, including 1,520 large plants, and 17 million people was a feat of amazing proportion, even if the majority of all assets were lost. By October 1941 75 percent of the entire airplane industry were on wheels. The transformation of the Eastern regions into the main industrial zones of the country also was a great accomplishment. These Eastern areas, which in 1941 had only an 18.5 percent share of arms production, by 1942 had a predominant 76.0 percent share. As Mark Harrison commented in his recent superb study of the Soviet war economy, despite the terrible problems,

> at the end of 1941 the first period of the Soviet war economy's development was complete. A decisive stage of evacuation, mobilization and conversion of the economy had been passed. A devastating blow had been absorbed and the next stage would be one of adjustment. In the next stage the economy would bring to bear its full war potential.[22]

The rest of the story is familiar and dealt with elsewhere. During 1942 Soviet industry stabilized and completed economic conversion by July. The economy began to move into high gear and completed the tasks of evacuation and relocation of industry and workers, transfer of workers and investment from civilian to military needs, and making workers work longer hours. During 1943 and 1944 the crisis was now past and the regime could go beyond emergency decrees to longer-range planning and economic reconstruction, especially beginning in the fall of 1943. In this success the highly effective Soviet system managed to completely centralize nearly all economic functions, ranging from production and planning to rationing goods and mobilizing, transferring, and training workers. The great Soviet successes in first absorbing enormous German punishment and then marching from Stalingrad to Berlin showed the strong capability of the Stalinist system in conducting the economic side of war.[23]

Not surprisingly, the United States, lacking the incentive of imminent danger or the regimented Soviet economy, did not carry out such sweeping centralized control of its economy. Given the enormous economic power of the United States even lenient policy was bound to bring forth great production—18.5 billion dollars of war output in 1941, 46.6 billion dollars of such output in 1942. From 1940 to 1944 raw materials output increased by 60 percent and industrial output increased by 300 percent. Only in the first six months of 1942 were a series of wartime boards with limited powers created, including ones for munitions, raw materials, shipping, production, and food. Not until the formation of the War Production Board and Controlled Materials Plan in the end of 1942 did the U.S. economy begin to feel the impact of more effective centralized control. Even here, though, this was limited. For example, the War Production Board allowed the army and navy to run their own military procurement and had only limited powers over industry. Only in the creation of the Office of War Mobilization in May 1943 and the full implementation of the Controlled Materials Plan in July 1943 did the U.S. economy achieve relatively centralized direction, albeit on a lower level than existing in the Soviet Union. Even then the pluralist forces so prominent in a liberal democratic capitalist economy prevented any full government control of the war effort.[24]

The outcome of World War II seemed to validate the economic systems of both nascent superpowers. For the Soviet Union, with vivid memories of the disasters of 1914–1917 and 1941–1942, the survival of the regime in the face of enormous threat, and its ultimate triumph in 1945 seemed to demonstrate the great advantages of the socialist system. At the point of greatest peril the Stalinist regime, through full mobilization of manpower and resources, had requested and obtained the total cooperation (both voluntary and coerced) of the Soviet people. They had sacrificed enormously and won a great victory, after seeing their way of life almost totally destroyed in the war.

By contrast, the United States, able to rely on Great Britain, the Soviet Union, and two great oceans for protection, carried out a much less severe mobilization for war. In the course of the war the enduring theme had not been sacrifice, which was limited to a very small proportion of the population, but prosperity and full employment, which held out great promise for the future postwar years. In 1945 the western half of the Soviet Union lay in ruins, as an exhausted and impoverished populace counted up its enormous sacrifice and gave thanks that peace had finally come. In the United States, too, the population rejoiced and hoped only that the wartime boom and prosperity would survive the transition to peacetime and not send the United States back into the dark days of the Great Depression.

NOTES

1, Lan, *SShA*, p.74; Clough, Moodie, and Moodie, editors, *Economic*, p.298; and Bergson and Heymann, *Soviet*, p.26.

2. In particular see Mark Harrison's fine and long-needed study of the Soviet war economy, *Soviet*, p.133. See also Ziemke, *Stalingrad*, p.23 and Volin, *Century*, p.275.

3. Linz, editor, *Impact*, pp.16–23, 189, 283–284; Moorsteen and Powell, *Soviet*, p.77; and Paterson, *Soviet-American*, p.34.

4. Harrison, *Soviet*, pp.124, 151, 578–579; Millar, *ABCs*, p.51; Zaleski, *Stalinist*, p.605; and Volin, *Century*, p.304.

5. *Statistical Handbook*, p.5; Bergson and Kuznets, editors, *Economic*, p.238; Zaleski, *Stalinist*, pp.328, 355; Linz, editor, *Impact*, p.81; Deane, *Strange*, p.37; McNeill, *America*, p.442; Werth, *Russia*, p.218; and *Istoriya velikoi*, v.1, p.63.

6. Bergson and Kuznets, editors, *Economic*, p.200; Nutter, *Growth*, pp.197, 455–459; and Zaleski, *Stalinist*, pp.580, 605.

7. See Werth's excellent account of the war, *Russia*.

8. Nove, "Soviet Peasantry in World War II," in Linz, editor, *Impact*, pp.262–278.

9. McNeill, *America*, pp.231–232.

10. Polenberg, *War*, p.131 and Blum, *V*, pp.190–192.

11. See the above fine works, in note 10, by Blum and Polenberg, as well as Perrett, *Days*.

12. For statistics see United Nations, *National Income*, p.243 and *Statistical History*, pp.139, 142, 178, 414. See also Perrett, *Days*, pp.339–340, 399.

13. Blum, *V*, pp.100, 117–140; *Statistical Handbook*, p.580; and Perrett, *Days*, p.402.

14. See Milward's fine volume *War*, p.22.

15. *Istoriya vtoroi*, v.7, p.41.

16. Zaleski, *Stalinist*, p.313; and Harrison, *Soviet*, pp.139, 145.

17. Zaleski, *Stalinist*, p.338; Bergson and Kuznets, editors, *Economic* p.86; Volin, *Century*, p.276; Erickson, *Road to Berlin* p.404; Linz, editor, *Impact*, p.139; and Jones, *Red*, p.99.

18. Lan, *SShA* p.116; Volin, *Century*, p.276; and Bergson and Kuznets, editors, *Economic*; p.86.

19. Hancock and Gowing, *British*, p.372 and Marwick, *War*, p.372.

20. See Zaleski, *Stalinist*.

21. *Ibid.*, p.315; Marwick, *War*, p.131; and Churchill, *Triumph*, p.272.

22. Harrison, *Soviet*, pp.93, 72–78, 84–88, 213.

23. *Ibid.*, pp.154, 192, 213; and Zaleski, *Stalinist*, pp.328–331.

24. Milward, *War*, pp.65, 112; and McNeill, *America*, pp.128–129, 226.

11

Conclusions

If wars are too important to be left to generals, then the study of wars is too significant to be left to military historians. With their focus on the purely technical side of war—the campaigns, battles, and technologies—the military historians have had little interest in the broader political, economic, and social aspects of war. Only recently, and tentatively, has this situation begun to change. This would not be significant except for the concomitant ignoring of wars and armies by most political scientists as well. Despite this common neglect of the nexus between wars, armies, and politics, it is undeniable that wars have had a powerful and independent impact on international politics and nation states.

Without the military destruction and occupation of Germany and Japan, and the Soviet occupation of Eastern Europe and East Germany by the end of World War II, the emergence of the Soviet Union as a superpower in the postwar era would have been well nigh impossible. The overwhelming U.S. role in the West after 1945 would have been unthinkable without the exhaustion of Great Britain, the paralysis of France, and the destruction of Germany. As Torbjorn Knutsen recently observed about new work in military history,

Interstate dynamics, expressed in military competition between territorial nation-states, have contributed more to the emergence and the development of the modern world system than analysts have hitherto assumed. Instead of only focusing on the means of production to explain the advent of the modern world, we ought to consider the impact of means of destruction as well. [1]

Wars also strongly impact the fate and nature of individual nation states. When Tsarist Russia was tested in World War I, it failed and disintegrated. Barely twenty months into the war its armies had lost any offensive capability against the German army. This occurred despite the fact that Imperial Germany was primarily involved on the Western front and had only secondary forces on the Eastern front. Only a year later the February Revolution would overthrow the Tsarist regime and effectively end Russian participation in the war. In March 1918 the capitulatory Treaty of Brest Litovsk would mark the nadir of Russia's fortunes. [2]

By sharp contrast, in World War II the Soviet Union absorbed the full shock of the attack of the vaunted Nazi legions, who invaded with an army roughly three times larger than the German forces in the East in World War I. For over 1,000 days, from June 1941 until June 1944, the Red Army suffered horribly at the hands of more than 3 million German and allied troops, who fought desperately to destroy the "Bolshevik menace." Despite various forms of Allied aid, from Lend Lease to attacks on the periphery of the Third Reich to air raids on Germany, the Red Army still stood relatively alone engaging the great bulk of active German land forces. And when it was over in June 1944, when a second front was finally formed, the Red Army had already destroyed most of the effectiveness of the Wehrmacht. Yet in the last year of the war, the Red Army would play a disproportionate role in the destruction of the Third Reich.

World War II, then, showed one thing: however much the West might detest Stalinism, the Soviet Union had passed the test of war with flying colors and shown the effectiveness and capabilities of its social and political system. And when, despite all the travail, the Red Army stood in Berlin, Vienna, Prague, and Budapest at the end of the war, who, remembering the tragic fate of Tsarist Russia, could deny the real achievements and accomplishments of the Soviet system? [3]

Furthermore, military capabilities reflect more than economic arrangements. The recurrent Israeli triumphs over the Arabs, the Soviet victories over the Germans in World War II, the Chinese successes in the Korean War in 1950 and early 1951, and the North Vietnamese march into Saigon in 1975 were not accompanied by any economic predominance of the victors over the vanquished. While economic arrangements are important in military success, so too are political and social factors, as well as purely military factors. The great victories of the United States and Soviet Union in World War II thereby demonstrated not only their impressive economic capabilities but also the soundness of their political and social arrangements and purely military organization.

World War II showed a great deal about Soviet and U.S. societies. The strong offensive capacity of the Soviet and U.S. armies demonstrated a high societal morale. This was especially noteworthy for the Soviet Union given the incredible devastation wreaked by the Germans there. The stronger reliance on coercion in the Red Army than the U.S. army mirrored the different political systems. The broad recruitment into the Soviet officer corps reflected the major changes that had occurred in Soviet society since the revolution. At the same time the heroic leadership displayed by Communist elements within the Red Army showed a major source of strength available to the Red Army that had no equivalent in the West.[4]

IMPORTANT QUESTIONS REVISITED

The first question in the introductory chapter concerned why the war took so long when the correlation of forces so overwhelmingly favored the Allies. Our answers have been primarily in the political and military realms. Politically, the Western Allies, by their appeasement of Nazi Germany and refusal to heed the Soviet calls of Litvinov for action against fascism, failed to contain Hitler and Mussolini when they were yet weak. Their tardy mobilization against the rearming (but not yet fully rearmed) Fascists gave the Nazis, with their superior military leadership and organization, a temporary "window of vulnerability." They brilliantly exploited this advantage in the first years of the war as they picked off their enemies one by one.

The absence of the United States from the struggle in the early days and the temporary Russo–German collaboration were devastating to the Allied cause. The United States, given its traditional isolationism, fine navy, geographic distance from the battlefield, and relative immunity from direct attack, was naturally slow to mobilize and get involved. And even when it did finally enter the war, its full-scale mobilization would be delayed by the absence of extensive peacetime preparations which were common in the European nations so much closer to the conflict. Similarly, the Soviet Union, remembering the devastating consequences for Russia of weakness in World War I, seeing the ineradicable hostility of the Axis powers, and failing to replicate the Triple Entente in 1939, was also understandably eager to deflect the German forces away from its borders in the Molotov-Ribbentrop Pact. But even though these actions were understandable politically, they were to have tragic consequences for the Allies in the early years of World War II.

Not only was the United States poorly prepared for war even by December 1941 but its military effort before June 1944 in the European theater was weak at best. Even in the final year of the war, despite massive air and naval superiority, the U.S. land effort remained mediocre, saved by the British and Soviet efforts and disintegration of the German foe. The U.S. military record, then, was a significant contributing factor to the prolongation of the war.

This answer also helps explain why the United States, despite its massive economic, political, and even military advantages, was unable to do better than divide the European continent with the Soviet Union. The Soviet Union, in tandem with the British Commonwealth, did mount large-scale and successful war efforts that left them thoroughly spent by the end of the war. The Soviet Union, threatened with extinction by Nazi Germany, effectively mobilized all of its resources for the war effort. It developed a workable labor-intensive strategy of warfare that destroyed the bulk of German land power in the East. The Stalinist leadership, the transformed economy, the improved army over time, the role of the party in the army, and the will to sacrifice marked this effort. The United States could afford not to mount such an effort because of the British and Soviet efforts and because the U.S. homeland was not threatened. Not mounting such an effort ensured a predominant role for the United States, with minimal casualties and a booming economy, after the war.

The Soviet accomplishment, of course, reflected the many positive accomplishments of the October Revolution and Stalin's "third revolution from above" of the 1930s. In the West it is fashionable to emphasize the many obvious deficiencies of Stalinism, from labor camps and show trials to collectivization and political repression. But it is important to see, as only a prolonged study of the fate of the Soviet Union in World War II can show, that Stalinism also contained the many positive elements that thrust a weak and discredited country in 1918 to superpower status by 1945.

We have examined some of the difficulties within the U.S. military that victory in the war concealed. The United States, by overly relying on air and naval power, failed to develop effective land power. The victory reinforced its belief in the magic of high technology and firepower, of quick and cheap victories that could be bought without serious casualties. Korea and Vietnam would show the problems therein quite clearly. While analysts frequently try to show the differences between the success in World War II and the problems and failures in the Korean and Vietnam wars, the simple truth is that there were far more similarities than differences.

Most importantly, the U.S. military naturally failed to admit the obvious: that until June 1944 its military role was very minor and, even after June 1944, it could win only under four conditions. These condition were that the German army had been largely decimated after three years of fighting in the East, the bulk of German forces were still being drawn off in the East in the last year, the Allies had overwhelming air and naval superiority, and the United States' Western allies would provide a force not far inferior to that of the United States in the West. By V-E Day, the United States would account for little more than 20 percent of the forces facing the Germans. And, with a low teeth-to-tail ratio, the quality of even this force would at times be in question.

The problem with failure to acknowledge the great limits to U.S. military capabilities in World War II was that it encouraged the United States to resort to its military in inappropriate settings in the postwar years. The frequent use of the military in the postwar era, and especially in Korea and Vietnam, flowed in part from this belief in U.S. power. The resultant frustrations and failures, especially when there were no other powerful countries to take the burden of the land fighting, would become a significant aspect of the postwar era.

The Soviet Union earned its great power status through a tremendous military performance. At the same time, this would lead to serious problems in the postwar era. Lacking the economic and political influence and capabilities of the United States, the Soviet Union would be hard pressed to maintain its status except through an ever-growing arsenal of weapons. But this military edge would have only limited applicability in peacetime, give the Soviet Union a militarist image among its neighbors, and retard development of the Soviet economy. The lack of good political and economic ties in Eastern Europe would leave the Soviet Union few alternatives but to resort to military force (as in 1953, 1956, 1968) or call in local secret police troops (in 1981 in Poland) when it felt its interests threatened. And with only sales of military weapons as its primary method of influence in the Third World, the Soviet Union inevitably would lag far behind the United States which had more powerful economic and political levers.

The United States, playing more of a supporting role, emerged from the war as the world's dominant economic and political power, with unquestioned high-technology superiority over the Soviet Union. Its more limited war effort also left the United States far better able to dominate the postwar era than the Soviet Union, with a shattered economy and polity.

ORIGINS OF THE COLD WAR

In the often heated debate on the origins of the Cold War, all sides to the ongoing controversy have usually downplayed military factors in favor of economic and diplomatic factors as explanatory variables. Equally interesting have been the often questionable military assumptions put forth by members of all three major feuding factions in the debate. The orthodox camp, in placing the basic blame for the Cold War on the Soviet Union, has portrayed vast Soviet military power and a weaker United States. Traditionally they have seen the Red Army as threatening to overrun Western Europe and lunge for the Atlantic. The revisionist camp, in mirror imaging, has placed the blame for the Cold War mainly on the United States. They inevitably have stressed the enormous U.S. military power, and especially the atomic bomb, relative to the weaker Soviet Union. Finally, the newer post-revisionist generation, while placing blame (or, more accurately, arguing that blame is irrelevant) on both sides, has tended to emphasize the greater military power of the United States.[5]

The two main military images of the three camps are only partially correct, reflecting only one aspect of the complex military reality of 1945. That this is so is hardly surprising. Not one of the major participants in the debate in any of the three camps is either a military historian or a political scientist with a strong interest in wars and armies. Very few of the participants in the debate are Soviet specialists. Beyond this, the reality of the military events of the war, as we have seen in this book, are complex and not easy to capture simply.[6]

Orthodox Camp

The view of the orthodox camp, that of a powerful Red Army ready to march to the Atlantic against weak Western defenses, is profoundly wrong. The one part of the reality that it does accurately capture is the superior land power of the Red Army to the Western armies during and after World War II and the Soviet geographic advantage of propinquity to Europe compared to the United States. In all other aspects it is deeply flawed. The Red Army could claim the greatest share of honor in destroying the Third Reich in World War II. While the United States suffered less than 300,000 military fatalities on both fronts in World War II, the Soviet Union suffered an astounding 7 million military fatalities, *plus* another 5.5 million soldiers taken prisoner by the German army. The bulk of German land power was destroyed in the East. By 1945 the Red Army had liberated all of Eastern Europe and taken Berlin, symbolic of its arrival as a powerful land army, the best in Europe. The great power of the Red Army, even if somewhat primitive, and the control of Eastern Europe and part of Germany thrust Soviet power right into the center of Europe. This, then, was the basis of the Soviet claim to superpower status, albeit of the second order, in the postwar era.

This in no way signified that the Red Army was ready to march on Western Europe, even though an impressed West was unwilling to risk this possibility. The Red Army was profoundly exhausted by the end of the war. No other army in history has ever suffered such staggering casualties. The last year of the war used up all its energies and cost the army over 1 million soldiers dead in the liberation of Eastern Europe, Belorussia, and the Baltics. In the final months of the war alone, in the drive from the Oder to Berlin, the Red Army lost more men than either the U.S. army or the British army lost in Europe in the entire war. Equipment losses were equally staggering. Discipline declined sharply with over 100,000 Red Army deserters in Eastern Europe alone. By V-E Day the Soviet Union was "exhausted . . . her huge armies were in a poor condition for fighting another war."[7]

After the war the Red Army faced other problems. The great bulk of the soldiers, who had survived such enormous carnage to finally seize Berlin, had but one thought: to go home. Fighting another war was the last thing on their minds. The Red Army also suffered from a serious shortage of mechanized transport, now that the Lend Lease pipeline had been shut down. This severely restricted the power projection capabilities of the Soviet Union in the West given the massive destruction of Soviet rail systems, industry, and communications west of the Urals.[8]

The desperate tiredness of the Red Army, the economic dictates of reconstruction, and the removal of any serious land threats to the Soviet Union from Japan and Germany pushed Stalin to massively demobilize the Red Army from 11.3 million men in 1945 to 2.8 million men in 1948. While still a large force, this demobilization of 75 percent of the manpower of the Red Army was hardly a sign of an aggressive Soviet posture, especially when the Red Army had enhanced responsibilities in Eastern Europe.[9]

Even more important, the Soviet land advantage in Europe was more than offset in this period by the U.S. possession of the atomic bomb, U.S. dominance of the air and sea, and U.S. allies in Europe. In 1945 the United States had the world's largest air force, with 15,000 long-range fighters and bombers, and largest navy, replete with 1,200 warships. From a strictly military view the United States could deal devastating conventional blows (not until the late 1940s would the bombers be equipped with atomic bombs) to the Soviet Union while the Soviet Union lacked any effective means of retaliation.[10]

The orthodox view also ignored the even more basic political and economic realities. Economically, the Soviet Union had been devastated by tremendous war losses that left 20 million people dead, 25 million people homeless, and 1,700 cities in ruins. European Soviet Union was a shambles and dire poverty was widespread. The Germans had destroyed between 25 percent–30 percent of the Soviet GNP before 1941. To rebuild all that had been lost would cost 8–10 years earnings of the 1945 labor force, or almost two five-year plans.[11]

By contrast, the U.S. economy in 1945 towered over a war shattered world. That year the United States produced nearly 50 percent of the world's GNP. In its vaults the United States held the majority of the world's gold and metals. The bulk of oil and coal in the world was produced in the United States, which owned the majority of all merchant ships in the world. The United States was the economic engine of the world, and especially the Western world. The remaining Western powers, including its only Western rival, Great Britain, would inevitably be heavily dependent on the United States for years for economic reconstruction from the enormous ravages of war. They all looked to the United States, and not to the socialist Soviet Union, to lead the postwar era.[12]

This gap would not soon close, given the slowness of the initial European recovery. This is not so surprising if one remembers that in June 1945 there were 30 million "displaced persons" in Europe including 11 million Germans expelled from the East. By 1950 the gold holdings of the United States (22.8 billion dollars) would be more than four times greater than that of France, Germany, Italy, and England combined (5.0 billion dollars). The U.S. GNP, having nearly doubled since 1938, was three times the size of the four major European powers combined.[13]

These statistics made dreary reading for Soviet leaders. In 1945 and 1950 the Soviet Union might well be the world's number two economic power (largely by default) but the distance separating it from the United States was a chasm. In 1945 the U.S. GNP was 4 times the Soviet GNP, in 1950 3 times. If the United States' Western European allies were added in, the Western economies were almost 6 times larger than the Soviet economy in 1945. While the U.S. GNP had almost doubled by 1945, the Soviet GNP had shrunk by 20 percent under the impact of the war. Soviet war losses consumed an enormous 20–25 percent of the capital assets and perhaps 30 percent of the GNP. As a result of this devastation of the Soviet economy and great expansion of the U.S. economy, U.S. tangible assets in 1945 were conservatively 10 times those of the Soviet Union.[14]

Politically, there was equally no contest. The United States emerged from the war as the unquestioned political leader of the Western allies. All of the world's other significant powers— Great Britain, France, West Germany (when it emerged as a state by 1950), Canada, Italy, and Japan (when it emerged from U.S. occupation)—would be aligned with the United States. In the late 1940s, by contrast, not one other major power sided with Moscow, and none would until the proclamation of the People's Republic of China in 1949. Weak, backward Eastern Europe, largely hostile to the Soviet Union, would be more of a burden (except in providing a buffer zone with the West) than an asset.[15]

The Kremlin leaders, on the other hand, faced serious internal political problems before they could even turn to the outside world. The tight controls of the Stalinist system had been severely disrupted by the war. Over 60 million Soviets had lived for several years under German control—and some had actively collaborated with the Nazis while many others had passively acquiesced to their rule. Another 7 million Red Army soldiers had marched into Eastern Europe and East Germany where, even in shambles, Eastern Europe had presented an alternative life-style to the soldiers. The vision of the Decembrists, who had led a revolt against Tsarism in 1825, was ever on Stalin's mind. Several million former slave laborers in the Third Reich had to be repatriated. The collective farmers had to be reminded that promises of a new and better life after the war were, unfortunately, not going to be honored. There were, as well, to be serious problems in the reintegration of an alien Baltics within the Soviet Union and great difficulties in the incorporation of an alien Eastern Europe into the Soviet sphere in the postwar years. Before the Soviet Union could ever turn confidently outwardly, there were enormous problems at home that would take many years to resolve.

Washington failed to see that Moscow, while having made significant gains as a result of the war was fatally flawed in the postwar era. What Moscow really needed was time—time to heal its massive human and economic losses, time to reintegrate the Soviet polity, time to absorb its new territorial gains, time to find its way in a new world order. No one appreciated the great U.S. power superiority over the Soviet Union better than Stalin. From a correlation of forces viewpoint, so beloved in the Kremlin, Washington enjoyed an enormous political and economic edge and significant military edge in all areas except land forces.

Revisionist and Postrevisionist Camps

The failure of the orthodox camp to understand the military reality of 1945, however, does *not* imply that the revisionist and postrevisionist camps have done any better. Their image of great U.S. military power also only reflects a limited part of the military reality of 1945. When William Appleman Williams, for example, spoke of "American omnipotence" and the United States as "confident in its vast economic and military superiority over Russia," he was only partially right.[16] The United States was economically dominant and militarily had air and naval superiority and the atomic bomb monopoly. But this view ignores a number of important aspects of the military history of World War II and its aftermath. As the war had so graphically demonstrated, the air and naval power of the United States had only limited applicability to power projection in Europe. Even in the last year of the war the Red Army, with a weak air force and even more pathetic navy, had still outperformed the U.S. army in the destruction of Nazi Germany. U.S. land power remained weak and unimpressive throughout the war, especially compared to Soviet land power. The U.S. monopoly of the atomic bomb was certainly significant but of limited value at this time. The United States had only two atomic weapons in August 1945, a very low rate of production that would not change for several years, and bombers not yet equipped to carry the new weapon.[17]

There were other military and political realities that further vitiate the perception of the revisionist and postrevisionist camps. The United States, by massively demobilizing its own armed forces in a manner akin to the Soviet Union, would rapidly destroy much of its limited power projection capabilities in Europe by 1948. The 12-million-man U.S. military of 1945 would shrink to a mere 1.5 million men by 1947. The military budget would collapse from 82.8 billion dollars in 1944 to only 15.5 billion dollars in 1948. This was the sole politically and economically feasible course open to the U.S. leaders at this time. In the wake of the protracted struggle of the war years there was minimal support for any confrontation against the former U.S. ally in Europe. Public clamor, troop protests and troop strikes hastened this process. By April 1948 the U.S. Congress would even reject a proposal to institute universal military training.[18]

Under these conditions the United States in the late 1940s was unable to pose an overwhelming military threat to the Soviet Union to match its awesome economic strength. It is also indicative of the true nature of the U.S. military in this period that its greatest problems were not the Soviet Union but rather a war-weary public demanding rapid demobilization of the armed forces and a military structure that needed rationalization and unification in the face of intense interservice rivalries.[19]

SOVIET-U.S. RELATIONS:
INTERACTION OR COACTION?

Perceptual problems were also very serious between the two sides. The two powers tended to see themselves as exemplars of a new world order, one far more progressive and modern than the old system. The United States passionately wanted to create a new liberal international capitalist order while the Soviet Union strongly wanted to create a new socialist international order. In each vision, they naturally put themselves at the center, seeing Washington and Moscow as the natural foci of the new order. Both countries were intensely nationalistic and chauvinistic, viewing the outside world as one of little interest to their welfare.

The level of contact between the two sides had been limited and often misleading. Washington had not even recognized the new government in Moscow for sixteen years, until 1933, and even then, relations had been generally cool. The level of knowledge of the other side was poor and often misinterpreted due to profound ideological differences. And the historical experiences of the two countries had been radically different, creating different national perspectives. The great U.S. experience had been colored by the feeling of exuberant power expanding outward against weak neighbors and by having no strong enemies. The predominant Soviet experience had been that of expansion in the East but, in less than two centuries, four major invasions from the West, conducted by the Swedes, French, and Germans.

There was almost no intersection between the two powers. Where the United States was strong economically and politically, the Soviet Union was strong militarily. Where U.S. military power was based on the navy and air force, Soviet military power was based on the army. Where U.S. power was worldwide, Soviet power was almost solely based on the Eurasian continent. Where the U.S. view, as befitting its war experience, was expansive and optimistic, the Soviet view, as reflecting its 20 million deaths in the war, was somber and defensive. Where the U.S. political system was liberal, democratic, and capitalist, the Soviet political system was authoritarian and socialist. Surely the Cold War was not inevitable—but some form of deep clash between two such radically different countries seems almost inevitable.

U.S. Perspective

The U.S. perception of the Soviet Union was hampered by several factors. First, the Soviet Union had been viewed as relatively unimportant before 1945. There were very few Soviet specialists, and no Soviet institutes, to add to the meager storehouse of knowledge. Second, the U.S. view of Moscow was very negative, influenced by the Soviet refusal to pay Tsarist war debts, Stalin's dictatorship, the Great Purges, and, later, the Soviet invasion of Finland. Third, the autarchical nature of the Soviet economy and the minimal Soviet participation in international trade aroused the deepest suspicions of the U.S. proponents of a new, free-trade-dominated international order. Finally, the small size of the U.S. government, even after the expansion of the New Deal and war years, limited the United States' ability to deal with the world. The U.S. view of the Soviet Union, then, was largely colored by the World War II experience, first of the nearly two years of Soviet–German collaboration and then the nearly four years of difficult Soviet–U.S. cooperation against Germany.[20]

The United States, despite Soviet and radical assertions to the contrary, was far from being a militantly expansionist power after the war. Rather, after 1945 the United States would dismantle the bulk of its great military might and by the late 1940s be again relatively weak and ineffective as a land power. This is hardly the course a powerful and expansive United States would have chosen against a weak and rebuilding Soviet Union. Ironically, the Soviet Union, due largely to its war record, would make many of its greatest gains in Eastern Europe at precisely the time of the greatest U.S. superiority over the Soviet Union in all areas of power indices.

The U.S. view of a powerful Soviet threat to a weakened Western Europe was very unrealistic and based solely on a worst-case-scenario. The last thing that Stalin needed after four years of war and destruction was more war and destruction—especially against a power with overwhelming air and sea power and sole possession of the atomic bomb. Americans also largely ignored the fact that, while they had choices in World War II, the Soviets had to fight the Germans. Why, then, should the Americans have expected Stalin to voluntarily choose another war?

Washington felt unable to grant Moscow what it wanted. It was unprepared to acknowledge the great Soviet role in the victory, seeing this as a denigration of its own role. To agree to confer great power status on the Soviet Union meant that the new political order would have, as its number-two member, a hostile and alien socialist country, run by a vicious dictator. To grant major aid to the Soviet Union would also serve to strengthen a regime seemingly destined to be the United States' main rival in the postwar era.

To grant the Soviet Union control over Eastern Europe, the main Soviet desire, would seriously interfere with U.S. efforts to create a new international order, aimed at the elimination of all Western colonies, special economic zones (as the sterling bloc), and spheres of influence. The closed nature of the Soviet economy and polity meant that Eastern Europe would now be lost to the new order. The Soviet moves into Eastern Europe during the war and the relatively harsh measures adopted in certain countries, such as Romania, aroused the deepest anxieties in U.S. leaders who were fearful of repeating the appeasement that had been so costly in the late 1930s. The United States, then, found it almost impossible to respond to the major Soviet desiderata of the postwar era.

The United States was viewing the world in fundamentally political and economic terms rather than military terms. This was a logical result of the far greater U.S. economic and political power than military power. And it also reflected a basic assessment that traditional U.S. military assets would suffice to handle any developing threats to peace. The United States also tended to believe, in an interesting form of Manchester liberalism, that economics heavily underlay politics. The closed economic blocs of the pre-World War II era had promoted economic rivalry that had led to war. Only by creating a new international economic order, with institutions to stabilize currencies, promote trade, and ease economic crises, could wars be averted.

In this world view, England, with its sterling bloc that controlled one-third of world trade before the war, was a greater threat to the United States than the Soviet Union. Fortunately for the United States, English power had been largely destroyed by the war and England could now be incorporated into the new order. The Soviet threat was more long term, since Moscow had been an extremely marginal participant in the international economic order before 1939. And with the immense war damage inflicted by the Germans on an already overburdened economy, the United States could believe that the Soviet Union would have no choice but to come to terms with the United States to gain the economic aid it so badly needed for rebuilding.[21]

Soviet Perspective

The Soviet view, based heavily on its war experience, was very different. It rivaled the U.S. view only in its degree of unrealism about the other budding superpower. Stalin, even near the end of World War II, still viewed England, and not the United States, as the Soviet Union's main rival. The level of Soviet knowledge of the United States was very weak. The Marxist filter made it difficult for Moscow to view the United States as anything other than a greedy, rapacious, imperialist capitalist state, eagerly vying with England for dominance in the capitalist world.

This negative view was certainly reinforced by the U.S. delay in opening a second main front in Europe until 1944. From the Soviet view, it seemed inconceivable that such a powerful economic force and huge country as the United States would not be able to field a significant force in Europe until almost five years after the beginning of the war. The only possible U.S. goal, from the Soviet viewpoint, was to completely exhaust and destroy the Red Army and Soviet economic resources in the struggle against fascism so that the United States could dominate the new postwar era.

The Soviet leaders had no grasp on the true nature of the U.S. political system. The Stalinist leadership, with its fixation on England, was almost bereft of U.S. experts. They failed to understand that the United States was truly run by the visible democratic electoral system, rather than a mysterious power elite. The Soviet leaders did not comprehend that the 1946 and 1948 congressional elections and the 1948 presidential election would, given the powerful public passion for normalcy after wartime restrictions, seriously restrict any possible elite desire to confront the Soviet Union. They failed to perceive that the massive demobilization of the armed forces would be a necessity, reinforced by economic and political considerations. And they never understood how their own tough actions would reinforce negative views of the Soviet Union that would further promote the deterioration of relations.

What Moscow hoped for from the West, but doubted it would ever obtain, were four things—major economic aid to overcome its enormous wartime losses, recognition of its powerful role in the wartime victory, acknowledgment of its great power status, and confirmation of its legitimate role in control of Eastern Europe. From the Soviet perspective all seemed perfectly reasonable. Did it not deserve U.S. aid in view of the fact that the Soviet Union had lost 20 million dead and the United States 300,000 dead in defeating Nazi Germany? Had it not earned recognition for its role in the war when for over 1,000 days, from June 1941 until June 1944, it, and it alone, had borne the brunt of the Nazi onslaught in the East while the United States engaged in small-scale operations on the periphery, in North Africa, Sicily, and Italy? Was the Soviet Union not now a great power, worthy of respect, as it divided the European continent, traditionally the center of international politics, between itself and the United States? After two German invasions of the Soviet Union and Tsarist Russia in the last thirty years, did it not deserve to control Eastern Europe (as the United States controlled Latin America) to prevent any further invasions? Did not the blood of over 1 million Soviet soldiers killed in the liberation of Eastern Europe (600,000 deaths in Poland alone) from Nazi tyranny alone consecrate the soil of Eastern Europe and earn Moscow the right to control the region? These, then, were the Soviet perspectives of the late 1940s.

Quite simply, the two nascent superpowers, hampered by strong perceptual difficulties in understanding the other side and restrained by serious substantive disagreements of policy issues, lumbered toward a Cold War that neither really desired.

LESSONS OF WORLD WAR II

The lessons of World War II are important and manifold, worthy of a separate volume in themselves.[22] There is little doubt that World War II had an even greater impact on the Soviet Union than on the United States. The cataclysmic events of World War II on the Eastern front—20 million dead, 25 million homeless, 1,700 towns destroyed, German occupation of territory on which 80 million Soviets lived before the war—numbed the Soviet mind and psyche. And yet from this endless horror and barbarism, from the overwhelming defeats of 1941 and 1942, there emerged great triumph and ultimate victory with the red flag hanging over the Reichstag in Berlin in 1945.

The Soviet experience in World War II was a tremendous, even overpowering, event of world historical importance. Much like the Holocaust (with which it overlapped) for the Jewish people, the victories of the German army early in the war seemed to call into question the very existence of the Soviet state or even the Soviet people. The survival and ultimate triumph of the Red Army after those horrifying early defeats and mass genocide practiced by the Germans made the war a formative event of deep emotional and substantive impact. The war is still very much with the Soviet people and its leaders. As Mohammed Heykal wrote in his recollections of the Nasser era in Egypt,

> Egyptian President Gamal Abdel Nasser once advised Third World leaders headed for Moscow to get themselves briefed about the details of World War II. "You must resign yourself to hearing over and over again about the experiences of your interlocutors in the Great Patriotic War." The Soviet leadership tries to do its best not only to keep that memory fresh but to shade martial reminiscences into contemplation of another conflict.[23]

There were many important legacies of this deeply traumatic experience but none more significant than the legitimizing of the regime. While the October Revolution and ensuing civil war divided the Soviet people and created a generation gap, the war effort unified them in a vast and ultimately sacred struggle for existence and final victory over the German barbarians. The massive contest and suffering touched and scarred almost every family. The great war victories legitimized the regime and unified the people around the Stalinist leadership. It showed the strength of the Soviet system of government and the powerful force of Soviet, and Russian, nationalism.

The war experience further validated the economic and administrative structures and the party itself, as well as the great transformation of Soviet society in the 1930s. The war generation found in it new sources of authority and values. Indeed, the postwar elite that ruled the Soviet Union for the next four decades after 1945 was heavily influenced by the war experiences, as was the general population.[24]

Despite changes in technology, domestic leadership and capabilities, and international politics, World War II has had an enduring impact on Soviet politics in general and the Soviet military in particular. The war literally transformed the Red Army, ousting the Horse Marshals and creating a new officer corps that predominated in the army until the 1980s. The heroes of the great victories from Moscow and Stalingrad to Kursk-Orel and Berlin would predominate in the army for decades. In this context the rebuilding of the army after the massive demobilization of the early postwar years would create an army profoundly influenced by the war experiences.

Despite Khrushchev's objections and the advent of the nuclear era, the war would promote a continuing major role for the ground forces, who had been so important in the attainment of final victory. The successful labor-intensive strategy of World War II ensured this result. In the postwar era of smaller, more mobile armies, the Soviet Union would retain a large, mass army with over 180 divisions, backed up by a large reserve force. It would maintain its belief in the efficacy of a huge quantity of material as well as men, with an enormous force of over 50,000 tanks, more than six times the number in the U.S. inventory.[25]

The war also deeply influenced military thought. Soviet military history remained mesmerized for the next four decades by the events of the war, which provided much of the raw data for Soviet military science. The military lessons of the war included a stress on the importance of surprise and preemption, blitzkrieg offensive warfare, and a strong, well-prepared defense. As Nathan Leites wrote in a chapter on "The Soviet Style of War,"

> The "lessons" of that war have since dominated Russian military writings and exercises. Today, comparisons are being drawn in the West between the German offensives of World War II and current Soviet capacities to "astonish" NATO. (Indeed, a newly confident and modernized Soviet military returning to German-style armored tactics that they had tried but were unable to adopt successfully in the past) . . . the Soviets believe there is much to learn from World War II. As the literature describes, modern decisions regarding training, deployment and an array of combat procedures are legitimized in the Soviet style of war because of their proven success in the battlefields four decades ago.[26]

The political legacy of the war was also substantial. For the bulk of party leaders into the 1980s—and most notably for Khrushchev and Brezhnev—the war was a central, formative experience and influence on their thinking. The huge war losses, enormous economic expense, and grave difficulties in achieving final victory would promote a conservative, calculated strategy in crisis situations. In numerous postwar crises, from Berlin and Yugoslavia in 1948 to the recurrent Middle East wars the Soviet Union would be extremely reluctant to use force. Only one time in the more than four decades since the end of the war would the Soviet Union be willing to use force outside the Warsaw Pact—and that was in Afghanistan in 1979, in a neighboring country with a long border with the Soviet Union that had traditionally been in the Soviet sphere of influence.[27]

The retention of Eastern Europe, purchased at the price of over 1 million soldiers' lives in the last year of the war, would become a very high Soviet priority. The near fatal consequences of allowing Nazi Germany to use Eastern Europe as an invasion corridor into the Soviet Union are not forgotten by Soviet decision makers. Neither is the fact that control of Eastern Europe has been important to the rise of the Soviet Union as a superpower. Here, unlike in the world in general, the Soviet Union has been willing to use force when necessary, as in Berlin in 1953, Hungary in 1956, and Czechoslovakia in 1968. However, even here, the conservative calculus of decision making has repeatedly searched for alternative solutions, as were found in Poland in 1956 and 1981.[28]

The enormous cost of the war would generate a strong Soviet desire to avoid any direct confrontation with the United States in the postwar era. This also reflected Moscow's awareness of how strongly the correlation of forces favored the West. As a consequence, one striking feature of the last forty-three years is that the conflict has always remained cold and never hot. Peace has remained an extremely high Soviet priority, given the extraordinarily wasteful and costly nature of war. The enormous economic cost of World War II was not only reflected in the huge immediate losses but in the long-run reduction of the system's capability to increase the labor force.

The war, by revealing the devastating consequences of military weakness, indelibly fixed in the minds of Soviet leaders the need for high investment in military spending and, if necessary, military overinsurance to protect a vulnerable country with long borders. Once the Stalin era was over, the impressive security imperatives would create a strong claim for a significant military role in Soviet politics. And its great role in the final triumph would ensure the Soviet military men the legitimacy to play a significant role in Soviet politics.

United States Lessons

As for the United States, the victories in World War II seemed to similarly vindicate its military system as well. The predominant emphasis on air and naval power would continue in the postwar era, highlighted by the creation of an independent air force in 1947. Only in Korea and Vietnam would the limits of air and naval power finally be revealed, as they already should have been in World War II.

Even by the 1980s the U.S. Army would remain weak and small, fielding but 16 divisions and perhaps 6,000 tanks. Not only is this vastly smaller than the Soviet army, but it is barely twice the size of any of five Middle Eastern armies, typically containing 400,000–800,000 men under arms and 3,000- 4,000 tanks. The weak performance of the U.S. army in Korea and Vietnam would merely continue a pattern already highly evident in World War II.[29] A great deal of U.S. military thinking remains quite influenced by the World War II experience. In the words of one author,

> Present-day U.S. military doctrine represents no more of a fundamental departure from the habits and practices of most (but not all) U.S. generals and armies during World War II than does the Soviet variety. . . . Today, while it is official U.S. policy to affirm that our forces are underequipped and outnumbered in the face of Soviet hordes, it is also official policy to fight as if the same aims and practices that led to victory in 1944–45 after a long drawn-out campaign still applied today.[30]

The great victory in World War II validated the U.S. style of war. Despite all the problems and inadequacies (which Americans were bound to forget in the flush of victory), the U.S. system had worked. The capital-intensive strategy produced great victory with minimum casualties and a popular war. The stress on high-technology warfare, on firepower and mechanical power, on achievement of victory by decisive offensive operations would be greatly reinforced by the events of the war. An expanded government, to which the U.S. citizens now looked for many more functions than before the war, would continue to expand in the postwar era.

The political legacy of the war on the United States was sharply different, as was the war experience. The United States had a "good war," reaping enormous political and economic gains at the cost of minimal casualties. Far from being the extremely sobering and restraining experience it was for the Soviets, World

War II was a heady experience promoting U.S. activism and even adventurism in the postwar world. For an isolationist nation to be thrust into a position of world dominance was an extraordinary experience. It is little wonder that the United States has been far more capable and willing to use military force in the postwar era in remote areas of the world (Korea, Vietnam) than the Soviet Union, which has confined itself to its borders. Only slowly and reluctantly has the United States learned the lesson that World War II was a unique experience, in which Soviet and British arms played a powerful role in enabling the United States to pick the fruits of victory.

To paraphrase General Douglas MacArthur, the world indeed has turned over many times since the Soviet and U.S. armies met on the Elbe in May 1945. The passage of time and evolution of the Cold War has dimmed our memories of what actually happened in that greatest military struggle in world history. But during and immediately after the war many Western leaders, in public and in private, were free to acknowledge what is rarely admitted today: that the Red Army played a powerful, even predominant, role in the destruction of the Wehrmacht. In December 1944, that fiery French patriot, General Charles de Gaulle, declared that "the French know what the Soviet Union has done for them and know that precisely Soviet Russia played the main role in their liberation."[31] Among the Americans, General George Marshall put the matter most directly in his report to the secretary of war in September 1945,

> The significance of these facts should be carefully considered. Even with two-thirds of the German Army engaged by Russia, it took every man the nation saw fit to mobilize to do our part of the job in Europe and at the same time keep the Japanese enemy under control in the Pacific. What would have been the result had the Red Army been defeated and the British Islands invaded, we can only guess. The possibility is rather terrifying.[32]

Only if we can rediscover what many conservative Western leaders well knew in 1945—the central role of the Red Army in victory in Europe, the great progress made by the Soviet regime over the weak and decaying Tsarist Russia, the difficulties experienced by the United States in translating its economic might into military power, the emergence of the United States as the one true superpower in 1945—can we truly understand and appreciate the origins and development of the postwar era.

NOTES

1. For a first-rate overview of recent military history, see Torbjorn Knutsen, "Old, Unhappy, Far-Off Things: The New Military History of Europe," *Journal of Peace Research*, Vol.24, No.1 (1987), pp.87–98. In this article he reviews recent works of "New Military History," such as those by Andre Corvisier, John Hale, and Geoffrey Best, which go beyond narration of events to analysis of the social and institutional context of warfare.

2. For the treatment of the nexus of war and politics, see Skocpol, *States*.

3. There is little question in the literature in the field of comparative revolutions of the strong connection between revolutions and greatly enhanced state power. Revolutions, including the Russian Revolution, have forged much stronger state institutions and incorporated the masses far more effectively into politics than the ancien regimes. Samuel Huntington has noted that the Russian Revolution, avoiding military dictatorship or monarchist restoration, "instead produced an entirely new system of party supremacy, 'democratic centralism,' and ideological legitimation which effectively consolidated and institutionalized the concentration of power and expansion of power produced by the revolution." See Huntington's classic, *Political Order*, p.314 and also Skocpol's *States*, p.161.

4. For interesting work on armies and societies see the journal *Armed Forces and Society*.

5. The Cold War has produced a huge body of work. For a classic orthodox view, see Spanier, *American*. For standard revisionist works, see Kolko, *Politics* and Williams, *Tragedy*. For the post-revisionist work see Pollard, *Economic*.

6. There is, as John Gaddis has observed, a great asymmetry in the documents available on the two sides that may influence the specialists as well. There is a vast treasure of U.S. documents and very few Soviet documents. See Gaddis, *United*.

7. See Vigor, *Soviet*, p.204.

8. *Ibid*.

9. See the dissertation by Cristann Gibson, "Patterns of Demobilization: The Soviet and American Cases," University of Denver, 1983.

10. Paterson, *Soviet–American*. p.8.

11. For an excellent view of the state of the Soviet Union in 1945 see Linz, editor, *Impact*.

12. Michel, *Second*, p.819.

13. Pollard, *Peaceful*, p.312; and Mueller, *Statistical Handbook*, pp.70, 232.

14. Nutter, *Growth*, p.215; Maddison, *Economic*, p.155; and Millar, *ABCs*, p.50.

15. The contrast between the prosperous Western Europe in the U.S.

orbit and the impoverished Eastern Europe in the Soviet orbit was overwhelming. As Derek Aldcroft has written, "In short, therefore, down to 1939 Eastern Europe remained a backward and predominantly agrarian based region. . . . It was potentially a rich region stocked with a poor people in which the maldistribution of poverty was the central feature." See Aldcroft, *European*, p.116.

16. See Williams, *Tragedy*, chapter 6.

17. Divine, editor, *Causes*, p.323.

18. See Paterson, *Soviet–American*, p.8; Kolko, *Limits*, p.480; and Bergson and Heymann, *Soviet*, p.99.

19. Kolko, *Limits*, p.91.

20. For an overall view, see Taubman, *Stalin's*.

21. Gaddis, *United*, pp.174–175; and Pollard, *Economic*.

22. See the forthcoming volume by Jonathan R. Adelman and Cristann Gibson, editors, *Past Imperative: The Lessons of World War II and Contemporary Soviet Military Affairs* (Winchester, Massachusetts : Allen and Unwin, 1988).

23. Heykal, *Sphinx*, p.27.

24. See the fine study by Harrison, *Soviet*, pp.x, 223. Also see Linz, editor, *Impact*, p.286.

25. See Jones' fine study, *Red*, p.217.

26. Leites, "Soviet Style of War," in Leebaert, editor, *Soviet*, p.219.

27. For more detailed consideration of this topic, see forthcoming works emanating from the study on superpower intervention in the postwar era being conducted by the author and his colleagues at the Graduate School of International Studies at the University of Denver in a two-year study supported by the Ford Foundation and Pew Charitable Trust.

28. See Adelman, editor, *Superpowers*.

29. Kolko, *Limits*, pp.92–93.

30. See Cockburn, *Threat*, p.182.

31. Harriman and Abel, *Special*, p.569.

32. *War Reports*, p.274.

Bibliography

This bibliography is not intended to be comprehensive but rather to serve as a guide to books in the field that were useful in the preparation of this work.

Adams, Arthur, *Imperial Russia After 1861* (Boston: D.C. Heath, 1965)

Adelman, Jonathan R., *The Revolutionary Armies* (Westport, Connecticut: Greenwood Press, 1980)

————, editor, *Communist Armies in Politics* (Boulder, Colorado: Westview Press, 1982)

————, *Revolution, Armies and War* (Boulder, Colorado: Lynne Rienner Publishers, 1985)

————, editor, *Superpowers and Revolution* (New York: Praeger, 1986)

Albrecht-Carrie, Rene, *The Meaning of the First World War* (Englewood Cliffs, New Jersey: Prentice-Hall, 1965)

Aldcroft, Derek, *The European Economy 1914–1970* (New York: St. Martin's Press, 1978)

Alperowitz, Gar, *Atomic Diplomacy: Hiroshima and Potsdam* (New York: Penguin, 1985)

Amann, Ronald, Julian Cooper, and R. W. Davies, editors, *The Technological Level of Soviet Industry,* (New Haven: Yale University Press, 1977)

Ambrose, Stephen, *Eisenhower and Berlin, 1945* (New York: W. W. Norton,1967)

————, *The Supreme Commander: The War Years of General Dwight D. Eisenhower* (Garden City, New York: Doubleday and Company, 1969)

Avrich, Paul, *Kronstadt 1921* (Princeton: Princeton University Press, 1970)

Bailes, Kendall, *Technology and Society Under Lenin and Stalin* (Princeton: Princeton University Press, 1978)

Balfour, Michael, *The Adversaries: America, Russia and the Open World 1941–62* (London: Routledge and Kegan Paul, 1981)

Barrett, Correlli, *The Swordbearers: Supreme Command in the First World War* (New York: William Morrow, 1964)

Baruch, Bernard, *The Public Years* (New York: Holt Rinehart and Winston, 1960)

Baylis, John and Gerald Segal, editors, *Soviet Strategy* (London: Croom Helm, 1981)

Beaver, Daniel, *Newton D. Baker and the American War Effort 1917–1919* (Lincoln: University of Nebraska Press, 1966)

Belchem, Major General David, *Victory in Normandy* (London: Chatto and Windus, 1981)

Bennett, Ralph, *Ultra in the West—The Normandy Campaign 1944–45* (London: Hutchinson, 1980)

Bergson, Abram, *Productivity and the Social System—The USSR and the West* (Cambridge: Harvard University Press, 1978)

———— and Hans Heymann, Jr., *Soviet National Income and Product 1940–48* (New York: Columbia University Press, 1954)

———— and Simon Kuznets, editors, *Economic Trends in the Soviet Union* (Cambridge: Harvard University Press, 1963)

Bialer, Seweryn, editor, *Stalin and His Generals* (London: Souvenir Press, 1970)

————, *Stalin's Successors* (Cambridge: Cambridge University Press, 1979)

Blackwell, William, editor, *Russian Economic Development From Peter the Great to Stalin* (New York: New Viewpoints, 1974)

Blond, Georges, *The Death of Hitler's Germany*, translated by Frances Frenaye, (New York: Pyramid Books, 1962)

Blum, John, *V Was for Victory: Politics and American Culture During World War II* (New York: Harcourt, Brace, Jovanovich, 1976)

Blumenson, Martin, *Mark Clark* (New York: Congden and Weed, 1984)

————, *The Patton Papers 1940–1945* (Boston: Houghton Mifflin, 1974)

Bradley, Omar, *A General's Life* (New York: Simon and Schuster, 1984)

————, *A Soldier's Story* (New York: Henry Holt and Company, 1951)

Brereton, Lewis, *The Brereton Diaries* (New York: William Morrow Company, 1946)

Breuer, William, *Storming Hitler's Rhine* (New York: St. Martin's Press, 1985)

Brook-Shepherd, Gordon, *November 1918: The Last Act of the Great War* (London: William Collins, 1981)

Brown, A. J. *Applied Economics: Aspects of the World Economy in War and Peace* (London: George Allen and Unwin, 1947)

Bruce, George, *Second Front Now! The Road to D Day* (London: Macdonald and Jane, 1979)

Bryant, Arthur, *Triumph in the West* (Garden City, New York: Doubleday and Company, 1959)

Brzezinski, Zbigniew and Samuel Huntington, *Political Power: U.S.A/U.S.S.R.* (New York: Viking Press, 1964)

Buchanan, A. Russell, *The United States and World War II*, Vol.II (New York: Harper and Row, 1964)

Butcher, Captain Harry, *My Three Years With Eisenhower* (New York: Simon and Schuster, 1946)

Carell, Paul, *Scorched Earth—The Russo-German War, 1943–1944,* translated by Ewald Osers (Boston: Little Brown, 1966)

Carr, E. H., *The October Revolution: Before and After* (New York: Vintage Books, 1971)

Chandler, Afred, Jr., editor, *The Papers of Dwight David Eisenhower: The War Years: III–IV* (Baltimore and London: Johns Hopkins Press, 1970)

Chorley, Katharine, *Armies and the Art of Revolution* (London: Faber and Faber, 1943)

Chuikov, Vasili, *The End of the Third Reich,* translated by Ruth Kisch (London: MacGibbon & Kee, 1967)

Churchill, Winston, *Triumph and Tragedy* (Boston: Houghton Mifflin, 1953)

———, *The Unknown War—The Eastern Front* (New York: Charles Scribner's Sons, 1931)

———, *The World Crisis*, Vol.4, (New York: Charles Scribner's Sons, 1927)

Clark, Alan, *Barbarossa—The Russo-German Conflict 1941–45* (New York: William Morrow and Company, 1965)

Clough, Shephard, Thomas Moodie, and Carol Moodie, editors, *Economic History of Europe: Twentieth Century* (New York: Walder and Company, 1968)

Coakley, Robert and Richard Leighton, *Global Logistics and Strategy* (Washington, D.C.: Government Printing Office, 1968)

Cockburn, Andrew, *The Threat Inside the Soviet Military Machine* (New York: Random House, 1983)

Coffman, Edward, *The War to End All Wars: The American Military Experience in World War I* (New York: Oxford University Press, 1968)

Cohen, Stephen, *Rethinking the Soviet Experience* (New York: Oxford University Press, 1985)

Collier, Basil, *The War in the West 1941–1945* (New York: William Morrow and Company, 1969)

———, *Hidden Weapons* (London: Hamish Hamilton, 1982)

Compton, James, *The Swastika and the Eagle: Hitler, the United States and the Origins of World War II* (Boston: Houghton Mifflin, 1967)

Costello, John, *The Pacific War* (New York: Rawson, Wade, 1981)

Craven, Wesley and James Cate, editors, *The Army Air Forces in World War II*, Vol.3, (Europe: *Argument to V-E Day, January 1944–May 1945*), (Chicago: University of Chicago Press, 1951)

Crowell, Benedict and Robert Wilson, *The Armies of Industry*, Vol.1 (New Haven: Yale University Press, 1921)

Dallin, Alexander, *German Rule in Russia, 1941–1945*, 2d ed. (Boulder, Colorado: Westview Press, 1981)

de Guingand, Major General Sir Francis, *Operation Victory* (New York: Charles Scribner's Sons, 1947)

Deane, John, *The Strange Alliance* (New York: Viking Press, 1947)

Denikin, Anton, *The Career of a Tsarist Officer: Memoirs 1872–1916*, translated by Margaret Patoski (Minneapolis: University of Minnesota Press, 1975)

DeWeerd, Harvey, *President Wilson Fights His War: World War I and the American Intervention* (New York: Macmillan, 1968)

Divine, Robert, editor, *Causes and Consequences of World War II* (Chicago: Quadrangle Books, 1969)

Doenitz, Admiral, *Memoirs*, translated by R. H. Stevene (Westport, Connecticut: Greenwood Press, 1976)

Downing, David, *The Devil's Virtuosos: German Generals At War 1940–5* (London: St. Martin's Press, 1977)

Dreisziger, N. F., *Mobilization for Total War—The Canadian, American and British Experience 1914–1918, 1939–1945* (Waterloo, Ontario: Wilfrid Laurier University Press, 1981)

Dunmore, Timothy, *The Stalinist Command Economy* (New York: St. Martin's Press, 1980)

Dunn, Walter, Jr., *Second Front Now 1943* (University, Alabama: University of Alabama Press, 1980)

Dupuy, R. Ernest, *World War II: A Compact History* (New York: Hawthorne Books, 1969)

Dupuy, Colonel Trevor and Paul Martell, *Great Battles on the Eastern Front* (Indianapolis: Bobbs-Merrill Company, 1982)

Dupuy, Colonel Trevor, *A Genius For War: The German Army and General Staff, 1807–1945* (Englewood Cliffs, New Jersey: Prentice-Hall Inc., 1977)

Edelman, Robert, *Gentry Politics on the Eve of the Russian Revolution* (New Brunswick: Rutgers University Press, 1980)

Edmonds, General James, *A Short History of World War I* (London: Oxford University Press, 1951)

Ehrmann, John, *Grand Strategy*, Vol. 6 (October 1944–August 1945) (London: Her Majesty's Stationery Office, 1956)

Eisenhower, David, *Eisenhower: At War 1943–1945* (New York: Random House, 1986)

Eisenhower, Dwight, *Crusade in Europe* (Garden City, New York: Doubleday, 1948)

Eisenhower, John, *Allies: Pearl Harbor to D-Day* (Garden City, New York: Doubleday and Company, 1982)

————, *The Bitter Woods* (New York: G.P.Putnam, 1969)

Eisenstadt, Murray, *The United States Foreign Relations 1890s–1970s* (New York: Oxford Book Company, 1971)

Ellis, John, *Armies in Revolution* (London: Croom Helm, 1973)

Ellis, Major L. F., *Victory in the West: The Battle of Normandy*, Vol.1 (London: Her Majesty's Stationery Office, 1962)

———— and Lt.Colonel A. E. Warhurst, *Victory in the West: The Defeat of Germany*, Vol.2 (London: Her Majesty's Stationery Office, 1968)

Elstob, Peter, *Hitler's Last Offensive* (New York: Macmillan, 1971)

Erickson, John, *The Road to Berlin* (Boulder, Colorado: Westview Press, 1984)

————, *The Road to Stalingrad* (Boulder, Colorado: Westview Press, 1979)

————and E. J. Feuchtwanger, editors, *Soviet Military Power and Performance* (London: Macmillan, 1979)

Erlich, Alexander, *The Soviet Industrialization Debate, 1924–1928* (Cambridge: Harvard University Press, 1960)

Eroshkin, N. P., *Istoriya gosudarstvennykh v chrezhdenii do revolyutsionnoi Rossii* (Moscow: Vyshaya Shkola, 1983)

Essame, Hubert, *The Battle for Germany* (New York: Charles Scribners, 1969)

Evans, Geoffrey, *Tannenberg: 1410:1914* (London: Hamish Hamilton Ltd., 1970)

Evans, Peter and Dietrich Rueschemeyer and Theda Skocpol, editors, *Bringing the State Back In* (Cambridge: Cambridge University Press, 1985)

Falls, Cyril, *The First World War* (London: Longmans, 1960)

Feis, Herbert, *Churchill, Roosevelt, Stalin* (Princeton: Princeton University Press, 1967)

Ferro, Marc, *The Great War 1914–1918*, translated by Nicole Stone (London: Routledge and Kegan Paul, 1973)

————, *The Russian Revolution of February 1917*, translated by J. L. Richards (Englewood Cliffs, New Jersey: Prentice-Hall, Inc., 1972)

Florinsky, Michael, *The End of the Russian Empire* (New Haven: Yale University Press, 1931)

Flower, Desmond and James Reeves, editors, *The Taste of Courage—The War, 1939–1945* (New York: Harper and Row, 1960)

Foreign Relations of the United States 1944, Vol. 4 (Washington, D.C.: Government Printing Office, 1966)

Forster, Gerhard, Heinz Helmert, and Helmut Schnitter, *Der zweite Weltkrieg* (Berlin: Militarverlag, 1972)

Freidel, Frank, *Over There* (New York: Bramhall House, 1964)

Friedlander, Saul, *Prelude to Downfall: Hitler and the United States, 1939–1941*, translated by Alina and Alexander Werth (New York: Alfred Knopf, 1967)

Fuller, J. F. C., *The Conduct of War 1789–1961* (New Brunswick: Rutgers University Press, 1961)

————, *The Second World War 1939–45* (New York: Duell, Sloan and Pearce, 1949)

Gabriel, Richard, *The Antagonists: A Comparative Combat Assessment of the Soviet and American Soldier* (Westport, Connecticut: Greenwood Press, 1984)

Gaddis, John, *Russia, the Soviet Union and the United States: An Interpretive History* (New York: John Wiley and Sons, 1978)

————, *The United States and the Origins of the Cold War 1941–1947* (New York: Columbia University Press, 1972)

Gardner, Lloyd, Arthur Schlesinger, Jr. and Hans Morgenthau, *The Origins of the Cold War* (Waltham, Massachusetts: Ginn and Company, 1970)

Gibson, Cristann, *Patterns of Demobilization: The US and USSR After World War II*, doctoral dissertation, University of Denver, 1983

Gilbert, Martin, *First World War Atlas* (New York: MacMillan, 1970)

————, *Russian History Atlas* (New York: Macmillan, 1972)

Gill, Graeme, *Peasants and Government in the Russian Revolution* (London: Harper and Row, 1979)

Goerlitz, Walter, *History of the German General Staff, 1647–1945*, translated by Brian Battershaw (New York: Praeger, 1953)

Golder, Frank, editor, *Documents of Russian History 1914–1917* (New York: Century, 1927)

Golovine, Nicholas, *The Russian Army in the World War* (New Haven: Yale University Press, 1931)

Goralski, Robert, *World War II Almanac 1931–1945* (New York: Bonanza Books, 1984)

Gourko, Vasili, *War and Revolution in Russia 1914–1917* (New York: Macmillan, 1919)

Grechko, Andrei, *The Armed Forces of the Soviet State*, translated by Yuri Sviridov (Moscow: Progress Publishers, 1977)

Greenfield, Kent, editor, *Command Decisions* (Washington, D.C.: Government Printing Office, 1947)

————, Robert Palmer, and Bell Wiley, *The Organization of Ground Combat Troops* (Washington, D.C.: Government Printing Office, 1947)

Gregory, Paul, *Socialist and Nonsocialist Industrialization Patterns: A Comparative Appraisal* (New York: Praeger, 1970)

————, *Russian National Income 1885–1913* (Cambridge: Cambridge University Press, 1982)

Grigg, John, *1943: The Victory That Never Was* (New York: Hill and Wang, 1980)

Guderian, Heinz, *Panzer Leader* (New York: Ballantine Books, n.d.)

Hancock, W. K. and M. M. Gowing, *British War Economy* (London: His Majesty's Stationery Office, 1949)

————, editor, *Statistical Digest of the War* (London: His Majesty's Stationery Office and Longmans Green and Company, 1951)

Harbord, James, *The American Army in France 1917–1919* (Boston: Little Brown, 1936)

Harriman, W. Averell, *America and Russia in a Changing World* (Garden City, New York: Doubleday, 1971)

────── and Elie Abel, *Special Envoy to Churchill and Stalin 1941–1946* (New York: Random House, 1975)

Harris, Mark, Franklin Mitchell, and Steven Schechter, *The Homefront: America During World War II* (New York: G. P. Putnam, 1984)

Harrison, Mark, *Soviet Planning in Peace and War 1938–1945* (Cambridge: Cambridge University Press, 1985)

Hastings, Max, *Overlord-D-Day and the Battle for Normandy* (New York: Simon and Schuster, 1984)

Haykal, Muhammad, *The Sphinx and the Commissar: The Rise and Fall of Soviet Influence in the Middle East* (New York: Harper and Row, 1978)

Herring, George, Jr., *Aid to Russia 1941–1946* (New York: Columbia University Press, 1973)

Hinsley, F. M., *British Intelligence in the Second World War*, Vol. 3, part 1 (Cambridge: Cambridge University Press, 1984)

Holloway, David, *The Soviet Union and the Arms Race* (New Haven: Yale University Press, 1983)

Howard, Michael, *War in European History* (London: Oxford University Press, 1976)

Huntington, Samuel, *Political Order in Changing Societies* (New Haven: Yale University Press, 1968)

Hurstfield, Julian, *America and the French Nation, 1939–1945* (Chapel Hill and London: University of North Carolina Press, 1986)

Huston, James, *The Sinews of War: Army Logistics 1775–1953* (Washington, D.C.: Government Printing Office, 1966)

Irving, David, *Hitler's War* (New York: Viking Press, 1977)

──────, *The War Between the Generals* (New York: Congdon and Lattes, 1981)

Issraeljan, Victor, *The Anti-Hitler Coalition*, translated by Dan Danemanis (Moscow: Progress Publishers 1971)

Istoriya grazhdanskoi voiny v SSSR, Vol. 1 (Moscow: Gosizdat, 1958)

Istoriya kommunisticheskoi partii Sovetskogo Soyuza, Vol. 5, book 1 (1938–1945) (Moscow: Partizdat, 1980)

Istoriya pervoi mirovoi voiny, 2 volumes (Moscow: Nauka, 1975)

Istoriya velikoi otechestvennoi voiny Sovetskogo Soyuza 1941–1945, 6 volumes (Moscow: Voenizdat, 1960)

Istoriya vtoroi mirovoi voina 1939–1945, 12 volumes (Moscow: Voenizdat, 1982)

Jacobsen, H. A. and J. Rohwer, editors, *Decisive Battles of World War II: The German View* (New York: G.P.Putnam's Sons, 1965)

Jasny, Naum, *Soviet Industrialization 1928–1952* (Chicago: University of Chicago Press, 1961)

Joint Economic Committee, *Soviet Economic Growth: A Comparison with the United States* (New York: Greenwood Press, 1968)

Jones, Ellen, *Red Army and Society* (Winchester, Mass: Allen and Unwin, 1985)

Jones, Robert, *The Roads to Russia: United States Lend Lease to the Soviet*

Union (Norman: University of Oklahoma Press, 1969)

Jung, Hermann, *Die Ardennen—Offensive 1944/45* (Frankfurt: Musterschmidt Gottingen, 1971)

Katkov, George, *Russia 1917—The February Revolution* (New York: Harper and Row, 1967)

Keegan, John, *Six Armies in Normandy* (New York: Viking Press, 1982)

Keitel, Field Marshal Wilhelm, *In the Service of the Reich*, translated by David Irving (New York: Stein and Day, 1979)

Kennedy, David, *Over Here: The First World War and American Society* (New York: Oxford University Press, 1980)

Kesselring, Albert, *A Soldier's Record*, translated by Lynton Hudson (New York: William Morrow and Company, 1954)

King, F. P., *The New Internationalism: Allied Policy and the European Peace 1939–1945* (London: David and Charles, 1973)

Kir'yan, M. M., *Voenno-tekhnicheskii progress i vooruzhennye sily SSSR* (Moscow: Voenizdat, 1982)

Knutsen, Torbjorn, "Old, Unhappy, Far-Off Things: The New Military History of Europe," *Journal of Peace Research*, Vol. 24, no. 1 (1987)

Kolko, Joyce and Gabriel, *The Limits of Power: The World and The United States Foreign Policy 1945–1953* (New York: Harper and Row, 1972)

Kolko, Gabriel, *The Politics of War: The World and the United States Foreign Policy 1943–1945* (New York: Random House, 1968)

Lafeber, Walter, *America, Russia and the Cold War 1945–1966* (New York: John Wiley and Sons, 1967)

Lamb, Richard, *Montgomery in Europe 1943–1945: Success or Failure?* (New York: Franklin Watts, 1984)

Lan, V.I., *SShA v voennye i poslevoennye gody* (Moscow: Nauka, 1978)

Leahy, Fleet Admiral William, *I Was There* (New York: Whittlesey House, 1950)

Leebaert, Derek, editor, *Soviet Military Thinking* (London: George Allen and Unwin, 1981)

The Letters of the Tsar to the Tsaritsa 1914–1917, translated by A. L. Hynes (Hattiesburg, Mississippi: Academic International Press, 1970

The Letters of the Tsaritsa to the Tsar 1914–1916, translated by A. L. Hynes (Hattiesburg, Mississippi: Academic International Press, 1970)

Lewin, Moshe, *Political Undercurrents in Soviet Economic Debates: From Bukharin to the Modern Reformers* (Princeton: Princeton University Press, 1974)

Lewin, Ronald, *Montgomery As Military Commander* (London: B. T. Batsford Ltd., 1971)

———, *Ultra Goes to War* (New York: McGraw-Hill, 1978)

Liddell Hart, Basil, *History of the Second World War* (London: Cassell, 1970)

———, *The Real War 1914–1918* (Boston: Little, Brown, 1930)

———, editor, *The Red Army* (New York: Harcourt, Brace, 1956)

Lider, Julian, *Correlation of Forces: An Analysis of Marxist–Leninist Concepts* (New York: St. Martins Press, 1986)

Liebman, Marcel, *The Russian Revolution*, translated by Arnold Pomerans (London: Jonathan Cape, 1970)

Link, Arthur, editor, *The Impact of World War I* (New York: Harper and Row, 1969)

Linz, Susan, editor, *The Impact of World War II on the Soviet Union* (Totowa, New Jersey: Rowman and Allanheld, 1985)

Lowenheim, Francis and Harold Langley and Manfred Jonas, editors, *Roosevelt and Churchill: Their Secret Wartime Correspondence* (New York: Saturday Review Press, 1975)

Lucas, James, *War on the Eastern Front 1941–1945* (New York: Bonanza Books, 1982)

———and James Barker, *The Battle of Normandy—The Falaise Gap* (New York: Holmes and Meier, 1978)

Lukacs, John, *1945: Year Zero* (Garden City, New York: Doubleday and Company, 1978)

Lutz, Ralph, *The Causes of the German Collapse in 1918* (New York: Archon Books, 1969)

MacDonald, Charles, *The Last Offensive* (Washington, D.C.: Government Printing Office, 1973)

———, *The Mighty Endeavor* (New York: Oxford University Press, 1969)

———, *The Siegfried Line Campaign* (Washington, D.C.: Government Printing Office, 1963)

Maddison, Angus, *Economic Growth in Japan and the USSR* (New York: W. W. Norton 1969)

——— *Economic Growth in the West* (New York: Twentieth Century Fund, 1964)

Maiskii, Ivan, *Memoirs of a Soviet Ambassador: The War 1939–43*, translated by Andrew Rothstein, (London: Hutchinson and Company, 1967)

Majdalany, Fred, *The Fall of Fortress Europe* (Garden City, New York: Doubleday and Company, 1968)

Marshall, George, *Memoirs of My Services in the World War 1917–1918* (Boston: Houghton Mifflin, 1976)

Marwick, Arthur, *Britain in the Century of Total War* (Boston: Little Brown, 1968)

———, *War and Social Change in the Twentieth Century* (New York: St. Martin's Press, 1974)

Mastny, Vojtech, *Russia's Road to the Cold War* (New York: Columbia University Press, 1979)

Matloff, Maurice, editor, *American Military History* (Washington, D.C.: Government Printing Office, 1969)

May, Ernest, editor, *Knowing One's Enemies: Intelligence Assessments Before the Two Major Wars* (Princeton: Princeton University Press, 1984)

McCauley, Martin, editor, *The Russian Revolution and the Soviet State 1917–1920* (London: Macmillan, 1975)

————, *Octobrists to Bolsheviks—Imperial Russia 1905–1917* (London: Edward Arnold, 1984)

McNeill, William, *America, Britain and Russia: Their Cooperation and Conflict 1941–1946* (London: Oxford University Press, 1953)

————, *The Pursuit of Power: Technology, Armed Forces and Society Since A.D. 1000* (Chicago: University of Chicago Press, 1982)

The Memoirs of Field Marshal the Viscount Montgomery of Alamein (Cleveland: World Publishing Company, 1958)

Messer, Robert, *The End of An Alliance: James F. Byrnes, Roosevelt, Truman and the Origins of the Cold War* (Chapel Hill: University of North Carolina, 1982)

Michel, Henri, *The Second World War*, translated by Douglas Parmee (London: Andre Deutsch Ltd., 1975)

Mickiewicz, Ellen, editor, *Handbook of Soviet Social Science Data* (New York: Free Press, 1973)

Middleton, Drew, *Crossroads of Modern Warfare* (Garden City, New York: Doubleday and Company, 1983)

Millar, James, *The ABCs of Soviet Socialism* (Urbana: University of Illinois Press, 1981)

Millett, Allan and Peter Maslowski, *For the Common Defense: A Military History of the United States of America* (New York: Free Press, 1984)

Milward, Alan, *War, Economy and Society, 1939–1945* (Berkeley and Los Angeles: University of California Press, 1977)

Mints, I. I., *Istoriya velikogo Oktyabrya*, Vol. 1 (Moscow: Nauka, 1977)

Mitcham, Samuel W., Jr., *Rommel's Last Battle—The Desert Fox and the Normandy Campaign* (New York: Stein and Day, 1983)

Montgomery, Field Marshal Viscount, *A History of Warfare* (Cleveland: World Publishing, 1968)

Montgomery, Field Marshal Bernard, *Normandy to the Baltic* (Boston: Houghton Mifflin, 1948)

Moore, Barrington, *Social Origins of Dictatorship and Democracy* (Boston: Beacon Press, 1966)

Moorsteen, Richard and Raymond Powell, *The Soviet Capital Stock 1928–1962* (Homewood, Illinois: Richard D. Irwin, 1966)

Morison, Samuel Eliot, *The Two Ocean War: A Short History of United States Navy in the Second World War* (Boston: Little Brown, 1963)

Mueller, Bernard, *A Statistical Handbook of the North Atlantic Area* (New York: Twentieth Century Fund, 1965)

Munting, Roger, *The Economic Development of the USSR* (New York: St. Martin's Press, 1982)

Neilson, Keith, *Strategy and Supply: The Anglo–Russian Alliance, 1914–17* (London: George Allen and Unwin, 1984)

Nicholas, H. G., editor, *Washington Despatches 1941–1945: Weekly*

Political Reports from the British Embassy (Chicago: University of Chicago Press, 1981)

Nikitinskii, I. N. and P. Sofinov, *Nemetskii shpionazh v Rossii vo vremya voiny 1914–1918 g.g.* (Moscow: Gosizdat, 1942)

Nolde, Baron Boris, *Russia in the Economic War* (New Haven: Yale University Press, 1928)

Nove, Alec, *An Economic History of the U.S.S.R.* (Hammondsworth, England: Penguin Books, 1975)

———, *Economic Rationality and Soviet Politics or Was Stalin Really Necessary?* (New York: Praeger, 1964)

Nutter, G. Warren, *Growth of Industrial Production in the Soviet Union* (Princeton: Princeton University Press, 1962)

Oldenburg, S. S., *Last Tsar: Nicholas II, His Reign and His Russia*, Vol. 4, translated by Leonid Mihalap and Patrick Rollins, (Gulf Breeze, Florida: Academic International Press, 1978)

Out of My Past—The Memoirs of Count Kokovtsov editor-M. M. Fisher (Stanford: Stanford University Press, 1935)

Palmer, Frederick, *Newton D. Baker: America At War* (New York: Dodd, Mead and Company, 1931)

Pares, Bernard, *Day by Day With the Russian Army 1914–1915* (New York: Houghton Mifflin, 1915)

———, *The Fall of the Russian Monarchy* (London: Jonathan Cape, 1939)

Paterson, Thomas, *Soviet–American Confrontation* (Baltimore: Johns Hopkins University Press, 1973)

Pearson, Raymond, *The Russian Moderates and the Crisis of Tsarism 1914–1917* (New York: Barnes and Noble, 1977)

Perrett, Geoffrey, *Days of Sadness, Years of Triumph: The American People 1939–1945* (New York: Coward, McCann and Geoghegan, 1973)

Pershing, John, *My Experiences in the World War*, Vols.1-2 (New York: Frederick Stokes and Company, 1931)

Pervaya mirovaya voina 1914–1918 (Moscow: Nauka, 1968)

Pinter, Walter and Don Rouney, editors, *Russian Officialdom* (Chapel Hill: University of North Carolina Press, 1980)

Pipes, Richard, editor, *Revolutionary Russia* (Cambridge: Harvard University Press, 1969)

Pogue, Forrest, *George C.Marshall: Organizer of Victory 1943–1945* (New York: Viking Press, 1973)

Polenberg, Richard, *War and Society: The United States 1941–1945* (Philadelphia: J. B. Lippincott, 1972)

Pollard, Robert, *Economic Security and the Origins of the Cold War 1945–1950* (New York: Columbia University Press, 1985)

Pollard, Sidney, *Peaceful Conquest: The Industrialization of Europe 1760–1970* (Oxford: Oxford University Press, 1981)

Porter, David, *The Seventy-Sixth Congress and World War II 1939–1940* (Columbia and London: University of Missouri Press, 1979)

Randall, Francis, *Stalin's Russia* (New York: Free Press, 1965)

Ready, J. Lee, *Forgotten Allies* (Jefferson, North Carolina: McFarland and Company, 1945)

Rigby, T. H., editor, *Stalin* (Englewood Cliffs, New Jersey: Prentice Hall, 1966)

Robbins, Keith, *The First World War* (Oxford: Oxford University Press, 1984)

Rodzianko, M. V., *The Reign of Rasputin: An Empire's Collapse*, translated by Catherine Zvegintzoff (London: A. M. Philpot Ltd, 1927)

Roper, H. R. Trevor, editor, *Blitzkrieg to Defeat: Hitler's War Directives 1939–1945* (New York: Holt Rinehart and Winston, 1964)

Ropp, Theodore, *War and the Modern World* (New York: Colliers, 1962)

Rose, Lisle, *The Long Shadow: Reflections on the Second World War Era* (Westport, Connecticut: Greenwood Press, 1978)

Rossiya v mirovoi voine 1914–1918 goda (v trifrakh) (Moscow: Central Statistical Administration, 1925)

Rostunov, I. I., *Russkii front pervoi mirovoi voiny* (Moscow: Nauka, 1976)

Rutherford, Ward, *The Russian Army in World War I* (London: Cremonesi Publishers, 1975)

Ryan, Cornelius, *The Last Battle* (New York: Simon and Schuster, 1966)

Ryan, Henry, *The Vision of Anglo–America: The US-UK Alliance and the Emerging Cold War, 1943–1946* (Cambridge: Cambridge University Press, 1987)

Samsonov, A. M., *Vtoraya mirovaya voina 1939–1945* (Moscow: Nauka, 1985)

Sazonov, Serge, *Fateful Years 1909–1916* (New York: Frederick A. Stokes, 1928)

Scherer, John L., editor, *USSR Facts and Figures Annual*, Vol.1 (Gulf Breeze, Fla: Academic International Press, 1977)

Schoenfeld, Maxwell, *The War Ministry of Winston Churchill* (Ames: Iowa State University Press, 1972)

Seaton, Albert, *The Fall of Fortress Europe 1943–1945* (New York: Holmes and Meier, 1981)

——, *The German Army 1933–45* (New York: St.Martin's Press, 1982)

——, *The Russo–German War 1941–45* (New York: Praeger, 1970)

The Service: The Memoirs of General Reinhard Gehlen, translated by David Irving (New York: World Publishing Company, 1972)

Seton-Watson, Hugh, *The Decline of Imperial Russia 1855–1914* (New York: Praeger, 1970)

Shifman, M. S., *Voina i ekonomika* (Moscow: Voenizdat, 1964)

Shigalin, G. I., *Voennaya ekonomika v pervuyu mirovuyu voinu (1914–1918)* (Moscow: Voenizdat, 1956)

Shoup, Paul, *The East European and Soviet Data Handbook: Political, Social and Developmental Indicators, 1945–1975* (New York: Columbia University Press, 1982)

Shtemenko, S. M., *The Last Six Months*, translated by Guy Daniels (Garden City, New York: Doubleday, 1977)

Shulman, Milton, *Defeat in the West* (New York: E. P. Dutton, 1948)

Siney, Marion, *The Allied Blockade of Germany 1914–1916* (Ann Arbor: University of Michigan Press, 1957)

Sivachev, Nikolai and Nikolai Yakovlev, *Russia and the United States*, translated by Olga Adler Titelbaum (Chicago: University of Chicago Press, 1979)

Skocpol, Theda, *States and Social Revolution* (Cambridge: Cambridge University Press, 1979)

Skowronek, Stephen, *Building A New American State: The Expansion of National Administrative Capacities 1877–1920* (Cambridge: Cambridge University Press, 1982)

Smith, Arthur, Jr., *Churchill's German Army* (Beverly Hills, California: Sage Publications, 1977)

Solzhenitsyn, Alexander, *August 1914*, translated by Michael Glenny (New York: Farrar, Straus and Giroux, 1971)

Sovetskaya voennaya entsiklopediya, Vols. 5 and 6 (Moscow: Voenizdat, 1978)

Spanier, John, *American Foreign Policy Since World War II* (New York: Praeger, 1977)

Spector, Ronald, *Eagle Against the Sun* (New York: Free Press, 1985)

Speer, Albert, *Inside the Third Reich*, translated by Richard and Clara Winston (New York: Macmillan, 1970)

Speidel, Lt. General Hans, *We Defended Normandy*, translated by Ian Colvin, (London: Herbert Jenkins Ltd., 1951)

Stacey, Colonel Charles, *The Canadian Army 1939–1945* (Ottawa: National Defense, 1948)

Stalin, Joseph, *The Great Patriotic War of the Soviet Union*, translation (New York: International Publishers, 1945)

Statistical Handbook of the U.S.S.R., translation (New York: Conference Board, 1957)

The Statistical History of the United States From Colonial Times to the Present (Stamford, Connecticut: Fairfield Publisher, 1965)

Statistical Yearbook of the League of Nations 1938–39 (Geneva, 1939)

Strawson, John, *Hitler As Military Commander* (London: B. T. Batsford, Ltd., 1971)

Stavrov, Theofanis, editor, *Russia Under the Last Tsar* (Minneapolis: University of Minnesota Press, 1969)

Stein, Arthur, *The Nation At War* (Baltimore: Johns Hopkins University Press, 1980)

Stoler, Mark, *The Politics of the Second Front: American Military Planning and Diplomacy in Coalition Warfare, 1941–1943* (Westport, Connecticut: Greenwood Press, 1977)

Stone, Norman, *The Eastern Front, 1914–1917* (New York: Charles Scribner's Sons, 1975)

Strachan, Hew, *European Armies and the Conduct of War* (London: George Allen and Unwin, 1983

Strokov, A. A., *Vooruzhennye sily i voennoe iskusstvo v pervoi mirovoi voine* (Moscow: Voenizdat, 1974)

Summersby, Kay, *Eisenhower Was My Boss* (New York: Prentice-Hall, 1948)

Suvorov, Viktor, *Inside the Soviet Army* (New York: Macmillan, 1982)

Talenskii, N. A., *Pervaya mirovaya voina (1914–1918 gg)* (Moscow: Gosizdat, 1944)

Taubman, William, *Stalin's American Policy: From Entente to Detente to Cold War* (New York: W. W. Norton, 1982)

Taylor, General Maxwell, *Swords and Plowshares* (New York: W. W. Norton, 1972)

Terkel, Studs, *The Good War* (New York: Pantheon Books, 1984)

Thorne, Christopher, *Allies of a Kind* (New York: Oxford University Press, 1978)

Timasheff, Nicholas, *War and Revolution* (New York: Sheed and Ward, 1965)

Toland, John, *The Last 100 Days* (New York: Random House, 1966)

Trevor–Roper, Hugh, editor, *Final Entries 1945—The Diaries of Joseph Goebbels*, translated by Richard Barry (New York: G. P. Putnam's Sons, 1978)

Turner, Gordon, editor, *A History of Military Affairs in Western Society Since the Eighteenth Century* (New York: Harcourt Brace, 1953)

Tucker, Robert, editor, *Stalinism—Essays in Historical Interpretation* (New York: W. W. Norton, 1977)

Ulam, Adam, *Expansion and Coexistence—Soviet Foreign Policy 1917–73* (New York: Praeger, 1974)

————, *The Rivals—America and Russia Since World War II* (New York: Viking Press, 1971)

Ukrainskaya SSR v velikoi otechestvennoi voine Sovetskogo Soyuza 1941–1945 gg, Vol. 3 (1944–1945) (Kiev: Politizdat Ukrainy, 1978)

United Nations, *National Income Statistics of Various Countries 1938–1948* (Lake Success, New York: Statistical Office of the United Nations, 1950)

————, *Statistical Yearbook 1948* (Lake Success, New York: United Nations, 1949)

————, Department of Economic Affairs, *A Survey of the Economic Situation Prospects of Europe* (Geneva, 1948)

Urlanis, B., *Wars and Population*, translated by Leo Lempert (Moscow: Progress Publishers, 1971)

van Creveld, Martin, *Command in War* (Cambridge: Harvard University Press, 1985)

————, *Fighting Power—German and United States Army Performance 1939–1945* (Westport, Connecticut: Greenwood Press, 1982)

————, *Supplying War* (Cambridge: Cambridge University Press, 1977)

Velikaya otechestvennaya voina Sovetskogo Soyuza 1941–1945: Kratkaya istoriya, 3rd edition (Moscow: Voenizdat, 1984)

Verzhkhovskii, D. V. and V. F. Lyakhov, *Pervaya mirovaya voina* (Moscow: Voenizdat, 1964)

Verrier, Anthony, *The Bomber Offensive* (New York: Macmillan, 1969)

Vigor, Peter, *The Soviet View of War, Peace and Neutrality* (London: Routledge and Kegan Paul, 1975)

Viorst, Milton, *Hostile Allies: F. D. R. and Charles de Gaulle* (New York: Macmillan, 1965)

Volin, Lazar, *A Century of Russian Agriculture: From Alexander II to Khrushchev* (Cambridge: Harvard University Press, 1970)

von Manstein, Erich, *Lost Victories*, edited and translated by Anthony G. Powell (Chicago: Henry Regnery, 1958)

Vorontsov, G. F., *Voennye koalitsii i koalitsionnye voiny* (Moscow: Voenizdat, 1976)

Voznesensky, Nikolai, *The Economy of the USSR During World War II*, translation (Washington, D.C.: Public Affairs Press, 1948)

Wade, Rex, *The Russian Search for Peace February-October 1917* (Stanford: Stanford University Press, 1969)

Waitley, Douglas, *America At War: World Wars I and II* (Encino, California: Glencoe Publishing Company, 1980)

War in the East: The Russo–German Conflict 1941–1945 (New York: Simulations Publications Inc., 1977)

The War Reports of General of Army George C. Marshall, General of Army H. H. Arnold and Fleet Admiral Ernest King (Philadelphia and New York: J. B. Lippincott, 1947)

Warlimont, Walter, *Inside Hitler's Headquarters 1939–45*, translated by R. H. Barry (New York: Praeger, 1964)

Webster, Charles and Noble Frankland, *The Strategic Air Offensive Against Germany 1939–1945*, Vol.3, part 5 (London: Her Majesty's Stationery Office, 1961)

Weigley, Russell, *The American Way of War* (New York: Macmillan, 1973)

————, *Eisenhower's Lieutenants* (Bloomington: Indiana University Press, 1981)

Werth, Alexander, *Russia at War 1941–1945* (New York: E. P. Dutton, 1964)

Westphal, Siegfried, *The German Army in the West* (London: Cassell and Company Limited, 1951)

White, D. Fedotoff, *The Growth of the Red Army* (Princeton: Princeton University Press, 1944)

Whiting, Charles, *Siegfried: The Nazis' Last Stand* (New York: Stein and Day, 1982)

————, *The End of the War* (New York: Stein and Day, 1973)

Wildman, Aaron, *The End of the Russian Imperial Army* (Princeton: Princeton University Press, 1980)

Williams, William Appleman, *American–Russian Relations 1781–1917* (New York: Rinehart and Company, 1952)

————, *The Tragedy of American Diplomacy* (Cleveland: World Publishing Company, 1959)

Willmott, H. P., *June 1944* (Poole: Blandford Press, 1984)

Wilmot, Chester, *The Struggle for Europe* (New York: Harper and Brothers, 1952)

Wright, Gordon, *The Ordeal of Total War* (New York: Harper and Row, 1968)

Yergin, Daniel, *Shattered Peace: The Origins of the Cold War and The National Security State* (Boston: Houghton Mifflin, 1977)

Zagorsky, S. O., *State Control of Industry in Russia During the War* (New Haven: Yale University Press, 1928)

Zaionchkovsky, A. M., *Mirovaya voina, 1914–1918* (Moscow: Voenizdat, 1981)

Zaleski, Eugene, *Stalinist Planning for Economic Growth 1933– 1952*, translated and edited by Marie-Christine MacAndrew and John Moore (Chapel Hill: University of North Carolina Press, 1980)

Zhilin, P. A., *O voine i voennoi istorii* (Moscow: Nauka, 1984)

Ziemke, Earl, *Stalingrad to Berlin: The German Defeat in the East* (Washington, D.C: Government Printing Office, 1968)

Index

Adelman, Jonathan R., 259n
Afghanistan, 255
Africa, 132, 134, 152
Afrika Corps, 155
Air power, 206
Aldcroft, Derek, 259n
Alekseyev, General Mikhail, 57
Alexander, General Harold, 157, 160, 162, 180
Algeria, 156
Algiers, 156
Allied Control Commission, 185
Allied armies, 31
Allied cause, 6
Allied coalition, 5
Allied intervention, 70
Allied occupation, 6
Allied shipping, 59
Allied strategic bombing, 187
Allied victory, 42
Allied war effort, 41
Allies, 13, 16, 29, 33, 35-40, 48, 53, 55, 57, 59-60, 62-63, 65-67, 69-71, 84, 89, 123, 126-127, 129-130, 132-134, 136-137, 139, 143-144, 152, 155-158, 160, 161-162, 170-171, 175, 177, 179-183, 186, 189, 191, 193-199n, 201, 203-205, 207, 210, 213-214, 238-239, 241
Alperovitz, Gar, 10
Alps, 162
America First Committee, 116
American Civil War, 7, 13, 61, 99
American Expeditionary Force, 33, 34, 35, 63, 180
American First Army, 65
Americans, 29, 32-33, 41, 43-44, 62, 67, 69, 70, 85, 124, 127, 132, 140-141, 157, 144, 171, 177, 179-180, 183, 188, 195, 203-204, 210-211, 223, 227-228, 249, 257; army, 62, 108; officers, 218; troops, 34
Amiens, 65
Anglo Saxon elites, 209
Anglo-American campaign, 193, 196

Anglo-American contribution, 170
Anglo-American decision, 177
Anglo-American divisions, 176, 179
Anglo-American forces, 6, 174, 195
Anglo-American relations, 141-142, 157, 179, 187, 189, 206, 208, 210
Anglo-French allies, 72
Anglo-United States relations, 123
Anglophobia, 210
Anti-Bolsheviks, 126
Anti-Communism, 102, 105
Anti-Semitism, 80
Antonescu brothers, 184
Antwerp, 183, 187-188
Anzio, 161
Apennine mountains, 162
April Theses, 56
Arab forces, 9
Arabs, 238
Ardahum, 59
Ardennes forest, Battle of, 172, 183, 188-189, 193-194, 196, 199n
Arkhangel'sk, 36
Armed forces, 196
Armenia, 55, 81
Armistice Day, 5
Army, 7, 9
Army Group Center, 177-179
Army Group North Ukraine, 178-179
Army Group Vistula, 191
Arnold, General Hap, 137
Arsenal of Democracy, 73, 127, 143
Aryans, 124
Asia, 6, 100, 125, 202, 205, 227
Atlantic, Battle of, 126, 133, 137, 161, 205
Atlantic Ocean, 2, 16, 86, 89, 126-127, 138, 147n, 156, 163, 205, 242-243
Atlantic Wall, 130, 136, 181
Atomic Diplomacy, 10
Augustów, 53
Australia, 134, 138, 202
Austria, 61, 72, 98
Austro-Hungary, 40; army, 49, 53, 64; disaster, 51; divisions, 41; empire, 8,

48, 55, 191; positions, 57; troops, 52
Avranches, 182
Axis, 2, 4, 14, 110, 112-113, 127, 135-136, 152, 155-156, 160-161, 191, 197n, 209, 240

Badoglio, Marshal Pietro, 160-161
Bagramyan, Marshal Ivan, 178
Baker, Secretary Newton, 62, 80
Baku, 154
Balance of power system, 210
Balfour, Lord Arthur, 40
Balkans, 40, 42, 175, 183-185, 189, 210
Ball, George, 208
Baltic states, 3
Baltics, 59, 70, 98, 159, 171, 178, 184, 243, 246
Baruch, Bernard, 80, 85
Bastogne, 169, 188
Batum, 59
Beaches, 180
Beatty, Admiral David, 86
Beaver, Daniel, 69
Belgium, 148, 52, 88, 214
Belgrade, 185
Beliayev, General Mikhail, 37
Belleau Wood, 65
Belorussia, 59, 70, 98, 159, 171, 177-178, 183, 243
Benelux, 14
Bergson, Abram, 106
Beria, Lavrentii, 231
Berlin, 6, 12, 15, 19, 29, 47, 52, 172-174, 178, 184, 189-191
Berlin, Battle of, 103, 145, 173, 195-196, 216, 233, 238, 243-244, 252, 255
Berlin, Treaty of, 3
Bessarabia, 3, 185
Bialer, Seweryn, 216
Black Hundreds group, 80
Blackwell, 90n
Blaskowitz, General Johannes, 183
Blitzkrieg warfare, 254
Blumentritt, General Gunther, 196
Blyukher, Marshal Vasilii, 112
Bodin, General Alexander, 215
Bolsheviks, 28, 58, 89, 97-98, 115, 124, 238
Bolshevism, 173, 191, 198n
Bonaparte, Napoleon, 115
Bradley, General Omar, 114, 157, 214-215
Brest Litovsk, Treaty of, 3, 6, 17, 30,

39, 59, 69, 70, 74n, 89, 96, 238
Bretton Woods accord, 211
Brezhnev, Leonid, 254
Britain, 3, 7, 14, 16, 18, 21, 30, 32, 34, 36, 42, 53, 65, 67-71, 86, 89, 101, 109, 113, 123-128, 131-138, 140-144, 146, 149-152, 156-157, 160-164, 170-171, 173, 174-175, 179-180, 185, 193, 196, 202, 205, 209, 213, 234, 237, 240, 245; army, 32, 65-67, 132, 243; intelligence, 66; military power, 17; navy, 62, 78, 101-102, 124, 127, 129, 132-133, 198; proposal, 194; rifle, 64; ships, 33; society, 8
Britain, Battle of, 124, 128, 133, 152
British Commonwealth, 5, 13, 19, 128-129, 132, 134-136, 149, 163, 170, 175-176, 178-180, 193, 197, 240
British Empire, 1, 128, 137, 144, 152, 160, 210
British Expeditionary Force, 40, 59, 66
British islands, 257
British isles, 179
British Royal Air Force, 86, 129, 133, 180, 207
British Royal Navy, 86, 205
British ships, 33
British War Cabinet, 34
British War Office, 37
Brody, 57
Brooke, Field Marshal Alan, 141, 199n
Browning automatic weapon, 64
Brusilov, General Aleksei, 55, 57-58
Brussels, 183
Brzezinski, Zbigniew, 11
Bucharest, 55, 185
Budapest, 6, 15, 53, 186, 189, 191, 238
Budenny, Marshal Semyon, 112
Buergermeister, 195
Bukovina, 55, 58, 185
Bulgaria, 2, 38, 40, 53, 83, 184-185
Bulgarian divisions, 41, 191
Bulge, Battle of, 15, 174
Butcher, Captain Harry, 131

Cabinet officers, 63
Cabinet, 81
Caen, 181
Canada, 134, 245
Canadian beaches, 180
Cantigny salient, 65
Caporetto, 42
Carpathian, 51-53, 58, 190
Casablanca conference, 157
Casablanca, 156

Central Europe, 14, 171
Central Powers, 40, 48, 52-53, 62
Central front, 189
Centralization, 231-234
Chaffee, General, 109
Chamberlain, Prime Minister Neville, 125
Channel islands, 186
Chantilly conference, 54
Chateau-Thierry, 65
Cherbourg, 182
Chernyakhovsky, General Ivan, 178, 190, 215
Chiang Kai-shek, 142
China, 8, 13, 31, 99-100, 139, 202, 238, 245
Chinese Civil War, 9
Chinese Revolution, 7
Churchill, Winston, 34, 137, 142-143, 152, 172, 179
Civil War, 3, 87
Clemenceau, Georges, 27
Coakley, Robert, 136, 139, 203
Cohen, Stephen, 17
Cold War, 10-11, 18, 21, 95, 105, 152, 209, 227, 242, 248, 252, 257
Comintern, 3, 70, 98, 117
Commissars, 215
Committee to Aid Russian POWs, 81
Communism, 17, 102, 216, 239
Confederacy, United States, 213
Congress of Vienna, 27
Congress, 62, 116-117, 247
Controlled Materials Plan, 233
Coral Sea, Battle of, 140
Correlation of forces, 23n
Costello, John, 140
Council of National Defense, 63
Council of War, 66
Creel, George, 79
Crimea, 159
Crimean War, 3
Cunningham, Admiral Andrew, 160
Czechoslovakia, 178, 255
Czernowitz, 54

D Day (1944), 14, 30, 127-128, 145, 164, 173, 179-182, 193
Dardanelles, 53
Dark Ages, 173
Darlan, Admiral Jean François, 156
De Gaulle, General Charles, 257
Deane, General John, 141, 152, 214
Decembrists, 246
Denikin, General Anton, 89, 97
Dniester, 58

Dovator, General Lev, 215
Duma, 80-82, 87
Dunn, Walter, 136
Dupuy, Colonel Trevor, 171

East, 5, 15-17, 27, 30-32, 40, 49, 52-53, 55, 59, 61, 69, 73n, 102, 128-130, 151, 152, 155, 158, 173-178, 187, 189-190, 193-198n, 225, 232, 238, 240-241, 243, 248, 252
East Galicia, 55
East Germany, 237, 246
East Prussia, 15, 39-40, 49, 51-53, 73n, 178, 189-191, 194
Eastern Europe, 6, 8, 13-14, 40, 42, 159, 163, 171, 175, 178, 183, 186, 237, 242-246, 249-250, 252, 255, 259n
Eastern European troops, 15
Eastern front, 4, 9, 12-15, 30, 40, 59, 129, 131, 146n, 149, 151, 157, 159, 161, 162, 164n, 172-173, 175-176, 179, 182, 199n, 202, 212, 238, 252
Eastern theater, 41
Ehrenburg, Ilya, 216
Eisenhower, General Dwight, 112, 131, 137, 156-157, 159-160, 173-174, 180, 186, 194-195, 199, 213-215
El Alamein, Battle of, 123, 128, 135, 155-156
Elbe, 2, 169, 173, 196, 257
England, 5-6, 11, 16, 32-33, 36-37, 40, 42, 44, 48, 60, 71, 83-84, 96, 106, 113, 118, 124, 127, 159, 198n, 245, 250-251
English Revolution, 7
English-speaking nations, 143
Erickson, John, 12, 164n, 190, 211
Espionage Act, 79
Eurasia, 115
Eurasian continent, 248
Eurocentric balance-of-power, 28
Europe First strategy, 138
Europe, 1-8, 11, 14-18, 21, 27-29, 33-35, 37-38, 43, 46-48, 60-62, 64, 67, 71-72, 75n, 79, 85-86, 88, 96, 98-99, 101, 103, 113, 118, 123-132, 134-135, 137, 138-142, 156-157, 159, 161-164, 169-170, 172, 177, 179, 183-185, 193, 196, 198n, 204-205, 207, 209, 211, 220, 227, 240, 244, 247, 251-252, 257; armies, 64; powers, 36, 44; recovery, 245; war, 213
European theater, 138-139, 202, 204, 211, 214

Falaise gap, 182
Far East, 132, 205
Fascism, 4, 8, 127, 239
Fatherland Front, 185
February Revolution, 8, 32, 37, 56, 78, 81, 88, 90n, 238
Ferdinand, Archduke, 61
Ferro, Marc, 56, 83
Filipino rebel, 63
Finland, 3, 59, 72, 98, 117, 125, 131, 175, 183-184, 249
Flanders, 42, 57
Foch, Marshal Ferdinand, 69
Folies Bergères, 214
Ford Foundation, 259n
Fort Leavenworth Staff College, 88
Fort Myer, 114
Fourteen Points, 70, 72
France, 1, 5-6, 9, 11, 13-14, 17, 21, 27, 30, 32-37, 40, 42, 44-45, 47-49, 51, 53, 60, 62-72, 83-86, 89, 101, 109-110, 113, 116, 118, 126-130, 134, 137, 152, 155, 159, 162, 170, 175-183, 186-188, 193, 196, 198n, 200n, 206, 208, 237, 245-246, 248; army, 32, 40, 65, 101, 108, 124-125; monarchy, 79
Franco, General Francisco, 4
Franco-Prussian War, 47
French Revolution, 7, 10, 79
Friessner, General Johannes, 184
Fuehrer, 171, 198n

Gabriel, Richard, 11
Gaddis, John, 258n
Galbraith, John Kenneth, 208
Galicia, 49, 51, 53-54, 58
Gallup Poll, 140
Genoa, 98
Genocide, 31
Germany, 1-6, 8-11, 13-19, 21, 27-33, 36-45, 47-55, 58, 62, 65-74n, 83, 87, 95, 96-98, 100-106, 108-109, 112-115, 117, 123-129, 131-133, 135-140, 142-143, 145, 150-152, 154-159, 161, 170-189, 191, 194-200n, 202, 205-210, 212-213, 220, 224-225, 233, 237, 239-240, 244-245, 248-250, 252-253; army, 4, 17, 47, 59, 61, 64-66, 88, 124-125, 127-130, 137, 152, 175, 187, 192-193, 204, 207, 223, 238, 241, 243, 253, 257; barbarism, 31; control, 246; economy, 219, 226; enemy, 218; invasion, 227, 229; navy, 127, 205;

offensive, 30, 254; resistance, 15
Geyer, Michael, 126
Gibson, Cristann, 259n
Goebbels, Joseph, 172
Gold, 180
Golitsyn, Nikolai, 81
Goremykin, Ivan, 81
Gorlice, 53
Graduate School of International Studies, 259n
Grant, General Ulysses S., 213
Great Britain. See Britain
Great Depression, 2-3, 14, 21, 90n, 95, 100-101, 103, 105, 108, 116, 118, 227, 229, 231, 234
Great Purges, 4, 14, 72, 101-102, 105, 107, 112, 117-118, 125, 216, 249
Great Russian nationalism, 81
Great War, 38-39, 44
Grigg, John, 136
Guadalcanal, 155
Guadalcanal, Battle of, 140
Guards units, Soviet, 212
Gumbinnen, 50
Guns of August, 43
Gustav line, 162

Hamburg, 196
Harbord, General James, 61, 87
Harriman, Ambassador Averell, 142, 198n
Harrison, Mark, 108, 232, 234n
Hart, Basil Liddell, 49
Hastings, Max, 23n, 171, 182
Heinrici, General Gerhard, 191
Heykal, Mohammed, 253
High Command, 48, 65
Hillman, Sidney, 229
Hindenburg line, 67, 68
Hiroshima, 225
Hitler, Adolph, 2, 102, 123-124, 126, 135, 142, 146n, 154, 163, 186, 191-193, 198n, 200n, 239
Hodges, General Courtney, 214-215
Holocaust, 12, 31, 253
Hong Kong, 100
Hopkins, Harry, 117
Horse Marshals, 102, 114, 253
Horthy, Admiral, 186
Hotel Britannique, 214
Hotel George V, 214
House, Colonel Edward, 80
Hughes, General Everett, 213
Hungary, 72, 131, 178, 185-186, 191, 194, 255
Huntington, Samuel, 11, 258n

Huston, James, 206
Imperial Germany, 8, 39, 60, 86, 238
Imperial Japan, 1, 115-116, 157, 202, 204
Imperial Russian army, 3
India, 7, 61, 99, 134
Indians, American, 114, 126
Inter-Allied conference, 37
International Monetary Fund, 211
Isolationism, 116-118
Israel, 9, 100, 238
Israeli army, 215
Italian theater, 180
Italy, 3, 6, 8, 10-11, 13-16, 19, 31, 33, 38, 42, 53, 55, 75n, 83, 109, 123, 127-131, 136, 138, 140, 149, 151-152, 155-156, 159-164, 170, 175, 177, 193, 197n, 245, 252
Iwo Jima, 204

Japan, 96-97, 102, 109-110, 113, 117, 123, 125-127, 136-142, 151, 161, 170, 202; barbarism, 31; navy, 117
Jews, 31, 81, 124, 253
Joffre, General Joseph, 54
Johnson Act (1934), 116
Johnson, General Hugh, 116
Jones, General L.E., 213
July Days, 58
Juno, Beach, 180

Kaiser Wilhelm, 27
Kars, 59
Kasserine Pass, Battle of, 137, 156
Katyusha, launchers, 191; rockets, 107, 220
Kennan, George, 82
Kerensky, Alexander, 56-58
Khalkin-Gol, Battle of, 102
Kharkov, Battle of, 154, 158
Khrushchev, Nikita, 254
Kiev, Battle of, 158
King, Admiral Ernest, 137
Kirponos, General Mikhail, 215
Knox, Alfred, 36
Knox, Secretary of State Frank, 142
Knutsen, Torbjorn, 237
Koenigsberg, 190, 191
Kolchak, Admiral, 97
Köln, 172
Komsomolites, 216
Konev, Marshal Ivan, 178, 190-191
Korea, 18, 197, 209, 220, 241, 256-257
Korean War, 238
Kornilov, General Lavr, 58
Kremlin, 115, 246

Krylenko, Nikolai, 59
Kurland, 59, 184
Kuropatkin, General Alexis, 54
Kursk-Orel, Battle of, 6, 15, 21, 29, 123, 129-130, 158, 254
Kuznets, Simon, 106
Kwangtung army, 204-205

Lake Balaton, 191
Lake Khasan, Battle of, 102
Land power, 206
Latin America, 252
League of Nations, 2-3, 7, 72, 96
Lebensraum, 102
Leigh-Mallory, Marshal Trafford, 180
Leighton, Richard, 136, 139, 203
Leites, Nathan, 254
Lend Lease, 3, 15, 116-117, 127, 134, 141-145, 147n, 150, 170, 201-202, 219-220, 223-224, 238, 244
Lenin, Vladimir, 27, 56, 69-70, 96-97
Leningrad, Battle of, 129, 154, 158, 225, 227
Leninist socialism, 28
Less Developed Countries (LDCs), 100
Lindbergh, Charles, 117
Lithuania, 54
Little Father, 82
Litvinov, Foreign Commissar Maxim, 101
Lodz, 52
Logistics, 205
London, 53, 84, 86, 180, 213
Lorraine, 188
Louisiana maneuvers, 109, 114
Low Countries, 181
Luftwaffe, 193, 195
Luxemburg, 188
Luzon, 204
Lvov, 53

MacArthur, General Douglas, 257
MacDonald, Charles, 194
Mackensen, General August, 52
Maginot line, 30, 101
Malenkov, Georgii, 231
Malinovsky, General Rodion, 184-185, 190
Manchester liberalism, 250
Manchuria, 16
Marne, Battle of, 27, 40, 51, 59, 66-67
Marseilles, 83
Marshall, General George 23n, 88, 112, 128, 137, 197n, 205, 213, 257
Marxism, 8, 102, 251
Marxist analysis, 11

Masurian lakes, 50, 51
Matloff, Maurice, 208, 213
Max, Prince, 66
May, Ernest, 126
McCormick, Robert, 117
McNair, General Lesley, 114, 182, 213, 215
McNeill, William, 173, 198n, 227
Mediterranean Sea, 15, 129, 133-134, 137, 143, 156-157, 162, 210
Mediterranean theater, 180
Messerschmidt fighter plane, 109
Method of Agreement, 23n
Method of Disagreement, 23n
Metz-Sedan-Mezeries, 68
Meuse-Argonne, Battle of, 7, 67-69
Mexicans, 114
Mexico, 7, 61-63, 126
Meyer, Major General Kurt, 198n
Michael, King, 184
Middle East, 40, 42, 53, 132-133, 138, 152, 156, 163, 170; armies, 256; wars, 255
Middle East, Battle of, 128
Midway, Battle of, 140, 203
Midwest, 61
Militarism, 8
Mill, John Stuart, 20, 23n
Millar, James, 12
Milner, Lord Alfred, 84
Milward, Alan, 207
Milyukov, Professor Pavel, 56
Model, Field Marshal Walther, 188, 195
Mogilev, 80
Molotov, Foreign Minister Vyacheslav, 141, 231
Molotov-Ribbentrop Nonaggression Pact, 14, 32, 101, 117, 124, 240
Montgomery, General Bernard, 38, 132, 156, 160-161, 172, 180, 186, 189, 194-196
Moore, Barrington, 20
More Developed Countries (MDCs), 100
Morgenthau, Henry, 135
Morocco, 156
Moscow, 3, 15, 29, 58, 80, 89, 100, 102-103, 105, 117, 123, 154, 178, 184, 227, 230, 245-246, 248-249, 251-255
Moselle, 67
Munich conference, 4, 14, 101
Murmansk, 36
Muscovy, medieval, 80
Mussolini, Benito, 161, 239

NATO, 254

Namur, 214
Nancy, 214
Naples, 161
Napoleonic France, 124
Narew, 51
Naroch, Lake, 54
Nasser, Gamal Abdel, 253
National Defense Act, 62
National Guard, 62, 63, 87
Nazi German weapons production, 113, 215, 219
Nazi Germany, 1, 2, 14, 21, 51, 101, 110-111, 114-116, 118, 123-124, 126, 128-129, 132, 134, 137, 141, 145-146, 149, 151, 157, 160, 164, 169-171, 173, 177, 186, 189, 193, 204, 211, 218, 230, 238-240, 247, 252, 255
Netherlands, 188
New Deal, 249
New Economic Plan, 99
New Guinea, 138, 203
New World, 95, 112
Nicholas, Grand Duke, 53
Nicholson, Lord, 40
Nile river, 156
Nimitz, Admiral Chester, 139
1905 Revolution, 82
Nitze, Paul, 208
Nivelle offensive, 55
Non-Russians, 87
Normandy, 14, 123, 127, 131, 139, 144-145, 151, 157, 159-161, 163, 169-170, 177, 179-183, 187, 198n-199n, 207, 213, 215
North Africa, 3, 15, 123, 127-128, 136-137, 149, 151-152, 155-156, 159-161, 163-164, 170, 252
North Vietnam, 238; forces, 9
Nove, Alec, 227
Nye Committee, 116
Nye, Gerald, 117

October Revolution, 3, 8, 32, 37, 58, 70, 72, 88, 105, 227, 240, 253
Oder river, 190, 243
Office of Production Management, United States, 109
Office of War Mobilization, United States, 233
Okinawa, 204
Omaha Beach, 179-181
Oosterbeek, 188
Operation ANVIL, 183; BAGRATION, 177, 179; BARBAROSSA, 123, 152; CITADEL, 157, 158; COBRA, 182,

199n; EPSON, 182; GOODWOOD, 182; GRENADE, 194; HUSKY, 157-160; MARKET-GARDEN, 187; OVERLORD, 137, 180; PLUNDER, 195; ROUNDUP, 155; SEA LION, 124; SLEDGEHAMMER, 155; TORCH, 137-138, 157; VARSITY, 195; VERITABLE, 194
Oran, 156
Orthodox camp, 10, 242-246
OSOAVIAKHIM, Soviet Union, 116
Ottoman Turkish Empire, 8, 48, 55
Overman Act, 85

Pacific Ocean, 2, 18, 125-126, 136-141, 147n, 151, 155, 162, 174, 201-204, 207, 213, 257
Palmer, Frederick, 62
Pancho Villa, 62
Panther tank, 109, 171
Panzer legions, 130, 142, 174, 179, 181, 188, 190, 199n
Paris, 3, 27, 40, 60, 65, 169, 183, 214
Pas de Calais, 181
Passchendaele, Battle of, 27, 29
Patton, General George, 114, 157, 160, 172, 180, 182, 188-189, 194-195, 214-215
Pax Americana, 16
Pearl Harbor, 113, 117, 123, 125, 127, 138, 140, 155, 157
People's Liberation Army, 9
Pershing, General John, 33-34, 61-64, 67-68, 74n, 82, 88
Petain, Marshal Henri, 33, 63, 156
Petrograd Soviet, 56, 58
Petrograd conference, 56, 84
Petrograd, 39, 56, 89
Pew Charitable Trust, 259n
Philippines, 63, 140, 204
Philippines, Battle of, 138
Ploesti oil fields, 207
Poland, 3, 36, 52, 54, 70, 98, 100, 117, 131, 158, 178, 180, 189-190, 242, 255
Polenberg, Richard, 227
Poles, 81
Polish salient, 51
Portugal, 112
Postrevisionist camp, 10, 242, 246-247
Prague, 6, 19, 238
Provisional Government, 56-58
Przemysl fortress, 53

RAF. See British Royal Air Force
RAINBOW war plans, 113

Rabat, 156
Rabaul, 203
Ramsay, Admiral Bertram, 180
Rapallo, Treaty of, 3
Rasputin, Grigorii, 80-81
Red Army, 4-6, 12, 14-17, 19, 21, 30, 53, 72, 97, 100, 102-103, 109-112, 115-116, 118, 125, 127-131, 144-145, 152, 154, 158-159, 161, 163, 169-170, 173-175, 177-179, 183-191, 193, 196, 238-239, 242-244, 246-247, 251, 253, 257
Red Cross, 214
Reichstag, 191, 252
Remagen, 169, 195
Rennenkampf, General Pavel, 50, 51
Republican forces, 3
Reserve Officer Training Corps, 62
Reserve, United States Army, 113
Revisionist camp, 10, 242, 246-247
Revolution, 7, 258n
Rhine, 169, 172-173, 194-195
Rickenbacker, Eddie, 117
Riga, 53-54, 58, 184, 194
Roaring Twenties, 99
Rokossovsky, Marshal Konstantin, 178, 190-191, 216
Romania, 2, 38, 55, 83, 98, 100, 110, 130, 154, 178, 184-185, 207, 250
Romanian positions, 154
Romanov monarchs, 79
Rome, 161-162, 177
Rommel, General Erwin, 133, 155, 181, 199n
Roosevelt, Elliott, 159
Roosevelt, President Franklin, 73n, 108-109, 113, 116-117, 135-137, 141-142, 152, 210, 228
Roosevelt, President Theodore, 61
Root, Secretary of War Elihu, 61, 64, 87
Rose, General Maurice, 215
Ruhr, 194-195
Russia, 2-3, 5, 8, 11, 21, 28, 30-32, 35-55, 57-58, 60, 62, 69-70, 74n, 77-78, 81, 83-84, 87, 89-90n, 95, 97, 115, 123, 152, 173, 175, 191, 196, 206, 238, 240, 247, 253, 257; army, 6, 27, 32, 34, 36-37, 40, 56, 59, 65, 86-87, 125, 152; front, 199n; monarchy, 79; navy, 86; people, 29, 32, 44, 128, 138, 227; socialism, 70
Russian Cabinet, 80, 81
Russian Civil War (1918-1920), 70, 115, 125
Russian Orthodox church, 81
Russian Poland, 53

Russian Revolution, 7, 89, 258
Russo-German collaboration, 239
Russo-German Neutrality Pact (1939), 116-117
Russo-German relations, 102
Russo-German war, 152
Russo-Japanese Neutrality Pact (1941), 117, 138
Russo-Japanese War (1904-1905), 3, 82, 102, 125

Saar, 172, 194
Saigon, 238
Salerno, 161
Samsonov, General Alexander, 50, 51
Scandinavia, 131, 175
Scheldt estuary, 187
Schlieffen Plan, 40, 48-49
Seaton, Albert, 164n
Second World War. *See* World War II
Second front, 141, 142, 210, 251
Sedition Act, 79
Seelow Heights, 191
Seine, 180, 183
Selective Service System, 79
Serbia, 38
Sevastopol, Battle of, 154
SHAEF, 186, 214
Shaposhnikov, Marshal Boris, 215
Sherman tank, 220
Siberia, 80, 173
Sicily, 123, 127, 159-161, 163, 170, 197n, 252
Siegfried line, 65, 183, 187-188
Silesia, 52
Singapore, 100
Sioux Indians, 63
Skocpol, Theda, 20-21, 24n
Smith, General Bedell, 180
Soissons, 66
Solomon Islands, 203
Solzhenitsyn, Alexander, 51
Somme, Battle of, 27, 29, 54
South Korea, 100
South Vietnamese Army, 9
South, 61
Southeast Asia 138-140
Southeast theaters, 173
Southwestern front, 176
Southwestern theaters, 173
Soviet Union economic production, 225
Soviet Union economy, 226
Soviet Union, 1-7, 9-11, 13-14, 16-23n, 27-28, 31-32, 69-72, 89-90n, 95-118, 123-130, 132, 133, 135-138, 140-142, 144-145, 149-152, 155, 157-158, 162-164162-164, 169-174, 17-178, 184-186, 189-191, 193-194, 196-198n, 201-202, 204-206, 210-211, 213-214, 216, 218, 223-227, 228-230, 232-234, 237-248, 250-258; army, 256-257; commanders, 215; economy, 219; leaders, 255; military power, 17; polity, 246; soldier, 216; specialists, 243; war production, 16; weaponry, 218, 219
Soviet-German collaboration, 249
Soviet-German front, 12
Soviet-U.S. relations, 117, 141, 148, 209
Spa, 214
Spain, 133, 156, 170; army, 63; empire, 7, 61
Spanish Civil War, 4, 102, 203
Spanish-American War (1898), 64, 87
Spector, Ronald, 203
Springfield rifle, 64
SS (Schutzstaffel), 195
St. Mihiel, Battle of, 34, 67-68
Stalin, Joseph, 16-17, 32, 72, 90n, 98, 100-103, 105-112, 114-118, 124, 142, 145, 154, 189, 197, 210, 226, 230-234, 238, 240-241, 244, 246, 249, 251, 253, 255
Stalingrad, Battle of, 6, 15, 21, 29, 123, 127-130, 135, 152-155, 157, 191, 216, 225, 233, 254
Stalluponen, 50
State Department, 142
Stavka, 55
Stein, Arthur, 8, 13
Sterling bloc, 210, 250
Stilwell, General Joseph, 213
Stimson, Secretary of War Harry, 61, 87
Stohr, Gauleiter, 172
Stoler, Mark, 211
Strategic air power, 208
Strategic bombing campaign, 207-208
Sturmer, Boris, 81, 84
Sukhomlinov, General Vladimir, 81
Swedes, 248
Sword Beach, 180

Taiwan, 100
Tannenberg, Battle of, 3, 32, 39-40
Tarawa, Battle of, 204
Tedder, Marshal Arthur 160, 180
Teheran conference, 142, 160, 177, 180, 210
Third Reich, 1, 9, 22, 32, 123-124, 128, 134, 145, 151, 157, 161-162, 169-171, 177, 183-185, 189, 191, 193,

196, 204, 206-208, 210, 216, 231,
238, 243, 246
Third World leaders, 253
Tiger tank, 109, 171
Tilsit, 3
Tito, Marshal Josip Broz, 185
Tokyo fire raid, 204
Tolbukhin, Marshal Fyodor, 184-185,
190-191, 214
Totalitarian theory, 17
Transcaucasus, 98
Transylvania, 185
Trepov, Alexander, 81
Trianon Hotel, 213
Triple Entente, 9, 48-49, 55, 240
Truk Islands, 203
Tsar Nicholas II, 27, 78-80, 82, 87
Tsar, 56, 82, 89
Tsarina Alexandra, 80-81, 87, 89
Tsarism, 3, 41, 51, 53, 56, 82, 87-88,
97-99, 105-106, 110, 117
Tsarist Russia, 8, 31, 42-46, 59-61, 77-
79, 83-84, 88, 90n, 103, 107, 227,
238, 249, 252; army, 3, 55, 88, 97;
polity, 81
Tukhachevsky, Marshal Mikhail, 111-
112, 125
Tunisia, 156, 197n
Turkey, 40, 41, 55, 59, 98
Turkish divisions, 41

U Bahn, 191
U-Boat, German, 48, 86, 126, 155, 171,
205
Ukraine, 59, 70, 81, 98, 158-159, 184
United Kingdom, 106
United Nations, 152, 211
United States, 1-6, 9-11, 13-18, 20-22,
23n, 27-28, 30-46, 48, 59-64, 66-
75n, 77-80, 83-86, 90n, 95-96, 98-
118, 123-127, 130-146, 149-152,
155-163, 169, 170, 172, 174-176,
178, 180, 185, 193-194, 196-197,
201-206, 208-211, 213, 218, 220,
223-224, 227-229, 231, 233-234,
239-252, 255-257, 259n; Air Force,
86, 138, 180, 189, 207-208; Army,
12, 20, 32-33, 64-66, 68, 70-71, 85,
87-88, 109, 110, 112, 113-114, 125-
126, 128-129, 161, 206, 209, 212-
213, 215, 239, 243, 256-257;
economic production, 225; economy,
226; Marines, 217; military, 63, 85-
86; Navy, 86, 127, 138-140, 205,
212, 216; soldier, 216; weapons
production, 219

University of Denver, 259n
Upper Rhine, 188
Urals, 244
Utah Beach, 180

V-E Day, 169, 193, 205, 241, 244
Van Creveld, Martin, 9
Vasilievsky, Marshal Alexander, 216
Verdun, 54
Verkhovsky, General Alexander, 58
Versailles, 21, 23, 96
Vichy France, 6, 133, 155-156, 159
Vienna, 6, 19, 191, 238
Vietnam War, 150
Vietnam, 8, 18, 197, 209, 216, 220,
241, 256-257
Vilna front, 214
Vilna, 53-54
Vistula, 50, 178
Volga river, 154
Volkssturm, 186, 195
Von Hindenburg, General Paul, 50, 71
Von Hoetzendorff, General Conrad, 51
Von Hutier, General Oskar, 58
Von Ludendorff, General Erich, 50-51,
65-66, 71
Von Mellenthin, General, 177
Von Paulus, General Friedrich, 154
Von Prittwitz, General Goffron, 49, 50
Von Rundstedt, General Gerd, 179, 186,
188
Voronov, Marshal Nikolai, 216
Voroshilov, Marshal Kliment, 112, 231

Wagner, Richard, 124
Wallace, Henry, 142
War Department, 33, 62, 85, 100, 113-
114
War Industries Board, 80, 85
War Production Board, 233
War of 1812, 7
Warsaw Pact, 255
Warsaw, 52-53, 178, 190
Washington, 3, 7, 33, 64, 85, 88, 100,
103, 162, 246, 248
Waterloo, 8
Wehrmacht, 31, 126, 129-130, 154,
163-164, 170-173, 175-176, 178-179,
186, 205, 194, 217, 238, 257
Weigley, Russell, 61, 134, 212, 218
Welles, Under Secretary of State Sumner,
142
Werth, Alexander, 227
West, 2-3, 10-12, 15-17, 20, 22, 32, 36-
37, 40, 48-50, 53, 55, 59, 61, 66,
72, 73n, 78, 88, 90n, 99-101, 103,

105, 115-116, 124, 129, 130, 142,
152, 155, 159, 163, 170-179, 181,
183, 186, 189-191, 193-198n, 239,
243, 246, 248, 251, 255
Western allies, 57, 59, 200n, 241
Western Europe, 37, 131, 171, 186, 193,
242-243, 245, 249, 259n
Western front, 15, 21, 30, 32, 36, 40,
42, 53, 59, 66, 86, 129, 172, 175-
176, 179, 191, 194, 238
Western leaders, 257
Western observers, 227
Western offensive, 54
Western powers, 14, 245
Western sources, 216
Westphalia, Treaty of, 1, 28
Whitehall, 210
Whites, 70, 97-98
Wilhelm, Kaiser, 47, 65
Williams, William Appleman, 246-247
Wilson, General Maitland, 180
Wilson, President Woodrow, 27, 60-63,
68, 70, 72, 78-80, 85, 96,
Wilsonian liberalism, 28
Window of vulnerability, 60
Winter War, Finnish, 3-4, 72, 102, 112,
117, 125

Wood, General Robert, 116
World Bank, 211
World War I, 1-3, 5-9, 13-14, 17, 21,
27-39, 41, 43-45, 47, 60, 62, 68, 70,
72-74n, 77, 79, 81-82, 84, 88-89,
95-96, 101-102, 108-109, 111, 115-
116, 124-126, 129-163, 206, 220,
238, 240
World War II, 1-6, 8-13, 16-22, 27-32,
37, 38, 47, 53, 73, 88, 99, 105, 109,
112, 116, 123-125, 129-130, 143,
151, 158, 164n, 169, 171, 173, 201-
202, 206, 212, 218, 227, 231, 233,
237-241, 243, 247, 249-251, 253-
257

Yakir, General Yona, 112
Yalta conference, 189
Yamamoto, Admiral Isoruku, 140
Ypres offensive, 57
Yudenich, General Nikolai, 89, 97
Yugoslavia, 13, 184-185, 255

Zemstvo, 82
Zero fighter plane, 109
Zhukov, Marshal Georgii, 190-191, 216

About the Book
and the Author

Prelude to the Cold War presents an original analysis of the roots of the protracted and dangerous rivalry between the United States and the Soviet Union. Jonathan Adelman explores, in a comparative framework, the military histories of the armies of the two future superpowers in World Wars I and II. This allows him to incorporate the military in the discussion of the origins of U.S.– Soviet tensions, a discussion more typically dominated by political, economic, and diplomatic approaches.

Adelman argues that the main theories of the Cold War have oversimplified a complex military reality. The United States, far from being all-powerful in World War II, was able to attain victory only with massive help from both the British Commonwealth and the Soviet Union and demonstrated relatively modest power-projection capabilities in Europe. The Soviet Union, after massive initial defeats, developed a strong, if primitive, land army with no more than modest ancillary capabilities.

The book concludes with an assessment of the impact of the sharply divergent military roles and capabilities of the two states on the development of the Cold War and on the lessons drawn from World War II by the Soviet Union and the United States.

Jonathan R. Adelman is associate professor in the Graduate School of International Studies, University of Denver. Among his numerous publications in this field are *Revolution, Armies, and War: A Political History* and *The Revolutionary Armies: The Russian and Chinese Communist Armies*.